Health for Life

Authors
Julius B. Richmond
John D. MacArthur Professor of
Health Policy
Director, Division of Health Policy
Research and Education
Harvard University
Advisor on Child Health Policy
Children's Hospital of Boston
Boston, Massachusetts

Elenore T. Pounds
Health Education Writer
Downers Grove, Illinois

Physical Fitness Author
Charles B. Corbin
Professor, Department of Health
and Physical Education
Arizona State University
Tempe, Arizona

Scott, Foresman and Company
Editorial Offices: Glenview, Illinois

Regional Offices: Sunnyvale, California • Tucker, Georgia • Glenview, Illinois • Oakland, New Jersey • Dallas, Texas

Authors

Julius B. Richmond, M.D., is the John D. MacArthur Professor of Health Policy and the Director of the Division of Health Policy Research and Education at Harvard University. He also is Advisor on Child Health Policy at the Children's Hospital of Boston. Dr. Richmond served as Surgeon General for the U.S. Public Health Service and as Assistant Secretary for Health from 1977–1981. Trained as a pediatrician, Dr. Richmond joined the faculty of the Harvard Medical School in 1971. He was professor of child psychiatry and human development before being appointed Surgeon General.

Elenore T. Pounds, M.A., is a health education writer and lecturer. A former elementary teacher, she served as directing editor of the Health and Personal Development Program. She is co-author of *Health and Growth, You and Your Health,* and other health publications.

Charles B. Corbin, Ph.D., is professor and coordinator of graduate studies in the Department of Health and Physical Education at Arizona State University. A former elementary physical education teacher, he previously served as professor and head of graduate studies in the Department of Health, Physical Education, and Recreation at Kansas State University. Dr. Corbin is the author of many research and professional publications, especially in the area of lifetime fitness.

ISBN: 0-673-29680-6

12345678910RRW9998979695949392919O

Consultants

Reading
Robert A. Pavlik, Ed.D.
Professor and Chairperson
Reading–Language Arts Department
Cardinal Stritch College
Milwaukee, Wisconsin

Medical
Jerry Newton, M.D.
Director, Health Services
San Antonio Independent School District
Clinical Professor, Pediatrics
University of Texas Medical School, San Antonio
San Antonio, Texas

Design
Design direction by Norman Perman
Graphic Designer and Art Consultant
Chicago, Illinois

Cover photograph by Zao Grimberg/Image Bank

Acknowledgments
The dental health information contained in Chapter 5 is considered by the American Dental Association to be in accord with current scientific knowledge, 1986.

For further acknowledgments, see page 320.

Content Specialists

Dental Health
Mary Banas
Program Specialist
Bureau of Health Education and Audiovisual Services
American Dental Association
Chicago, Illinois

Drug Education
Chwee Lye Chng
Assistant Professor
Division of Health Education
North Texas State University
Denton, Texas

Merita Thompson
Professor
Department of Health Education
Eastern Kentucky University
Richmond, Kentucky

Family Life Education
Linda Berne
Professor
Department of Health and Physical Education
The University of North Carolina
Charlotte, North Carolina

Nutrition
Jean Mayer
President
Tufts University
Medford, Massachusetts

Safety and First Aid
Janice Sutkus
Technical Specialist
National Safety Council
Chicago, Illinois

Reviewers and Contributors

Lourdes Alcorta-Rogover
Educational Consultant
Former Teacher
Miami, Florida

Ruth Ann Althaus
Professor of Public Health
Master of Public Health Program
Illinois Benedictine College
Lisle, Illinois

Matthew Bustamante
Bilingual/Cross-Cultural Education Specialist
Bandini Elementary School
Montebello, California

Judi Coffey
Educational Consultant
Learning Disabilities Specialist
Jonesboro, Arkansas

Bryan Cooke
Professor
Department of Community Health
College of Health and Human Services
University of Northern Colorado
Greeley, Colorado

Gail Daud
Teacher in Gifted Education
Spring Shadows Elementary School
Houston, Texas

Bo Fernhall
Director, Fitness and Cardiac Rehabilitation
Department of Physical Education
Northern Illinois University
DeKalb, Illinois

Linda Froschauer
Teacher
Weston Public Schools
Weston, Connecticut

Rosalyn Gantt
Teacher
Midway Elementary School
Cincinnati, Ohio

Jon Hisgen
School Health Coordinator
Pewaukee Public Schools
Pewaukee, Wisconsin

Peter Loudis
Teacher of Gifted and Talented
Spring Branch Junior High School
Houston, Texas

Jeanne Mannings
Teacher
Adamsville Elementary School
Atlanta, Georgia

Nancy Henry Morrison
Teacher
Edwin J. Kiest Elementary School
Dallas, Texas

Wanda Nottingham-Brooks
Learning Disabilities Teacher
Morrisonville Junior and Senior High School
Morrisonville, Illinois

Bert Pearlman
Director, Curriculum Research and Evaluation
Office of the County Superintendent of Schools
Santa Barbara, California

Candace Purdy
Health Teacher
Maine South High School
Park Ridge, Illinois

Joan Salmon
School Nurse
Greenwood School Corporation
Greenwood, Indiana

Deborah J. Schoenecke
Teacher
Ella Iles Elementary School
Lubbock, Texas

Betty Smith
Teacher of Talented and Gifted
Kiest/Urban Parks Elementary School
Dallas, Texas

David R. Stronck
Associate Professor of Health Education
Department of Teacher Education
California State University, Hayward
Hayward, California

Shirley Van Sickle
Health Teacher
DeVeaux Junior High School
Toledo, Ohio

Chapter 2 How Your Body Works 40

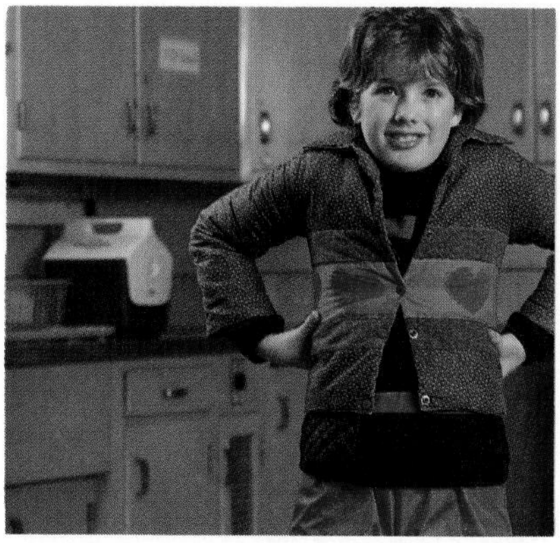

Chapter 3 Keeping Yourself Fit 68

Chapter 4 Knowing How to Be Safe 94

Chapter 5 Taking Care of Your Body 118

Chapter 6 Food and Your Body 146

Chapter 7 Medicines and Other Drugs 172

Chapter 8 Preventing Disease 200

Why Learn About Health

"When you have your health, you have just about everything." You might have heard this saying before. What does it mean to you? Most people agree that good health is one of the most important things a person could have. When you are healthy, you can enjoy life more fully. Good health helps you think clearly and get along with others at school. Good health keeps your body working properly so you can enjoy your play. Good health helps you look and feel your best.

Learning about health is important because you are making more and more decisions about your own health. For example, you might decide what to eat for lunch or where to play after school.

To make the wisest decisions, you need good information. Then you need to know how to use this information. Finally, you need to develop *skills for life.* These skills will help you deal with events in your life in good and healthful ways. Scott, Foresman's *Health for Life* gives you the tools that can improve your health, but it is up to you to use them. Make good health a part of your day and a part of your life, now and in the years to come.

When You Read This Book

1. Read the question.

4. Learn the health word.

2. Look at the picture.

pedestrian
(pə des′trē ən), a person who travels by walking.

Did You Know?
By law, a car or bus driver must stop for a pedestrian in a crosswalk, even if the crossing has no traffic light. However, a careful pedestrian must always check that no cars are coming before crossing any street.

1 What Should Careful Pedestrians Do?

The children in the picture walk to school. They are **pedestrians**, people who walk on a street or sidewalk. At times you are a pedestrian too. If you follow the safety rules on page 97, you will be a safe pedestrian.

Some pedestrians are not safe. Maybe you have heard the word *jaywalker.* A person who is a jaywalker is not a careful pedestrian. Jaywalkers often walk or cross streets without paying attention to safety rules. They might not look carefully for cars before crossing a street. Jaywalkers often have or cause accidents.

3. Find the answers.

When the sign for walk lights up, what should you do before you cross?

How Can You Walk Safely?

The rules below describe ways to walk safely. Which of these rules are the students in the picture following?

- Before you cross a street, look to the left, then right, and left again. Look for cars that might turn in front of you. Cross only when no cars are coming toward you.
- Obey traffic lights and signs. Know and follow signs for pedestrians.
- Always stop at the curb or outside edge of a parked car before entering the street. Wait on the sidewalk, not in the street, for cars that are turning to pass.
- Be careful whenever you cross a street, even when you cross at a corner or in a marked crosswalk. Be sure the driver of any oncoming car sees you.
- Walk on the left side of the street or road if the road or street has no sidewalk. You will face the traffic and can see oncoming cars. Walk one behind the other if you walk with others.
- Wear light-colored clothing and carry a light if you walk at night.

Think Back • *Study on your own with Study Guide page 256.*

1. What are five rules for crossing streets safely?
2. Where and how should a person walk if a road or street has no sidewalk?
3. What should a pedestrian do when walking on a street or road at night?

5. Use what you learned.

97

Chapter 1

Getting to Know Yourself and Others

What hobbies do you have? The boy in the picture makes puppets and puts on puppet shows as a hobby. You might have different hobbies. Each person is different in many ways.

This chapter will help you understand differences in people. You will learn to understand yourself and others better. You will also learn how to make wise decisions that will help you all through your life.

Health Watch Notebook

Gather pictures of yourself doing activities you like or from different times in your life. Tape them in your notebook. Write captions describing yourself under each picture.

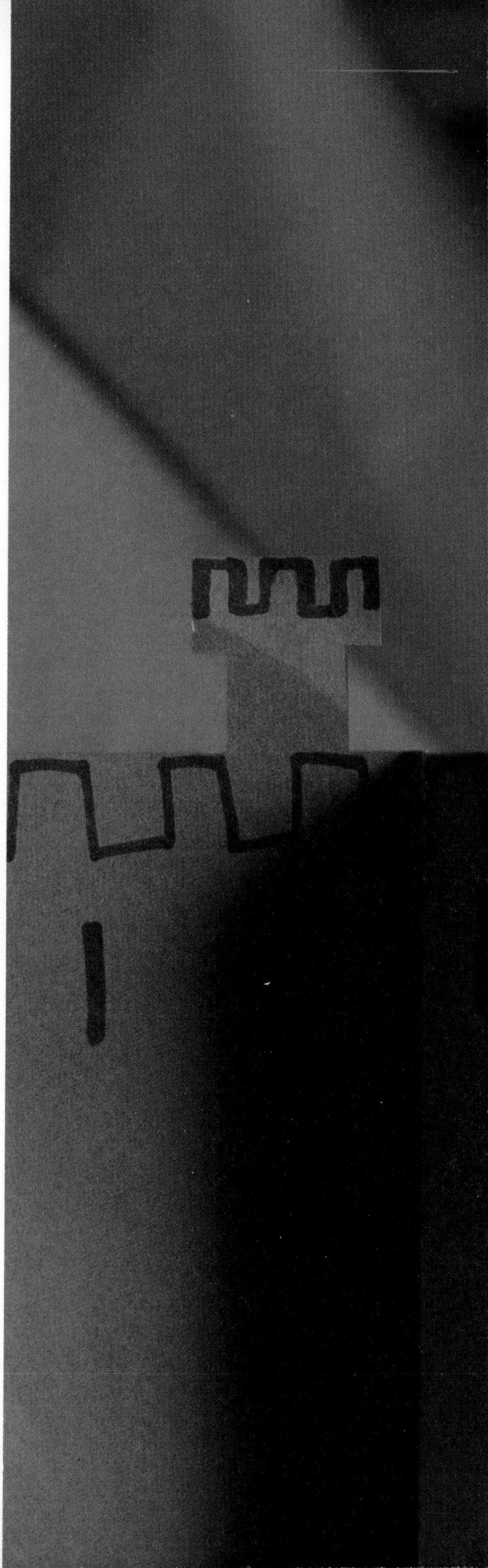

strength, something a person is strong in or can do well.

self-image (self′im′ij), the way a person sees or feels about himself or herself.

What do you notice about the students below? What makes the picture on page 19 more interesting?

1 How Can Understanding Yourself and Others Help You?

Look at the pictures on these two pages. Most people would say the picture on page 19 is more interesting. The differences in how the students look help make each person special.

Understanding some of the ways you are special can help you feel good about yourself. Your appearance helps make you special. No one else looks exactly like you. **Strengths**—what you do well—also help make you special. For example, you might write or sing well.

Knowing your strengths helps you understand yourself. When you know you can do something well, you feel good about yourself. You have a good **self-image.**

People with a good self-image like themselves. They accept themselves the way they are. This means knowing they have weaknesses, or things they do not do very well. People with a good self-image try to improve in what they do not do very well. However, sometimes weaknesses cannot be changed very much. For example, some people cannot sing or draw very well. A person with a good self-image can accept the fact that he or she has some weaknesses.

Having a good self-image can help you get along well with others. You do not expect to be just like others. You do not expect others to be just like you. Differences make life more interesting. For example, what would a baseball team be like if all the players were only good pitchers?

On Your Own
Find out how your classmates are special. Think of three people you know. List a strength each person has. Are the strengths all the same? Write your ideas about how each strength makes the person special.

How Can Appreciating Differences Help You and Others?

Suppose a new girl moves into your neighborhood. She comes from another country and speaks a language different from yours. How would you try to make friends with her?

In the picture on this page George is making friends with Mary, a new girl in the neighborhood. George and the other children in the neighborhood cannot talk to Mary easily because she cannot speak much English. As they play here, Mary is teaching George some words in her language. George is also teaching English words to Mary. The two children can get to know each other better when they can speak to each other more easily. Mary and the others will also enjoy playing together and learning from each other.

Learning from different people is one way to appreciate differences in others.

The children had learned to **appreciate** differences in each other. When you appreciate someone, you think well of him or her. Appreciating differences in others helps you get along better with them. You also understand others better when you appreciate some of the ways they are special.

appreciate (ə prē′shē āt), to think well of someone or something.

Later, appreciating differences helped the neighborhood children again. Bob, a boy who is deaf, joined their group. Bob communicates one way by using sign language. The picture shows Bob teaching his new friends some signs.

How might being able to communicate with Bob help others learn to appreciate him better?

Think Back • *Study on your own with Study Guide page 250.*

1. What makes a person special?
2. What is a person's self-image?
3. How can a good self-image help a person?
4. How can it be helpful to learn to appreciate differences in other people?

Health Activities Workshop

Appreciating Differences in People

1. You use one or two hands to make a word or an idea in sign language. Look at these pictures. Learn how to sign the words. Look in the library for a sign-language dictionary for the deaf. Learn more signs. Then show them to your class.

2. Find out how you and your classmates are alike or different. On your own paper list five things you like. List five things you dislike. One or more classmates can do the same. Look at the lists. Do you like some of the same things as your classmates?

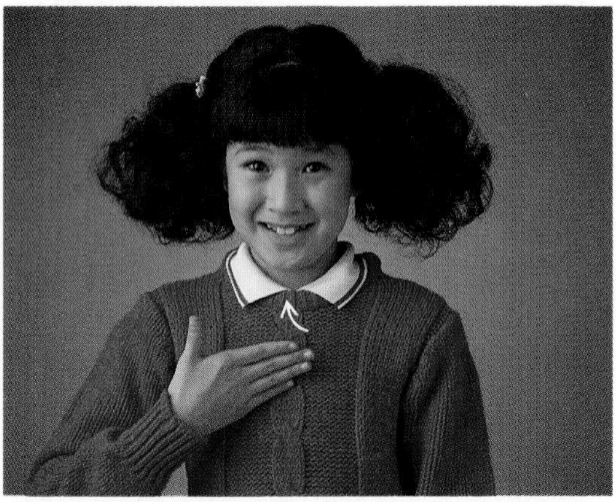

happy

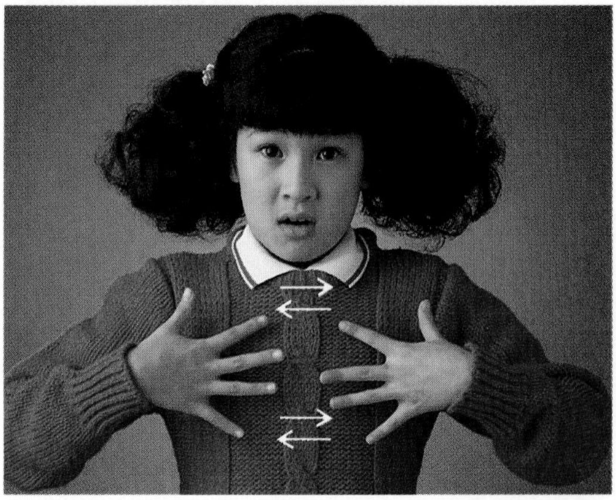

afraid

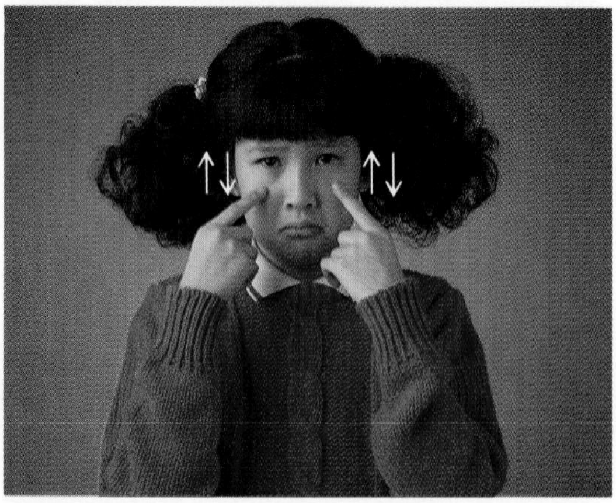

cry

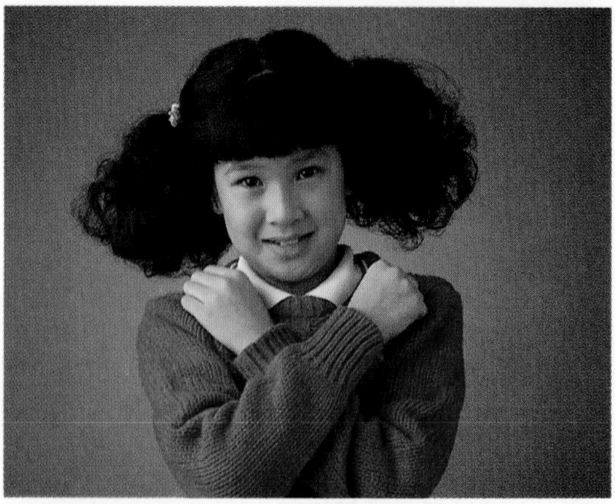

love

3. Draw three pictures of yourself, each one showing one of your strengths. Keep your pictures to remind you of how you are special.

4. Write three or more sentences about some of your strengths. Think of things you do fairly well. One student wrote the sentences that follow. What will you write?

- I think I make friends easily.
- I take good care of my cat.
- I like to put together model cars and I am good at it.
- I do well on the weekly spelling tests most of the time.

5. Look at the puzzle. Read from left to right. Find four words telling how people are special. Write the words on your own paper.

X J U M R A P L V E R S C H

K L B D I F F E R E N C E S

C N M O O X C G K Y K L E Z

L M A P P E A R A N C E S B

K L B T R S B O O I C S L O

B N N A N S T R E N G T H S

L W E A K N E S S E S G G L

2 How Can Your Feelings Affect You?

Laura is just about to give a report to her class. She has worked hard on the report. Now she wonders if it will be good enough. She notices that her hands are sweaty. Her heart is beating faster than it usually does.

Feelings can affect how your body works. For example, feelings of worry or fear or anger can make your heart beat faster. The feelings can also make you breathe faster. Feelings of excitement or surprise can cause these body changes too. Sometimes these feelings can make your muscles tremble.

People who speak or perform in front of others often feel a little worried or fearful. Sometimes the feelings help the people do their best. Because of the worried feelings, the people prepare what they will do extra carefully.

Worried, scared, or angry feelings can affect your stomach. These feelings can make the work of the stomach speed up or slow down.

Feelings do not affect everyone's body the same way. The body changes you might have could be different from those others have. Many people notice how feelings cause changes in their bodies. Other people might not notice changes as much. People are different.

Most feelings that cause body changes do not last very long. The changes in the body do not last long either. If upset feelings last for a long time, they might cause problems such as headaches.

Laura's worried feelings started to go away as she began her report. Later, she felt a little surprised and pleased that the report turned out fairly well. Next time giving a report might seem easier because Laura knows that she can give a report and do it well.

Think Back • *Study on your own with Study Guide page 250.*

1. What are some feelings everyone has at times?
2. What changes can feelings cause in the way parts of the body work?
3. How long do body changes caused by feelings usually last?

Laura is happy she has given her report. She and her teacher talk over the report and discuss ways to make giving her next report easier.

3 What Can You Do About Angry Feelings?

The person who drew this picture about angry feelings found that drawing the picture helped get rid of the feelings.

Susan feels angry because her friend Cathy blamed her for something she did not do. Then Cathy went off to play with other friends. Susan feels that Cathy is treating her unfairly.

Like Susan, everyone feels angry at times. People usually have good reasons for being angry. Thinking they are being treated unfairly makes most people feel angry. Not being included in a game with friends could cause angry feelings. What else could make people feel angry?

You know that angry feelings can cause changes in the way your body works. Angry feelings might make your head ache or your stomach hurt.

You can learn helpful ways to deal with angry feelings. Talking things over is one good way to deal with angry feelings. Talking things over with a family member or friend can help you feel better. What do you think Susan is telling her mother about in the picture on page 27?

Suppose you keep your angry feelings to yourself and the feelings do not soon go away. Sooner or later they will show up. Then you might get angry at people who had nothing to do with your first angry feelings. You might act or speak unkindly to others. For example, you might shout at a younger brother or sister for no reason.

Sometimes you have no one to talk with about your angry feelings. Doing some activity you like might help you feel less angry. Maybe you could play an active game with friends. You might ride a bicycle or run for a while. You might talk with a friend on the telephone or read a book. If you feel like crying, sometimes that helps. Writing about your angry feelings or drawing a picture, such as the one shown here, can also help.

Think Back • *Study on your own with Study Guide page 251.*

1. What are some reasons for getting rid of angry feelings?
2. What are some helpful ways to deal with angry feelings?

Did You Know?
Sometimes relaxing for only two or three minutes can help a person get rid of angry feelings. You can relax by taking a deep breath and letting it out slowly while counting to ten. Repeat several times.

Telling her mother how angry she is at her friend helps make Susan feel better.

disagreement (dis′ə grē′mənt), a difference in what people think.

4 What Can You Do If You Have a Disagreement?

Why do people sometimes disagree? They disagree because people are not the same. Different people have different ideas about what they like and dislike. Even people who like each other very much can have **disagreements.** People who have disagreements think differently from one another.

You can learn from disagreements. When you learn how to settle disagreements, you are learning how to work out problems and difficulties. Often you can work out a problem by sharing or taking turns.

Talking things over can sometimes help settle a disagreement. Suppose you want to buy a pair of white shoes, but an adult in your family says no. The adult thinks you should buy brown shoes. What do you do then? You can accept the decision, or you might politely explain why you want the white shoes. You might have a good reason. The adult might have a good reason too. When you disagree with someone, be willing to listen to the other person's reasons. Try to talk about the problem without getting angry. You can disagree with others without arguing with them.

Some disagreements cannot be settled, such as disagreements about what people like best. If you have this kind of disagreement, you could agree not to argue. For example, the children in the picture have agreed not to argue about liking a dog or a cat better.

You can prevent some disagreements from happening. Often, a disagreement need not happen if you learn to accept certain family rules. For example, you might prevent a disagreement with adults at home by following rules about bedtime hours.

Think Back • *Study on your own with Study Guide page 251.*

1. What can cause disagreements?
2. What can be learned from settling disagreements?
3. What are some ways to settle a disagreement?
4. What are some ways to prevent some disagreements from happening?

This girl and boy have agreed not to argue about what animal makes the better pet.

Health Activities Workshop

Dealing with Angry Feelings

1. Work with others to act out some good ways to settle the following disagreement:

A family is making plans about what to do together on a Saturday. Some family members want to have a picnic in the park. Others want to go to a museum. Act out how the family worked out the problem.

2. Pretend you and other family members have a disagreement about who helps clean up after dinner. The picture shows one way to solve the problem. What way is shown? What might be another way?

	Clear Table	Rinse Dishes
Sunday	Joe	Mom
Monday	Grandmom	Tina
Tuesday	Tina	Dad
Wednesday	Mom	Grandmom
Thursday	Dad	Joe
Friday	Joe	Mom
Saturday	Grandmom	Tina

3. Find out what happens when you cry. Look in an encyclopedia or a library book about the eye. Look under such words as *eye, tears,* or *tear glands.* Find out what tear glands do. Find out how tears get from tear glands to the eyes. Find out where tears from the eyes can go. Explain to others what you learn. Use a picture to help you explain.

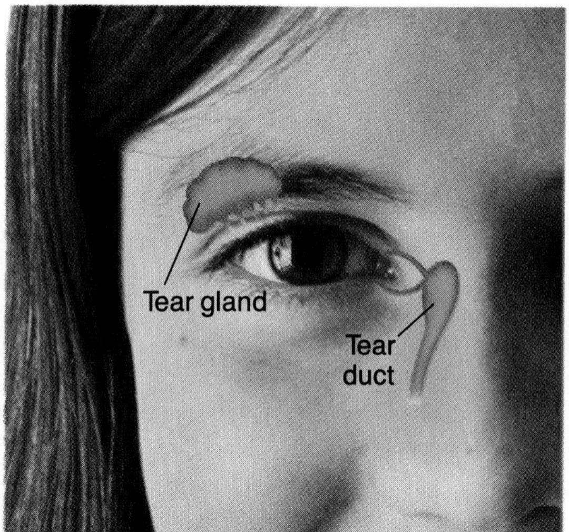

4. Draw a picture of an angry person. Next to the picture, write some body changes that angry feelings might cause.

5. Make a picture collage showing activities you could do to help when you are angry. You can find pictures in magazines or draw the pictures yourself.

Looking at Careers

6. Everyone has troubled feelings at times. Some people can deal with these troubled feelings by themselves. Other people need help, especially if troubled feelings last a long time. Several kinds of health workers help people with troubled feelings. A **psychologist** is one of these workers.

A psychologist can help people deal with problems that result from feelings. A psychologist works to help people understand themselves better.

A person who wants to be a psychologist must continue studying after graduating from college. He or she also gets more training by working with other psychologists.

The picture shows a psychologist at work. Describe what you might like about a psychologist's job.

5 How Can You Make Wise Decisions?

Everyone has to make decisions. The pictures show some decisions Brian often has to make.

Brian has another decision to make too. He just had a spelling test, and he made many mistakes. Brian does not like spelling and did not study very hard for the spelling test. Still, Brian knows he needs to decide about improving his schoolwork. He also knows that deciding to improve his schoolwork is more important than deciding what to wear to school. What can help Brian make a wise decision about his schoolwork? The steps in the chart on the next page show one good way.

What could help Brian in the decisions he is making? What kinds of decisions do you need to make?

Steps in Decision Making

Step 1. Realize that a decision is needed.

Step 2. List the possible choices.

Step 3. List the possible results of each choice.

Step 4. Decide which choice is best.

Step 5. Judge the decision.

Did You Know?
When you make a decision, it helps to follow certain guidelines to help you pick out a responsible choice. Below are guidelines for decision-making:

1. The choice should be safe and promote health.
2. The choice should be legal and follow the rules of school and community.
3. The choice would be acceptable to parents and other family members.
4. The choice shows respect for self and others.

How Can You Use the Steps to Make a Decision?

Brian will use the steps in the following way to help him make a decision about the way to improve his spelling. You can use the steps when you need to make a decision. Part of growing up is knowing how to make wise decisions on your own. If you need help in making important decisions, parents and teachers can help you.

Step 1. Understand that a decision is needed.

Brian knows that he needs to decide how to improve his spelling.

Step 2. List the possible choices.

Brian lists his choices.

- He could study at home each night for fifteen minutes by himself.
- He could ask his friend Joe to help him study for the next spelling test. Joe likes spelling and is a good speller.

Step 3. List the possible results of each choice.

Brian lists good and bad results of each choice. These might be results of studying on his own.

- Brian will improve in spelling.
- Brian will learn how to study on his own.
- Brian will feel good about himself because he improved his spelling on his own.
- Brian will not be able to improve his spelling on his own.

These might be the results of studying with Joe.

- Joe will help him, and Brian will improve in spelling.
- Brian will learn to like spelling more, and he will have fun with Joe.
- Brian and Joe might play instead of studying and Brian's spelling will not improve.
- Brian will not learn how to study on his own.

Step 4. Decide which choice is best.

The picture shows Brian's decision. What did he decide to do?

Step 5. Judge the decision.

Brian makes fewer mistakes on his next spelling test. He thinks he made the right choice.

Now use the steps to make a decision for Tina. She promised her friend Jill she would go bicycling with her Saturday morning. Then Karen asked Tina to come over the same morning to play a video game. Tina will have to decide what to do. What decision do you think Tina would make?

On Your Own
Think about a decision you need to make. Then use the steps to help make your decision. Write what you would do at each step.

Think Back • *Study on your own with Study Guide page 251.*

1. What does making wise decisions have to do with growing up?
2. What five steps can be followed to make a wise decision?

Brian can use the steps now and for many other decisions in his life.

Puppets Come to Life

A puppet rolled out on the stage in a wheelchair. He had big eyes and a mop of hair sticking out beneath his hockey helmet. Other puppets on the stage were blind, or had only one arm, or were deaf. What was this puppet show all about?

This life-size puppet is used in the show.

A teacher named Barbara Aiello began making these puppets in 1977. She called them "The Kids on the Block." She wanted to help people understand the daily lives of children with disabilities. By understanding more about disabled children, people learn about the special strengths such children have.

The puppet with one arm is named Sarah Michaux. She is thirteen and loves sports. She even plays catcher for her softball team. If you were watching the puppet show, you could ask Sarah how she catches the ball or how she feels when someone stares at her. By meeting Sarah as a puppet, children can ask questions they might not ask disabled people they meet. By talking to the puppets, the children can learn to accept differences in others.

How do disabled children like the show? Barbara Aiello says "they are our biggest fans." They like it when people understand them better.

Talk About It

1. Why did Barbara Aiello make the puppets of children with disabilities?
2. How do you think the puppets help people appreciate others?

Health at Home

Learning About Family Differences

You have learned that you can enjoy meeting people who are different from you. You can learn new and interesting things from them. The members of your family are different from you. What interesting things could you learn from them?

You might look at a family picture album with an adult in your family. You might ask the adult to show you pictures that help answer questions such as these:

- What did you like to do when you were my age?
- Where did you live when you were my age?
- How did you decide to do the work that you do?

Reading at Home

Making Up Your Own Mind by Joy Wilt. Word, 1978. Learn how to make decisions and solve problems.

People by Peter Spier. Doubleday, 1980. Find out about many ways people are different.

Chapter 1 Review

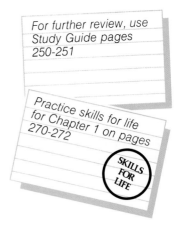

For further review, use Study Guide pages 250-251

Practice skills for life for Chapter 1 on pages 270-272

SKILLS FOR LIFE

Reviewing Lesson Objectives

1. Tell how having a good self-image and learning to appreciate differences in people can help a person. (pages 18–21)
2. Describe how feelings can cause changes in the way parts of the body work. (pages 24–25)
3. Explain how to feel better about oneself by using healthy ways to deal with anger. (pages 26–27)
4. Explain why disagreements can happen, and tell some ways to settle a disagreement. (pages 28–29)
5. List the five steps to follow when making a decision and tell how following these steps can help a person feel better about himself or herself. (pages 32–35)

Checking Health Vocabulary

Number your paper from 1–4. Match each definition in Column I with the correct word or words in Column II.

Column I

1. something a person does well
2. the way a person thinks of and sees himself or herself
3. to think well of someone or something
4. a difference in what people think

Column II

a. appreciate
b. disagreement
c. self-image
d. strength

Number your paper from 5–9. Next to each number write the word that best completes the sentence. Choose the words from the list below.

decisions	self-image
settle	weaknesses
appreciate	

5. If you like yourself, you likely have a good ____.
6. Getting to know many people might be a way to learn to ____ differences in people.
7. Talking things over is one way to ____ a disagreement.
8. People can make wise ____ by using the five steps.
9. A person usually has both strengths and ____.

Reviewing Health Ideas

Number your paper from 1–13. Next to each number write the word that best completes the sentence. Choose the words from the list.

alike	interesting
angry	result
appearance	self-image
choices	stomach
decisions	strength
different	weaknesses
feelings	

1. Every person looks and is ____.
2. A person's ____ makes that person look special.
3. Being able to draw pictures well might be a ____.
4. Knowing what you do well helps you have a good ____.
5. People who have a good self-image accept their ____.
6. Knowing people different from you helps make life ____.
7. Different ____ can cause changes in a person's body.
8. Feeling excited might affect the work of the ____.
9. Talking things over is a way to get rid of ____ feelings.
10. People disagree because all people are not ____.
11. Every person needs to know how to make wise ____.
12. One step in making a decision is to list the possible ____.
13. One ____ of a wise decision about studying might be doing better schoolwork.

Understanding Health Ideas

Number your paper from 14–24. Next to each number write the word or words that best answer the question.

14. What helps make people special?
15. What is self-image?
16. How do people with a good self-image feel about themselves?
17. What does it mean to appreciate someone?
18. How does the feeling of anger affect the heartbeat?
19. How does being treated unfairly make most people feel?
20. What is a good way to get rid of angry feelings?
21. What is one way to settle disagreements?
22. What is one kind of disagreement that cannot be settled?
23. What is the first step in making a decision?
24. What is the last step in making a decision?

Thinking Critically

Write the answers on your paper. Use complete sentences.

1. How might feeling good about yourself show in your appearance?
2. How can friends help each other improve in what they do not do very well? Give an example, such as finishing homework.

Chapter 2

How Your Body Works

Why will this girl have to stop wearing her favorite jacket? Have you ever had to stop wearing a favorite piece of clothing because it became too small?

This chapter will explain how your body grows and works. You will learn what your body is made of and how different parts work. Knowing how your body works and grows can help you take good care of your body. It can help you stay healthy now and all through your life.

Health Watch Notebook

Interview a relative or other adult who has heart disease. Ask the person how he or she found out about the problem and how it has affected his or her life. Also ask how he or she now copes with heart disease. Write what you have learned in your notebook.

cell (sel), the smallest part that makes up a living thing.

tissue (tish′ü), cells of the same kind grouped together.

organ (ôr′gən), several kinds of tissues that work together for a special purpose.

Bone cell

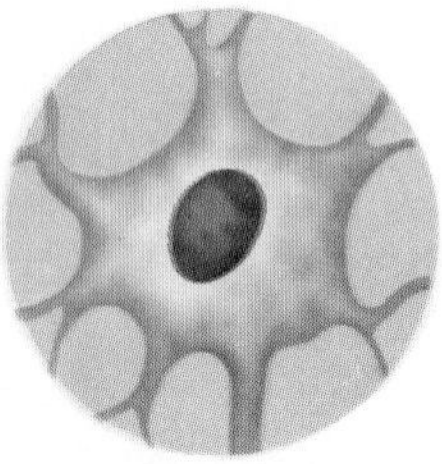

Nerve cell

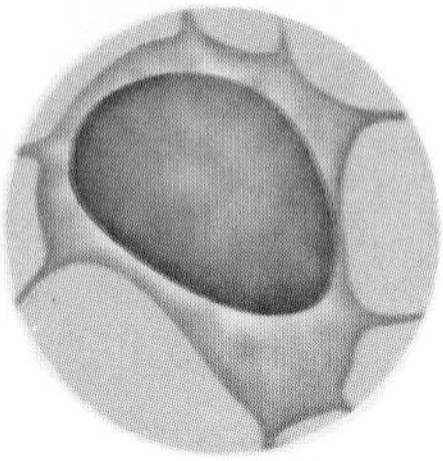

Skin cell

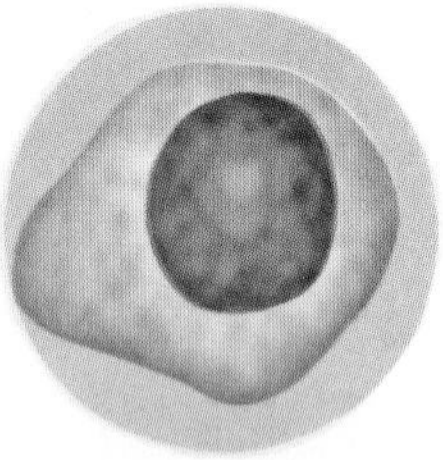

Fat cell

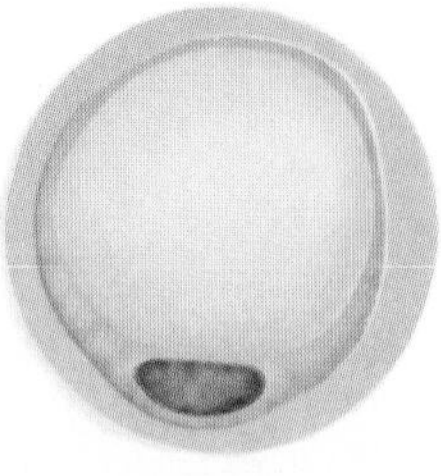

1 What Is Your Body Made Of?

Suppose someone asks you, "What are you made of?" By now you know some of the answer. You might say you are made of many parts, including skin, fat, muscles, nerves, bones, and blood.

The parts of your body look different and work differently. However, all parts of your body are alike in one way. All parts are made of tiny **cells.** Cells are the smallest living parts of your body. Since cells make up all parts of your body, they are often called the body's building blocks.

Find skin, fat, nerve, and bone cells in the pictures. Notice that different kinds of cells look different. Each kind of cell looks different because it does a different job in the body.

Cells of the same kind group together to form body **tissue.** Many nerve cells group together to form nerve tissue, or nerves. Bundles of muscle cells form muscle tissue. What do groups of bone cells form?

Two or more kinds of tissue grouped together form an **organ.** In a body organ the different tissues work together for a special purpose. The eye is an organ. Look at the picture on the next page to see some tissues that make up the eye. Nerve tissue in your eyes sends messages about light to your brain. Muscle tissue in your eyes moves your eyeballs. Nerve and muscle tissues in your eyes work together so you can see.

Some other organs in your body are your brain, heart, lungs, and stomach. Each organ is made of several different kinds of tissues. Each organ does special work to keep you alive and healthy.

Left: Different kinds of cells in your body look different. Cells of the same kind form body tissue.

Right: What different kinds of cells make up tissues in the eye?

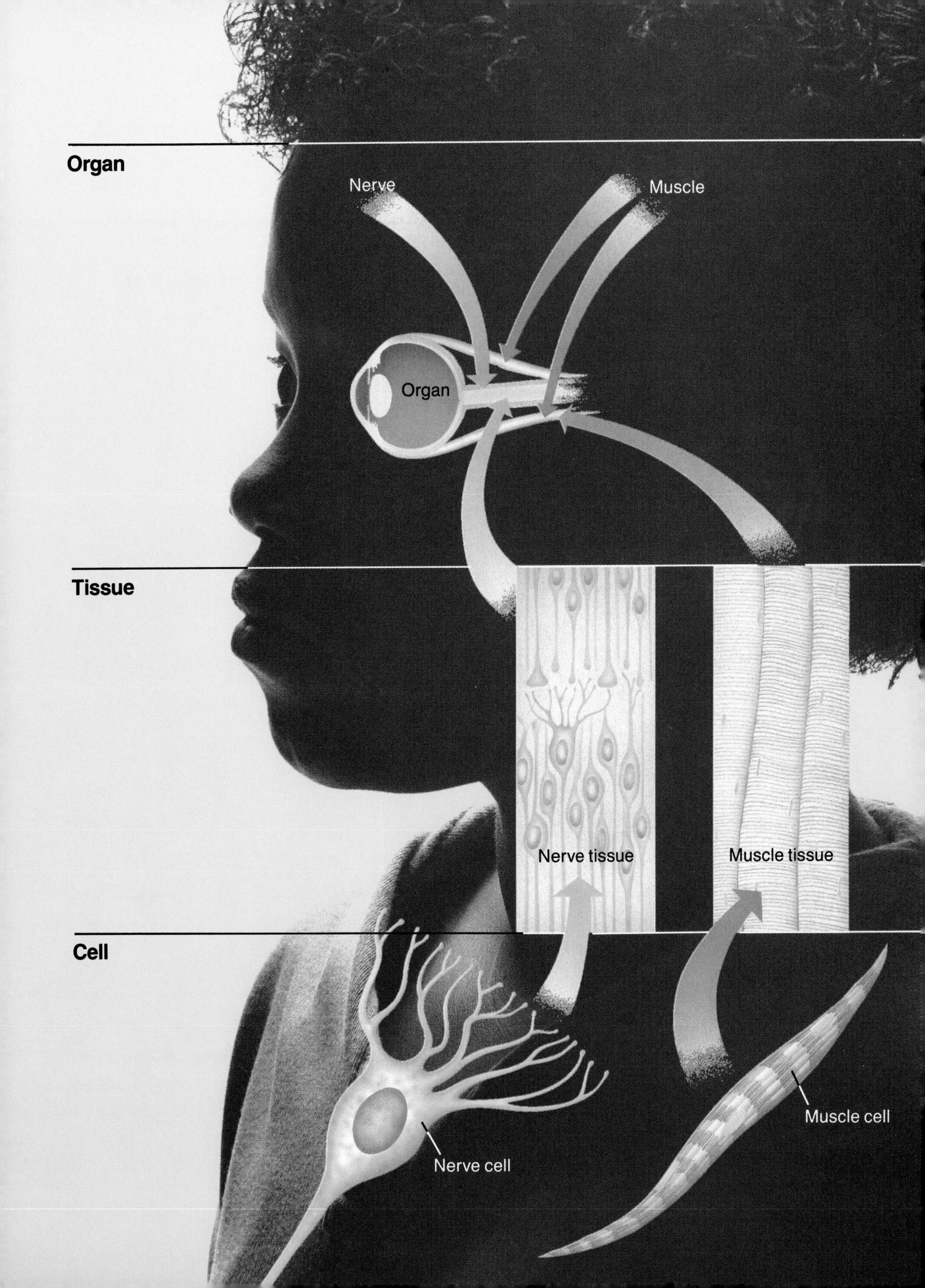
Organ
Nerve
Muscle
Organ
Tissue
Nerve tissue
Muscle tissue
Cell
Nerve cell
Muscle cell

system (sis′təm), a group of organs and body parts that work together to perform a job.

What Is a Body System?

Sometimes several organs and body parts work together to do a job. For example, your stomach and several more body parts work together to change food into a form cells can use. Your brain, nerves, and other body parts work together to help you think.

A group of body organs and parts that work together is a body **system.** Each system works to keep you alive and healthy. You can see four body systems on these two pages. What systems do the pictures show?

The digestive system changes food you eat.

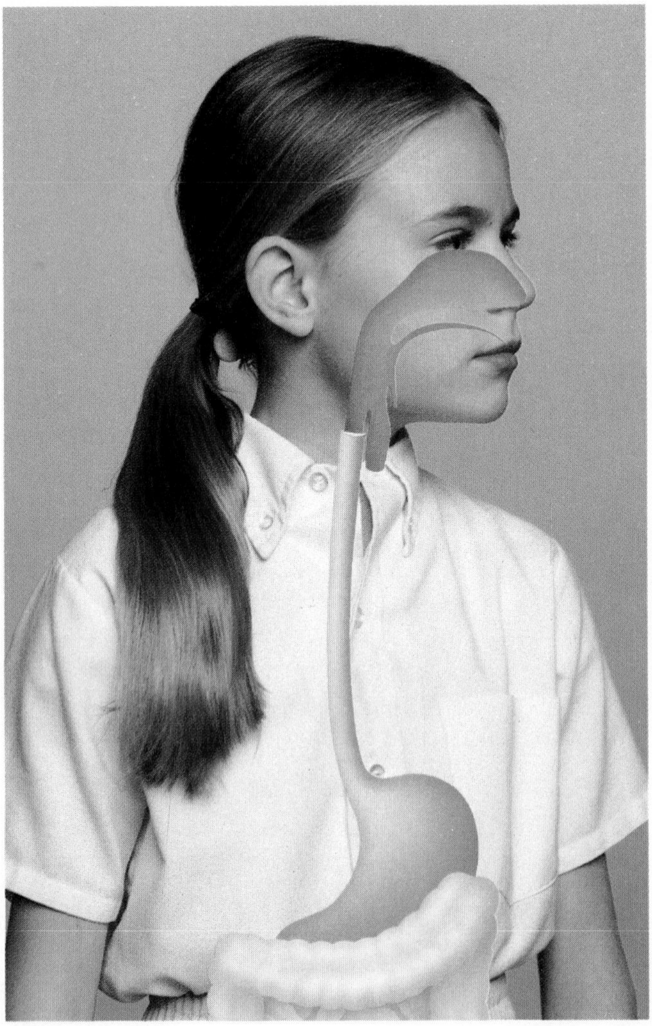

The circulatory system moves blood around your body.

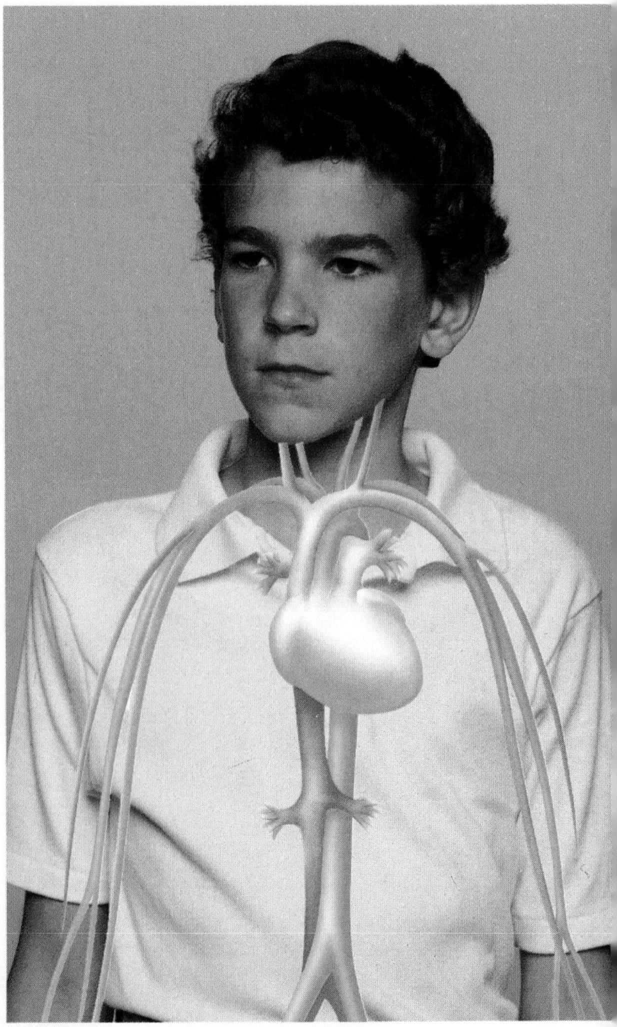

One body system helps you breathe. One changes food into a form your cells can use. Another makes it possible for you to think and act. Still another moves blood all around your body. Look at some of the organs and body parts that make up each system.

Think Back • *Study on your own with Study Guide page 252.*

1. What is a cell?
2. What is body tissue?
3. What is a body organ?
4. What is a body system?

The respiratory system helps you breathe.

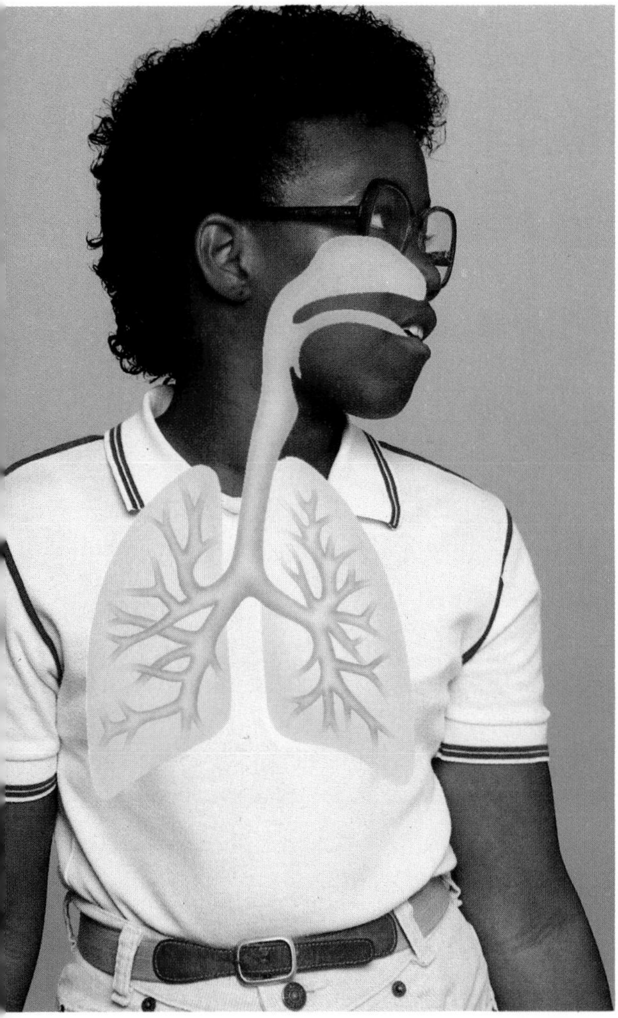

The nervous system helps you think and act.

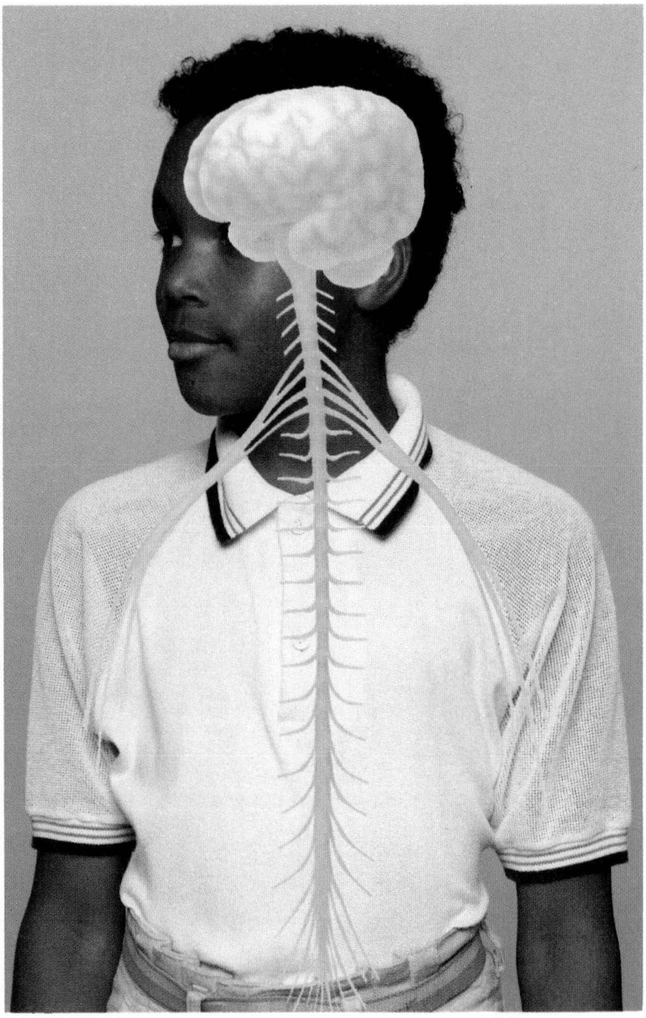

circulatory system
(ser′kyə lə tôr′ē sis′ təm)
the body system made up of the heart, blood, and blood vessels. This system moves materials to and from body cells.

Did You Know?
Day and night, your heart beats about ninety times a minute. An adult's heart beats about seventy to eighty times a minute. Your heart could beat three billion times in your life.

2 What Happens When Your Heart Beats?

You know your heart must beat all the time. Do you know why it must beat? Your heart is made of a certain kind of muscle. The heart muscle can contract. When the heart contracts, it gets smaller. Then the heart relaxes and becomes larger again. A heartbeat takes place each time the heart muscle moves this way.

Blood moves inside your body when your heart beats. Blood can move through the heart because the heart has spaces in it. When your heart gets smaller, blood is squeezed out. Each time the heart beats, blood is pumped out into tubes called blood vessels. Blood moves in the blood vessels all through your body.

You can feel your heartbeat. You can feel it by putting your hand on your chest. You can also feel your pulse—the push of blood through certain blood vessels. You can feel it at places where certain blood vessels are near the skin. Try to feel your pulse on the inside of your wrist. Then try to feel it at your neck.

Your heart, blood, and blood vessels make up the **circulatory system.** This system moves blood around and around in your body. Blood carries needed materials to every body cell. Blood carries wastes away from all body cells. You can see the parts of the circulatory system in the picture on the next page.

Notice how the outside of the heart looks in the large picture. See how the blood vessels lead into the heart.

Circulatory System

What is the job of the circulatory system?

Large blood vessels lead from your heart to all parts of your body.

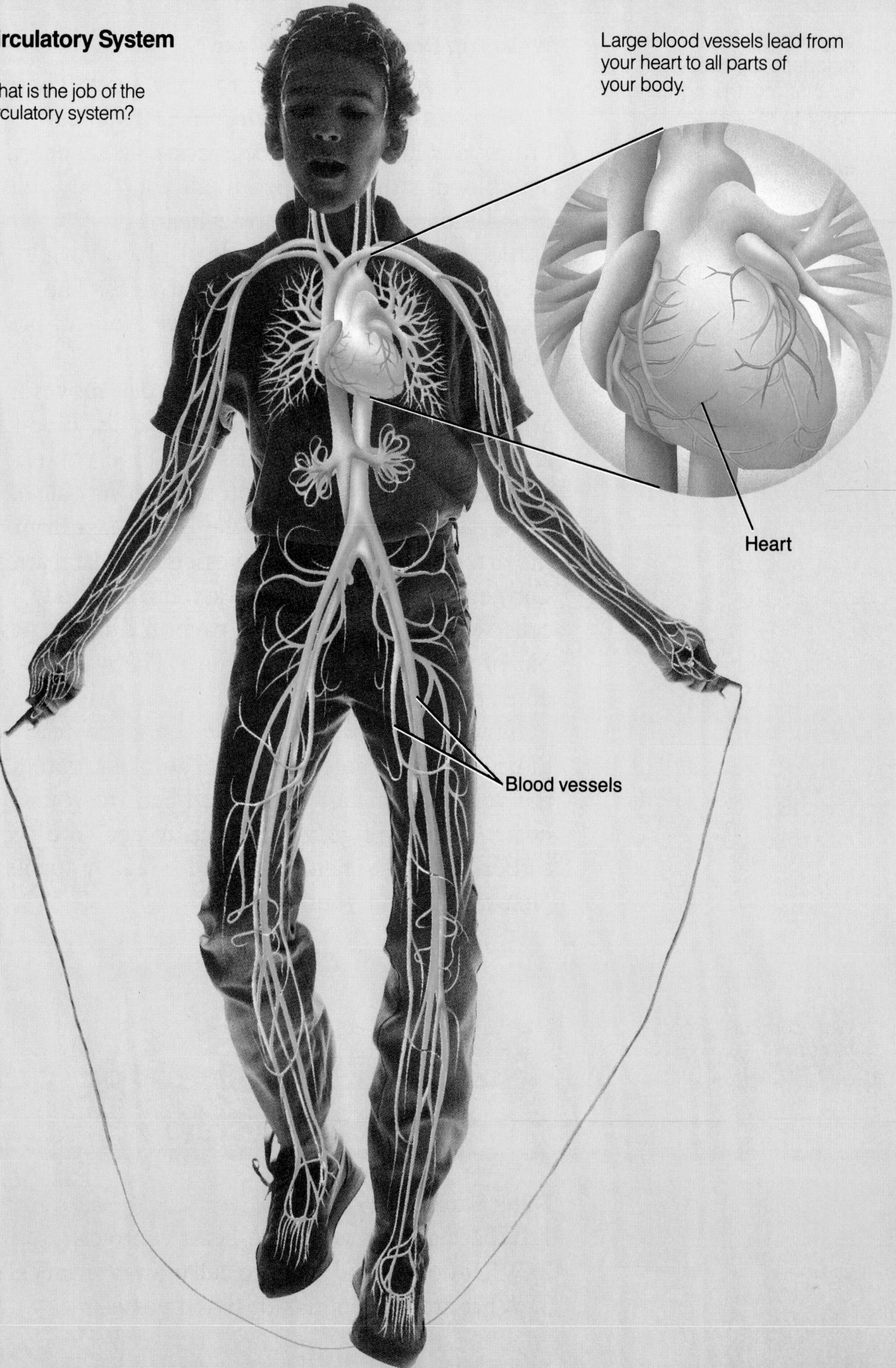

oxygen (ok′sə jen), a colorless, odorless gas in air that most living things need to stay alive.

carbon dioxide (kär′bən dī ok′sīd), a colorless, odorless gas that is a waste product of body cells.

What Trip Does the Blood Take?

Your heart pumps blood to your lungs. There, blood picks up **oxygen,** which is a gas in air. From your lungs blood goes back to your heart. The blood is then pumped to all your body cells. Blood then goes back to your heart.

Blood travels in three kinds of blood vessels, which are arteries, capillaries, and veins. The picture below shows how the three kinds of blood vessels are connected.

Blood with a fresh supply of oxygen moves in arteries from the heart to the body cells. Blood in arteries also carries nutrients from food you eat. Nutrients are substances you need to stay alive.

Oxygen and nutrients in the blood pass from the arteries into the tiniest vessels, the capillaries. Oxygen and nutrients then pass into the body cells. Wastes such as the gas **carbon dioxide** pass out of the cells at the same time. The wastes enter the blood.

Now the blood, which has taken up the carbon dioxide, leaves the capillaries. The blood enters the veins, which carry the blood back to your heart. Blood will go to the lungs to get rid of carbon dioxide. Then blood will be ready for its next trip around your body.

What connects arteries to veins?

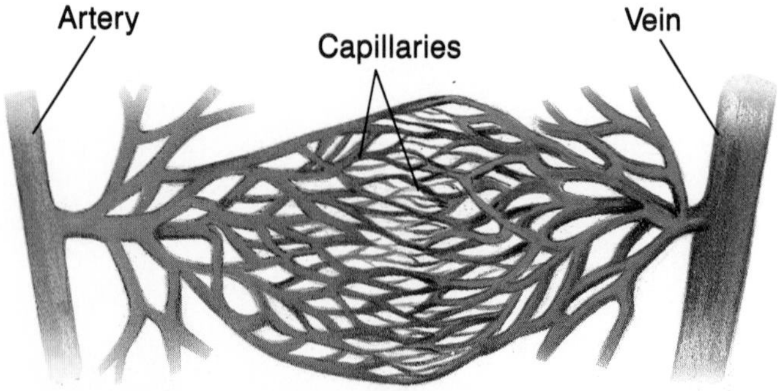

Think Back • *Study on your own with Study Guide page 252.*

1. What happens when the heart contracts?
2. What does blood carry to cells? away from cells?
3. What are three kinds of blood vessels?

Learning How Parts of the Body Work

1. Use an old hollow rubber ball with a small hole in it. Think about this ball as your heart. Then fill the ball with water through the hole. What does the water in the ball stand for?

Now squeeze the ball. Notice how the water spurts out of the hole each time you squeeze. What do you show each time you squeeze the ball?

2. Look in the puzzle below. Find the names of six parts of the body you learned about in your study of the circulatory system. Use your own paper and write the six words on it. Then tell what you know about each part.

T	R	Y	S	V	E	I	N	S	X	Y	Z	L
B	C	A	R	M	N	O	C	R	P	U	D	K
V	S	R	A	R	T	E	R	I	E	S	F	J
X	C	A	P	I	L	L	A	R	I	E	S	A
I	F	G	A	Z	R	V	X	P	U	L	S	E
H	E	A	R	T	O	B	B	L	O	O	D	T

3. Find your pulse at your wrist, neck, or at the side of your head. Count the number of pulse beats in one minute. Run in place twenty times. Then count the number of pulse beats for one minute again. What has happened to your pulse? What can you tell about how the pulse changes during exercise?

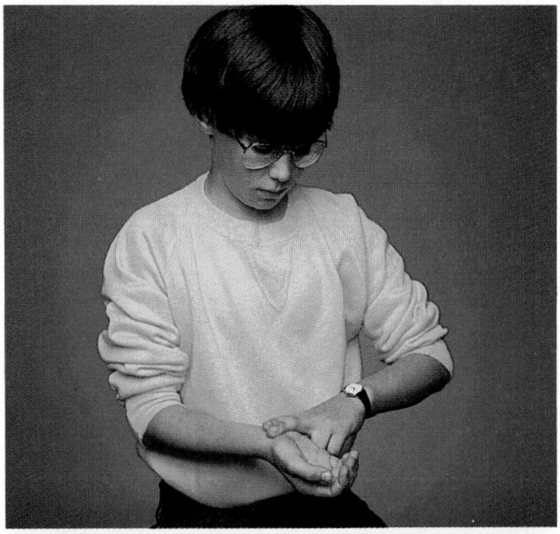

digestive system
(də jes′tiv sis′təm)
all the organs and body parts that help change food into a form cells can use.

On Your Own
Suppose you ate an apple. Write several paragraphs telling how the apple would be changed by different parts of your digestive system. Begin with your teeth biting into the apple. Use the picture on page 51 for help.

3 What Happens to Food You Eat?

You must have food to stay alive. All the body's cells need food to stay alive and do their work. First the food must be changed into a form cells can use. This changing of food is called digestion. Your body's **digestive system** does this job.

Digestion starts in the mouth. Your teeth break food into small pieces. Your tongue mixes the food with saliva. This liquid wets the food and starts to change it. The food you swallow goes down your food tube into your stomach. The food mixes with digestive juices that come from the walls of your stomach.

Before long, the food is partly digested. It now looks like a thick soup. The stomach squeezes this food into the small intestine. Juices from the small intestine and nearby organs finish digesting most of the food. The food now looks like a thin, watery soup. The thin liquid contains nutrients from the food you ate. The food has been changed to a form the cells can use. The thin liquid with nutrients goes into the capillaries that line the walls of the small intestine. From there the liquid passes into the blood and is carried to body cells.

Not all foods can be digested. Skins and seeds from fruits and vegetables are not digested. Such undigested food moves into the large intestine. Muscles in the large intestine then move this material and other wastes out of the body. The movement is called a bowel movement.

Think Back • *Study on your own with Study Guide page 252.*

1. What happens to food in your mouth?
2. What happens to food in your stomach and small intestine?
3. What does digested food have that cells need?

Digestive System

How do the organs and body parts shown help digest food you eat?

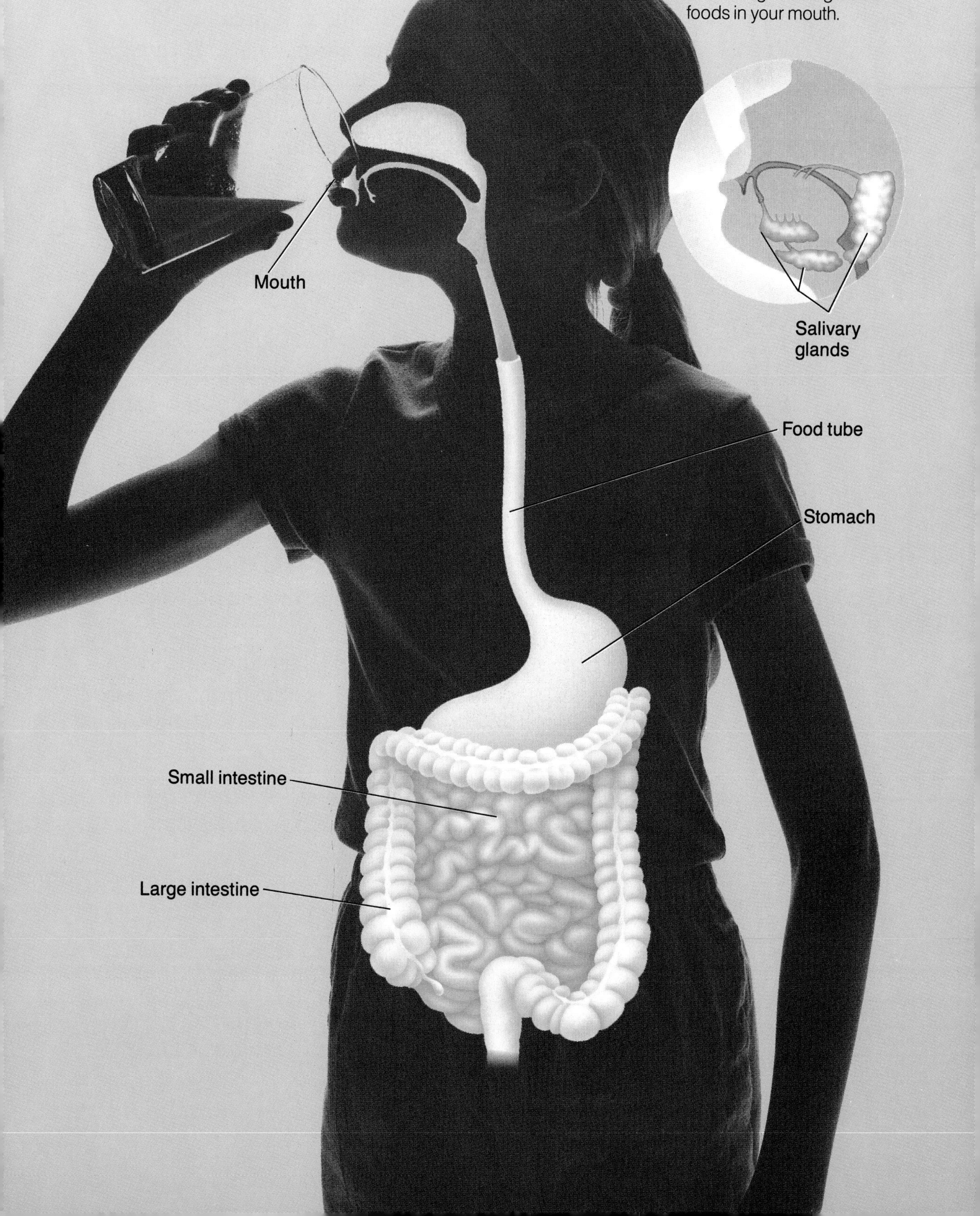

respiratory system
(res′pər ə tôr′ē sis′ təm)
all the organs and body parts that help the body take in oxygen and get rid of carbon dioxide.

Did You Know?
Lungs in adults are the size of footballs. They fill the chest from the bottom of the neck to the bottom of the ribs.

4 What Happens When You Breathe?

You must breathe if you are to stay alive. Your cells need oxygen in the air you breathe. You need to breathe, but you do not have to think about it. A part of your brain keeps you breathing all the time.

You breathe air into your body through your nose and often your mouth. Air is drawn into your lungs through a long tube called the windpipe. The windpipe goes down through your neck and then divides into two tubes. One tube leads into each lung.

The tubes divide into smaller and smaller parts that end in air sacs. Air sacs look like tiny balloons. They fill up with air when you breathe in. Air leaves them when you breathe out.

What happens in the lungs? Oxygen from the air you breathe passes through the walls of the air sacs. Then it passes into tiny blood vessels around the air sacs. The blood carries this oxygen to the heart. The heart then pumps this blood to all the body cells.

Something else happens in the lungs. Carbon dioxide leaves the blood. It passes from the blood into the air sacs. Then it leaves the body when you breathe out.

You can see the organs and body parts of the **respiratory system** on page 53. This system has two main jobs. What are they?

Think Back • *Study on your own with Study Guide page 253.*

1. What path does air take to your lungs?
2. What passes into the blood when it gets to your lungs?
3. What leaves blood when it is in your lungs?

Respiratory System

How does oxygen reach cells in your body?

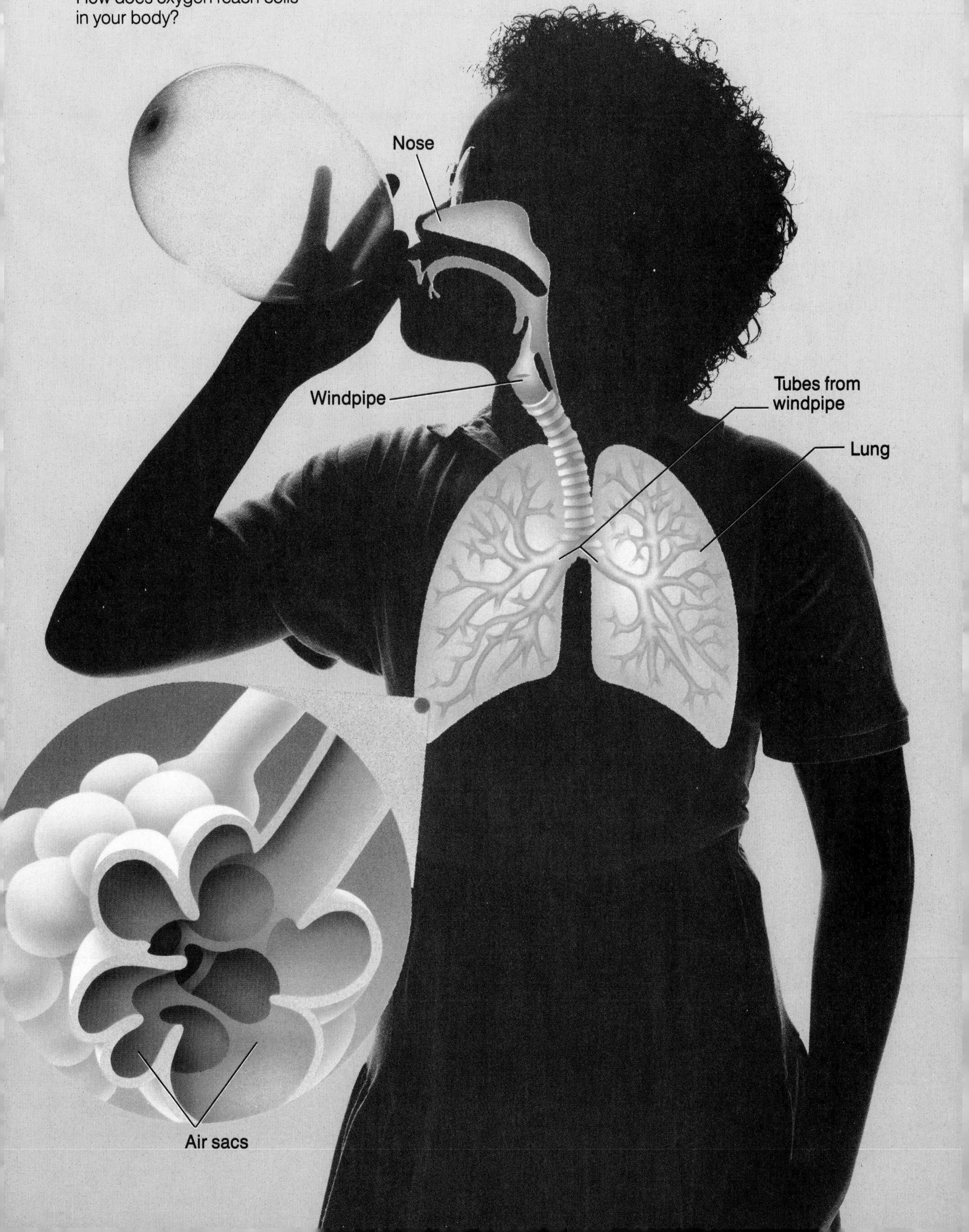

Health Activities Workshop

Learning More About How Your Body Works

1. Find out how exercise affects your breathing. Work with a partner. Ask your partner to watch as you sit and breathe in a normal way. Ask your partner to count the number of times your chest rises in one minute. Record this number on a sheet of paper. Now run in place twenty-five times. Sit down and ask your partner to count again the number of times your chest rises in one minute. Did the number of breaths you took in one minute change? If so, what reason can you suggest to explain the difference?

2. Find out about how teeth affect digestion by breaking food into bits. Get two lumps of sugar and two glasses of water. Put a whole lump of sugar in one glass. Crush the other lump of sugar and put it in the other glass. Watch to see in which glass the sugar dissolves more quickly. Suppose the water were saliva. How does saliva help prepare food so the body can use it?

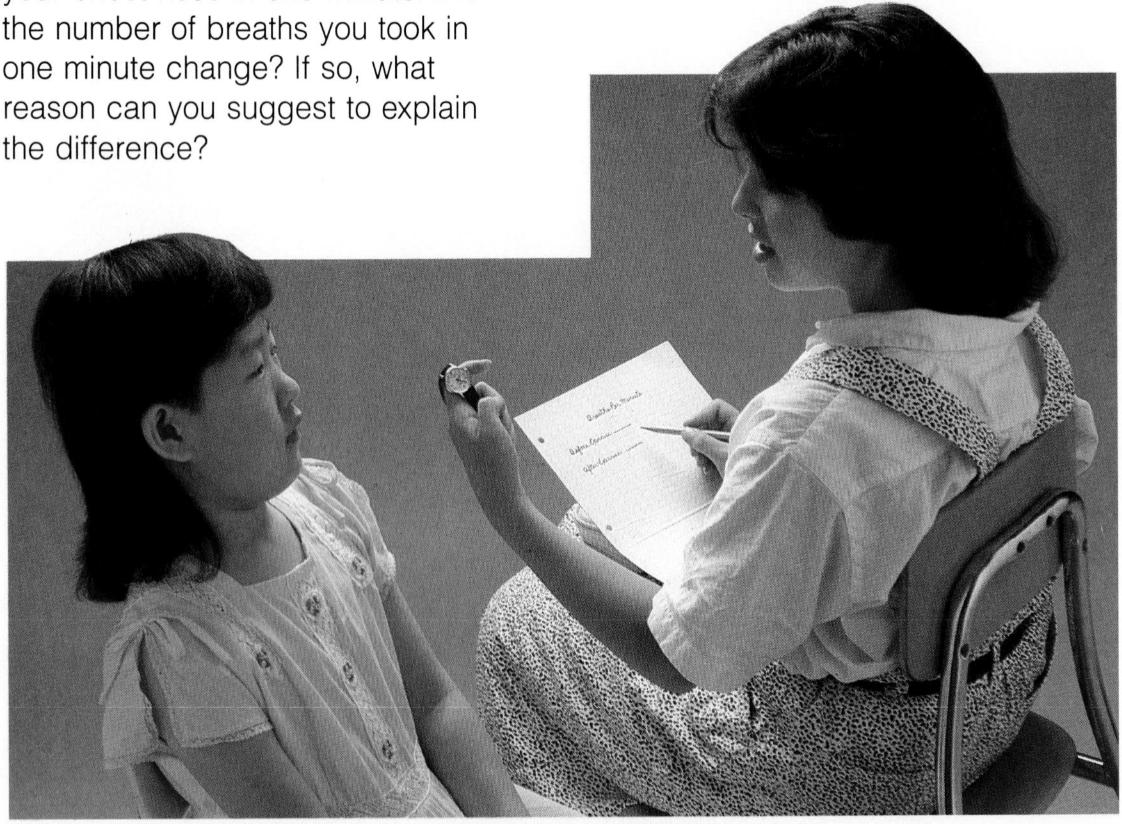

3. Look in the library for information about Dr. William Beaumont. Look in an encyclopedia or in the card catalog. Read about how this army doctor worked over a hundred and fifty years ago. He learned how the stomach worked before X rays were discovered.

Dr. Beaumont studied a man who had a hole in his side and stomach. The doctor could lift up a flap of skin and see the stomach at work. Find out how the stomach worked when the man was happy. Find out how the stomach worked when the man was sad. Learn what Dr. Beaumont found out about how long foods stay in the stomach.

Make up a play with others or write a story about what you have learned.

Looking at Careers

4. Do you think you would enjoy using a microscope to see how cells look and work? If so, you might like to be a **certified laboratory assistant.** A person with this job often works with a doctor or a medical technologist. A laboratory assistant looks at blood cells under a microscope. He or she keeps careful records of any tests made.

To be a certified laboratory assistant, a person studies for a year after finishing high school. Write a paragraph about the work of a certified laboratory assistant. What strengths might help a person in this job?

5 What Do Your Brain and Nerves Do?

Suppose you walk into a room one day and see an animal. Before you really know what animal it is, something must happen. Messages go from your eyes to your brain. Your brain then tells you the animal is a cat.

Did You Know?
Your brain is soft, spongy, and made of millions of tiny brain cells. Your brain is well protected by three covers. They are the outer, middle, and inner covers. A liquid between the middle and inner covers helps protect the brain against blows.

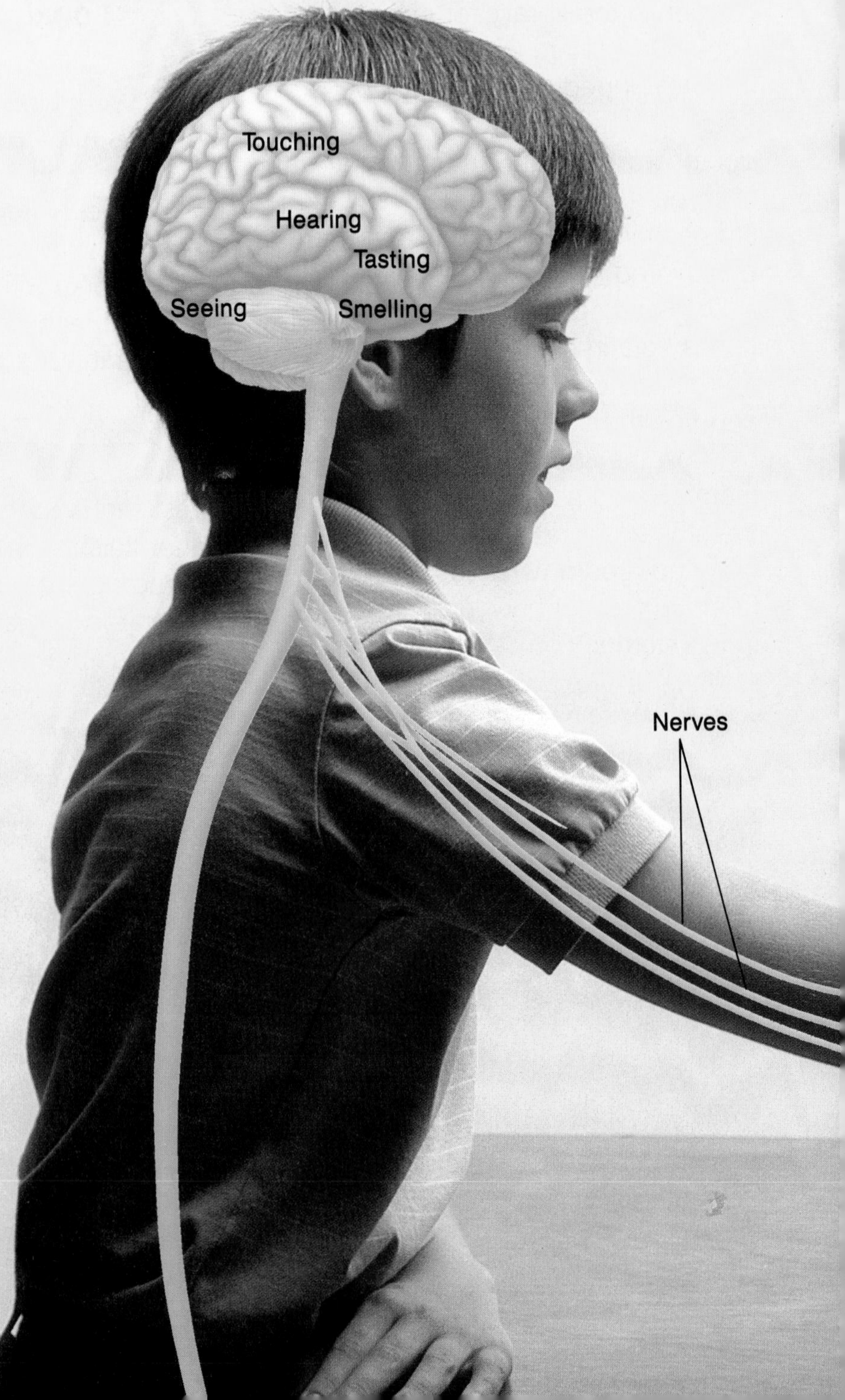

How will messages about how soft and furry the cat feels reach this girl's brain?

Suppose you want to pet the cat. Your brain sends messages to muscles in your back and arms. The messages tell your muscles to move so you can reach over. Your brain sends messages to muscles in your fingers telling how to move finger bones. Then you can pet the cat.

Your brain takes in information from all your senses. Your five main senses are seeing, hearing, touching, tasting, and smelling. Sensory nerves carry messages from sense organs to the brain. Your skin is a sense organ. What are the four other main sense organs?

Messages from sense organs go to special centers in your brain. For example, messages from the ears go to the hearing center. Notice the centers for hearing and the other senses in the picture.

What happens after messages come to the centers? The brain thinks about what to do. The brain might decide that nothing should be done. Suppose there is a need to do something. Then the brain sends messages to muscles. The messages go from the brain over motor nerves. These messages tell your muscles how and when to move.

nervous system (nėr′vəs sis′ təm) all the organs and body parts that control actions you direct and actions you do not direct.

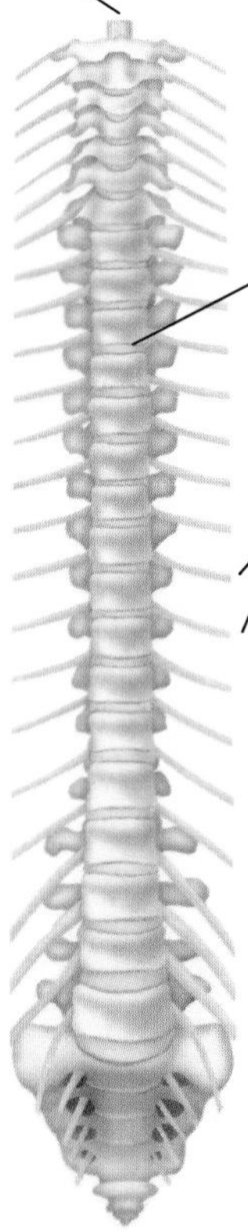

Why do you think the spinal cord is so well protected?

What Is the Nervous System?

Your brain, spinal cord, and nerves make up your **nervous system.** The spinal cord is a long cord of nerve tissue that extends from the brain down the length of your back. The picture on this page shows the chain of bones that encloses the spinal cord. This chain of bones is called the backbone, or spine. Run your finger down the middle of your back. Feel the bones that protect your spinal cord.

The spinal cord is a passageway for nerves. Sensory nerves carry messages through the spinal cord to the brain. Motor nerves carry messages from the brain through the spinal cord to the muscles. Notice in the picture on the next page that many nerves branch off from the spinal cord. Nerves divide and divide again. They reach all parts of your body. Nerves pass through all your body organs.

You can do things you want to do because of your nervous system. Your nervous system allows you to do things you must think about and direct.

Your nervous system also takes care of actions that you do not have to think about. These actions are called automatic actions. For example, you do not have to tell yourself to digest food. You do not have to direct your heart to pump blood. A special part of your nervous system controls automatic actions.

Think Back • *Study on your own with Study Guide page 253.*

1. How does your brain get information to think and act?
2. How do messages travel to and from your brain?
3. What automatic actions does the brain control?

Nervous System

The nervous system takes care of actions you direct, such as moving. The nervous system takes care of other actions you do not direct, such as digestion.

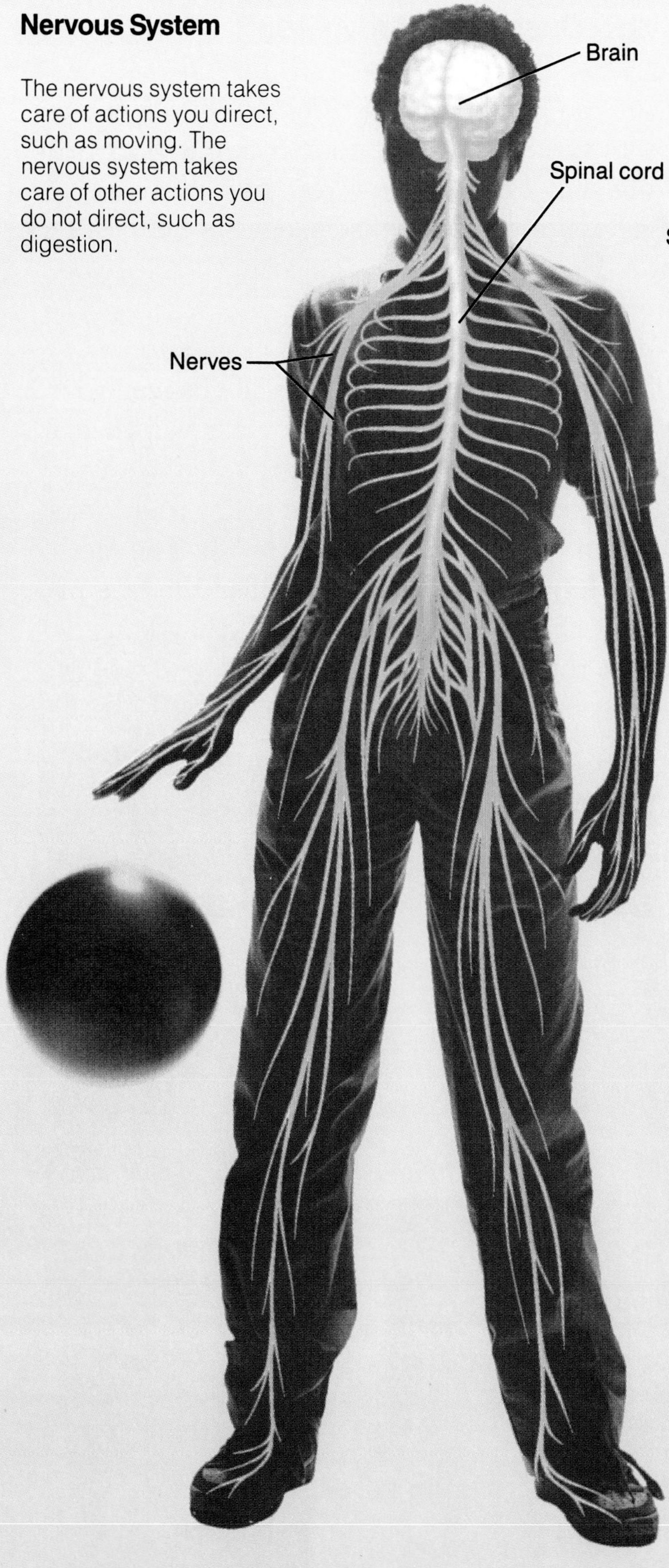

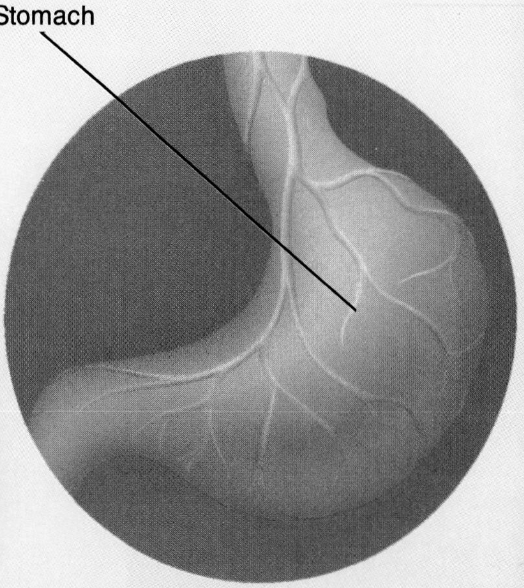

Each body organ has nerves that connect the organ with the brain. The brain then sends messages to control the work of the organ. What organ is shown here?

6 How Does Your Body Grow?

Can you match each person with his or her baby picture? Could someone pick out your baby picture only knowing how you look today?

The way a person looks changes as he or she grows. How have your looks changed since you were very young?

You will change more as you grow into an adult. The shape of your body will change. Your appearance will change. Some organs will change.

You get taller and heavier partly because your body makes more bone and fat cells. Your looks change in other ways as you grow up. The face of a baby, for example, is rounder than the face of an older child. An adult's face is usually longer and less round than a child's face.

The chart below shows ways your body has changed since you were born. The chart also shows ways you will change as you keep growing.

Notice how different parts of the body change. How does your head change in size as you grow from a baby to an adult? How does each leg grow? The trunk is the part of the body from the neck to the top of the legs. How much bigger is an adult's trunk than a baby's?

You do not stop growing when you have reached your adult size. You just grow more slowly and in different ways. Bones grow longer during childhood and the teen years. Bones stop growing longer when adult height is reached. Bones grow heavier for about twenty years after you reach adult size.

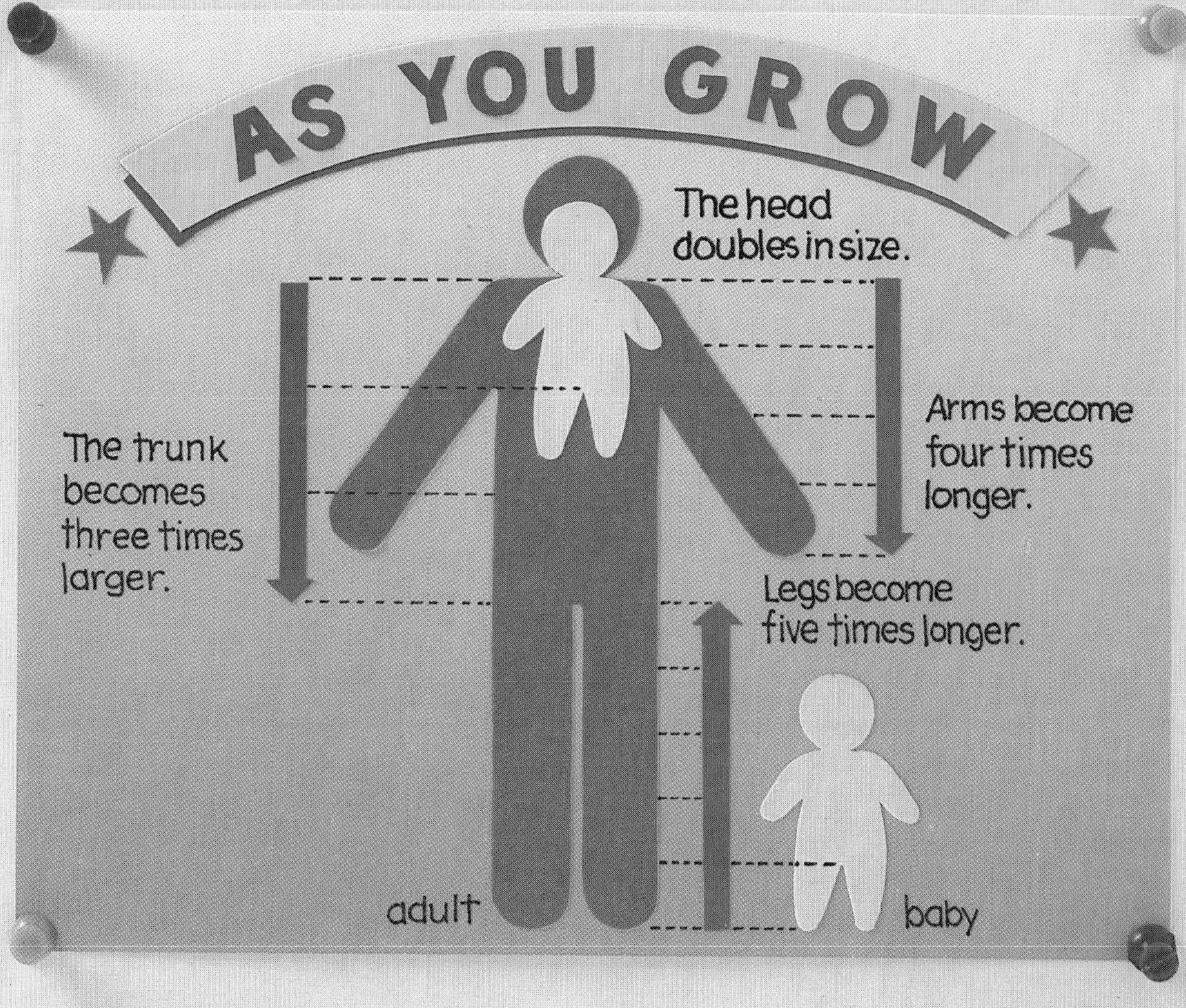
AS YOU GROW
The head doubles in size.
The trunk becomes three times larger.
Arms become four times longer.
Legs become five times longer.
adult
baby

What Is Special About How You Grow?

Could you pick out your best friend in a crowd of people? Of course you could. Your best friend has his or her own special looks. Unless you have an identical twin, you also have your own special looks. Only identical twins look almost just like each other.

Each person also grows in his or her own special way. You have a special size and shape. Other people have their special sizes and shapes. The children in the picture are all about the same age. Yet none is the same height and weight. Each one has a different body shape. One young person has a small, slim body. Another young person has a larger, rounder body.

Now, or in the next few years, you will grow taller and heavier very rapidly. A rapid gain in height or weight is called a growth spurt.

Each boy and girl is about the same age. Notice that each person has a size and shape special to that person. Each person will keep growing in the way that is right for him or her.

Everyone has a growth spurt. During the period of rapid growth, you will reach almost full adult height. You will grow into the adult shape that is right for you. Not everyone begins the growth spurt at the same age. Not everyone grows the same amount during a growth spurt.

Girls usually start to grow heavier and taller between ages nine and thirteen. Boys usually start to grow heavier and taller between the ages of eleven and fifteen. The growth spurt means you are starting to have the body of an adult.

You can help keep your body healthy as you grow. You can eat the right foods and get the rest and exercise you need. Keeping healthy helps your body grow as it should.

On Your Own
Write one or two paragraphs telling how a baby will change during life. Describe ways the baby's body will change as he or she grows. You might describe other ways the baby will change too, such as new skills the baby will learn.

Think Back • *Study on your own with Study Guide page 253.*

1. What causes the body to get taller and heavier?
2. How do a baby's head and legs change as he or she grows?

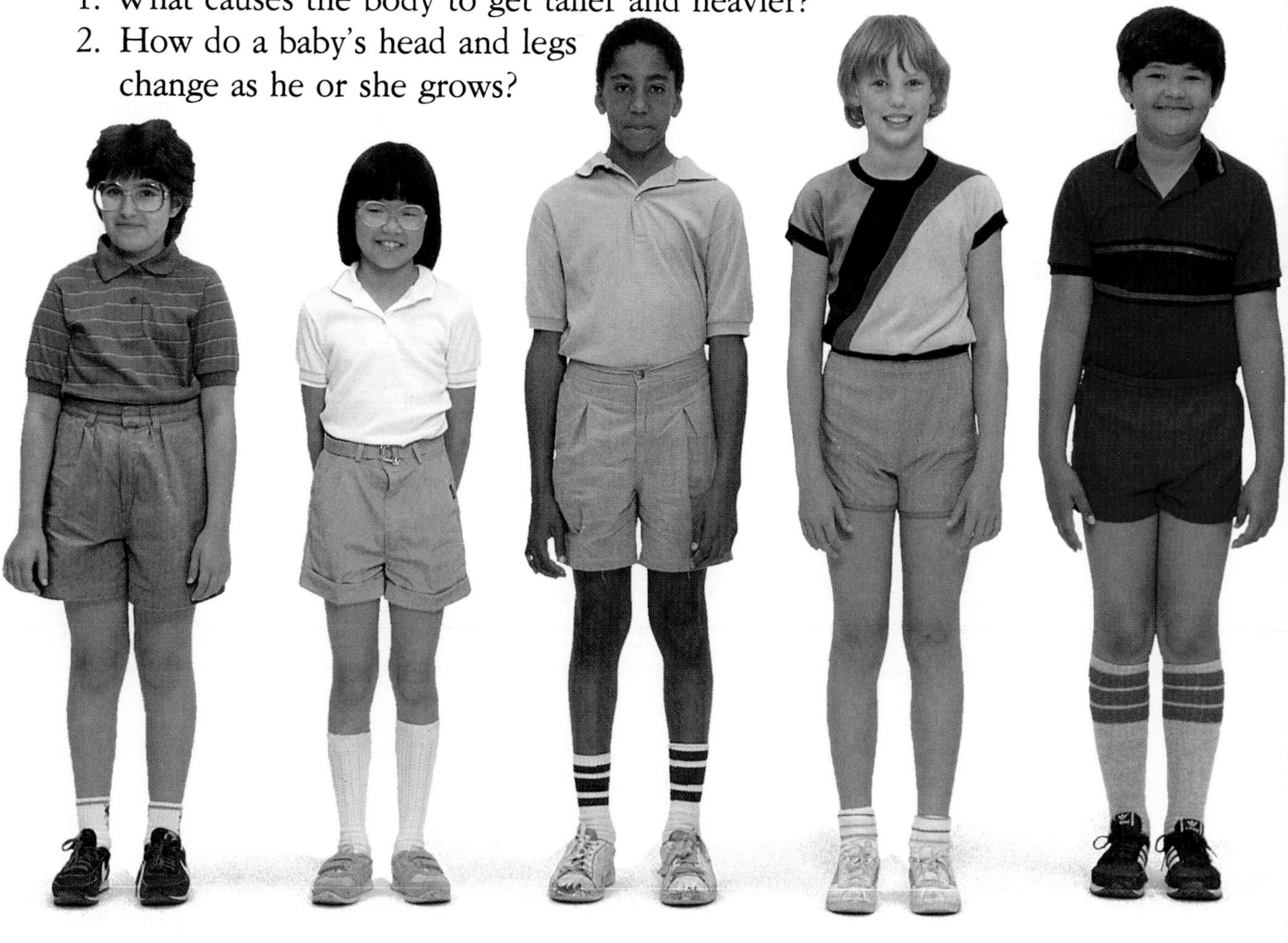

Health Focus

Dr. Laënnec and the First Stethoscope

Over a hundred and fifty years ago, a French doctor named René Laënnec had a problem. He was taking care of a sick person who was very fat. He thought something was wrong with the person's heart. However, the only way he could hear the person's heartbeat was by putting his ear on the person's chest. He could not hear the heartbeat through the fat.

About that time the doctor saw some children playing with a hollow log. One child was scratching the end of the log with a pin. The other child was listening at the other end of the log. This child was laughing and saying, "I can hear that pin scratch."

The children's game gave the doctor an idea. He rolled up a sheet of paper very tightly. He put one end of the rolled paper on the sick person's chest. He put the other end against his own ear. Now the doctor could hear the heart, even through the person's fat.

Dr. Laënnec later made a tool he used to listen to hearts. The tool was a stethoscope. Doctors today use a stethoscope like the one shown here.

Talk About It

1. What did Dr. Laënnec use for his first stethoscope?
2. How did the invention of the stethoscope help people's health?

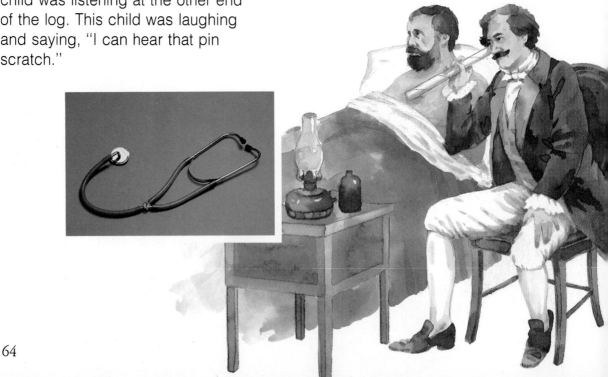

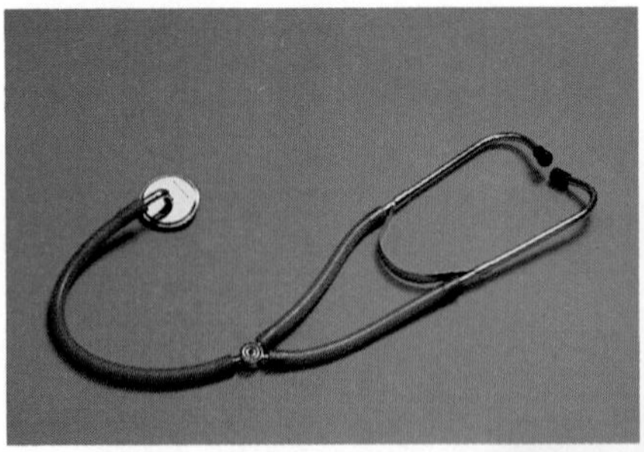

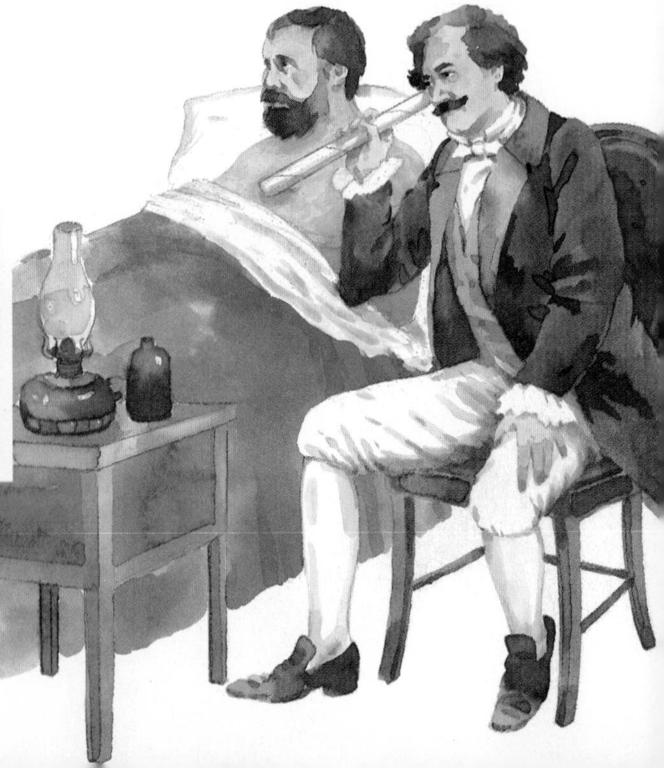

Sharing Information about the Heart

These ideas tell about how to take care of your heart. You might want to discuss these ideas with your family.

- Get plenty of exercise.
Exercise helps your heart become stronger. It helps your heart work better.

- Avoid being overweight.
Your heart must work harder when you are overweight.

- Get plenty of sleep.
When you sleep, your heartbeat slows down. Your heart gets a chance to rest.

Talk over the kinds of activities you and your family like to do. Which activities might help keep your heart healthy? Try to think of ways you and your family can do these activities regularly.

Reading at Home

Brain Power, Secrets of a Winning Team by Pat Sharp. Lothrop, 1984. Read more about how the brain works.

Breathing by John Gaskin. Watts, 1984. Find out how you use air to make sounds, cough, and sneeze.

Chapter 2 Review

Reviewing Lesson Objectives

1. Tell what tissues, organs, and systems are. (pages 42–45)
2. Explain what a heartbeat is. Tell what blood carries to and away from cells. (pages 46–48)
3. Explain the job of the digestive system. (pages 50–51)
4. Explain what happens inside the lungs to the oxygen you breathe. (pages 52–53)
5. Explain how the brain gets information to act on. Tell how messages get to and from the brain. (pages 56–59)
6. Describe ways people change as they grow. (pages 60–63)

For further review, use Study Guide pages 252-253

Practice skills for life for Chapter 2 on pages 273-274

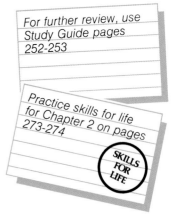

SKILLS FOR LIFE

Checking Health Vocabulary

Number your paper from 1–14. Match each meaning in Column I with the correct word or words in Column II.

Column I

1. the system that takes in oxygen and gets rid of carbon dioxide
2. similar cells grouped together
3. a substance in food the body needs
4. the system that takes care of actions you direct and actions you do not direct
5. the system that carries food and oxygen to cells
6. the smallest living part of the body
7. several kinds of tissues that work together
8. a group of organs and body parts that work together
9. a gas that is a waste product of most cells
10. the system that changes food into a form cells can use
11. a gas in air that people need to stay alive
12. a time of very rapid growth
13. the blood vessels that connect arteries and veins
14. the passageway for nerves leading to and away from the brain

Column II

a. capillaries
b. carbon dioxide
c. cell
d. circulatory system
e. digestive system
f. growth spurt
g. nervous system
h. nutrient
i. organ
j. oxygen
k. respiratory system
l. spinal cord
m. system
n. tissue

Reviewing Health Ideas

Number your paper from 1–14. Next to each number write the word or words that best complete the sentence. Choose the words from the list.

blood	heartbeat
bones	lungs
brain	mouth
carbon dioxide	organs
cells	sense organs
food tube	small intestine
head	windpipe

1. ___ make up all body parts.
2. Body parts and ___ make up a system.
3. Blood leaves the heart during a ___.
4. Blood goes to the ___ to pick up oxygen.
5. Digestion starts in the ___.
6. Food moves down the ___ into the stomach.
7. Most digestion takes place in the ___.
8. The ___ carries digested food to all body cells.
9. Oxygen is drawn down the ___ into the lungs.
10. ___ leaves the body when a person breathes out.
11. The spinal cord connects the ___ to all body nerves.
12. Eyes and the other ___ send information to the brain.
13. During childhood and teen years, ___ grow longer.
14. A child's ___ doubles in size as he or she grows.

Understanding Health Ideas

Number your paper from 15–26. Next to each number write the word or words that best answer the question.

15. What kind of cells form muscle tissue?
16. What are two kinds of tissues in your eye?
17. What are the names of two systems in your body?
18. What carries blood in the body?
19. What are the tiniest blood vessels in the body?
20. What liquid starts digesting food in the mouth?
21. Where does partly digested food go when it leaves the small intestine?
22. Which parts of the body can breathe in air?
23. What nerves carry messages from the brain through the spinal cord to the muscles?
24. What is the chain of bones that encloses the spinal cord?
25. What is an example of an automatic action?
26. What is the time of rapid growth around the teen years called?

Thinking Critically

Write the answers on your paper. Use complete sentences.

1. Your alarm clock rings. What happens in your body before you can turn the alarm off?
2. How can you help parts of your body work together as they should?

Chapter 3

Keeping Yourself Fit

The boy in the picture plays an active game after school. Do you know how the game helps keep him healthy? Being active helps keep people physically fit, which is important for staying healthy.

This chapter will explain how being fit helps keep parts of the body healthy, especially the heart and muscles. You will also learn new exercises to help you become more fit now and keep you healthy as you grow older.

Health Watch Notebook

Collect news or magazine articles about athletes you admire. Put the articles in your notebook. For each athlete, write down what types of fitness his or her sport builds, and why you admire that person.

1 How Can Physical Fitness Help You?
2 How Can Having Muscle Fitness Help You?
3 How Can You Build Physical Fitness?
4 How Do Sports Skills Help You?
5 How Can You Enjoy Playing Sports and Games?

physical (fiz′ə kəl) **fitness,** the ability to exercise, play, and work without getting tired or injured easily.

Did You Know?
Your body needs a certain amount of fat to work properly. The body stores some vitamins in body fat, including vitamins A and D. Body fat helps protect the body against injuries and protects muscles and organs. Body fat also helps keep the body warm and stores energy.

Being fit can help keep you from having too much body fat, which might harm your health. When you do not have too much body fat you look better and you can play and do activities easier.

1 How Can Physical Fitness Help You?

Look at the young people shown on the next page. Which person needs to be fit? You are right if you guessed all of them. **Physical fitness** helps people work and play all day. Physical fitness also helps keep people healthy.

Maybe you enjoy playing games with your friends or being active by yourself. With physical fitness, you can play without getting too tired and without injuring yourself easily. You can do more activities with less effort. You can climb, run, jump, and use your muscles for many activities. Your muscles can also move freely and easily.

Being fit helps keep your heart healthy. Your heart is a muscle that grows stronger with regular exercise. The heart of a fit person pumps more blood with less work than the heart of a less fit person. Keeping the heart strong through regular exercise also helps prevent heart diseases.

Being fit also helps people have healthy lungs. Blood picks up oxygen in the lungs and carries it to the muscles. Regular exercise helps oxygen get from the lungs to the muscles.

Everyone in the pictures is fit. Their strong muscles move easily and freely. They can work and play for a long time without getting tired. How might being fit help them feel good about themselves?

Think Back • *Study on your own with Study Guide page 254.*

1. What can fitness help a person do?
2. In what ways can physical fitness help a person stay healthy?

Each person can work, play, and exercise a long time without getting tired because each person is fit.

flexibility
(flex′sə bil′ə tē), the ability of muscles to move easily and freely.

2 How Can Having Muscle Fitness Help You?

A person with good physical fitness has good muscle fitness. Flexibility, strength, and endurance are the three kinds of muscle fitness. People who want to be healthy want to have all three kinds of muscle fitness.

Did You Know?
Exercises that cause you to bounce when you stretch might make your muscles sore. To build flexibility, you should do stretching exercises slowly without bouncing.

What Is Flexibility?

Flexibility is the ability to move the body easily. You can move easily in many different ways if your muscles have flexibility. For example, a dancer who bends, twists, and turns easily has flexibility. A plumber who bends and reaches into out-of-the-way places also has flexibility. The boy in the picture is testing his flexibility by doing an exercise called sit and reach.

People with flexibility are less likely to have sore and injured muscles. Their muscles are used to being stretched and moved. You can help your own flexibility by using and stretching all your muscles. Playing active games is one way to use and stretch your muscles.

Sit and Reach
Tape a ruler to a large box as shown. The six-inch (15.24 cm) mark should be even with the edge of the box closest to you. Rest your feet against the box and keep your legs straight. Put one hand on top of the other so the tips of your middle fingers are even. Slowly reach forward and try to touch the ruler. Hold for three seconds. The farther you reach, the better the flexibility in your legs and back.

What Is Muscle Strength?

Muscle strength is how much force a muscle can produce. A person with muscle strength can lift, carry, push, or pull heavy objects without feeling tired or sore. Think about a person who carries large trays of food in a restaurant. He or she needs muscle strength to work without feeling tired or sore. Muscle strength helps you jump and climb when you play. What activities do you enjoy that need muscle strength?

Using your muscles keeps them from getting weak. If you have weak muscles, you might find it hard to do everyday jobs or play actively. The girl in the picture is doing sit-ups to find out about her muscle strength.

You can build strength by using your muscles to push, carry, and move objects. Getting regular exercise in active play also helps a person build muscle strength.

muscle strength (strengkth), the ability of muscles to produce a great deal of force.

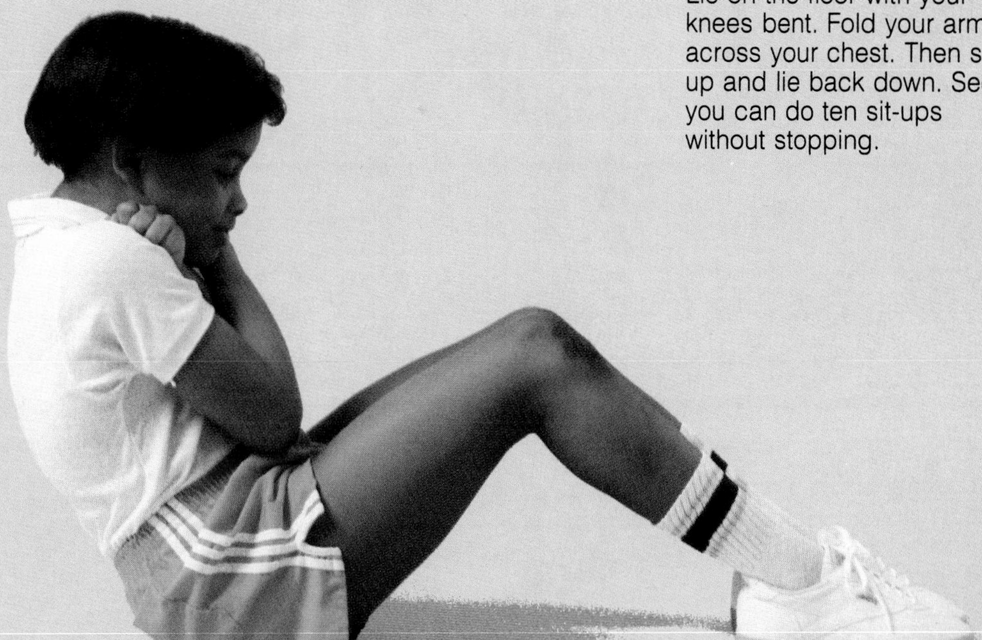

Sit-Up
Lie on the floor with your knees bent. Fold your arms across your chest. Then sit up and lie back down. See if you can do ten sit-ups without stopping.

muscle endurance (en dür′əns), the ability to use muscles for a long time without getting tired.

On Your Own
Think of two jobs you might like to have when you grow up. Write a paragraph for each job describing how having muscle fitness would help you in the job.

What Is Muscle Endurance?

Have you ever gone hiking with a group? Who could hike the longest without needing to rest? A person with good endurance can hike for a long time without having tired muscles. **Muscle endurance** is the ability of muscles to exercise a long time without getting tired.

Muscle endurance helps people work and play. For example, a person who puts stock on shelves in a supermarket needs to bend and reach a long time without getting tired. A person who cuts hair needs to stand and work a long time without getting tired. You can ride a bicycle or row a boat for a long time without getting tired if you have good muscle endurance. The boy in the picture is testing his endurance by doing the stride jump.

Stride Jump
Stand with your right leg forward and your left leg back. Put your left arm out in front of you and your right arm out in back of you. Jump up, moving your left foot forward and your right foot back. As your legs change places, move your left arm back and your right arm forward. Try to repeat the stride jump for one minute without stopping.

Endurance also helps people have good **posture.** Your posture is the way you hold your body when you stand, walk, or sit. Endurance, as well as muscle strength, helps you hold your body in a balanced but comfortable way. The girl in the pictures has good posture. She can sit, stand, and walk for a long time without feeling tired.

posture (pos′chər), the way a person holds the body while sitting, standing, or walking.

Think Back • *Study on your own with Study Guide page 254.*

1. What are three kinds of muscle fitness?
2. How can each kind of muscle fitness help people?
3. How can having good posture help a person?

People with good posture often have fewer muscle problems, such as backaches.

Health Activities Workshop

Checking Your Fitness

1. Read again how to do the tests for flexibility, muscle strength, and muscle endurance on pages 72, 73, and 74. If possible, take these tests. You can take them at school or at home. You might want to ask someone to watch you and possibly help you.

2. Find out about how active you are. Make a chart like the one shown here. For one week, write on your chart how much time you spend playing active games and exercising. Write how much time you spend watching TV. Look at your chart at the end of the week. Compare the amount of time you spent watching TV and the amount of time you spent playing games and exercising. Write a sentence or two about how watching too much TV might keep a person from being fit.

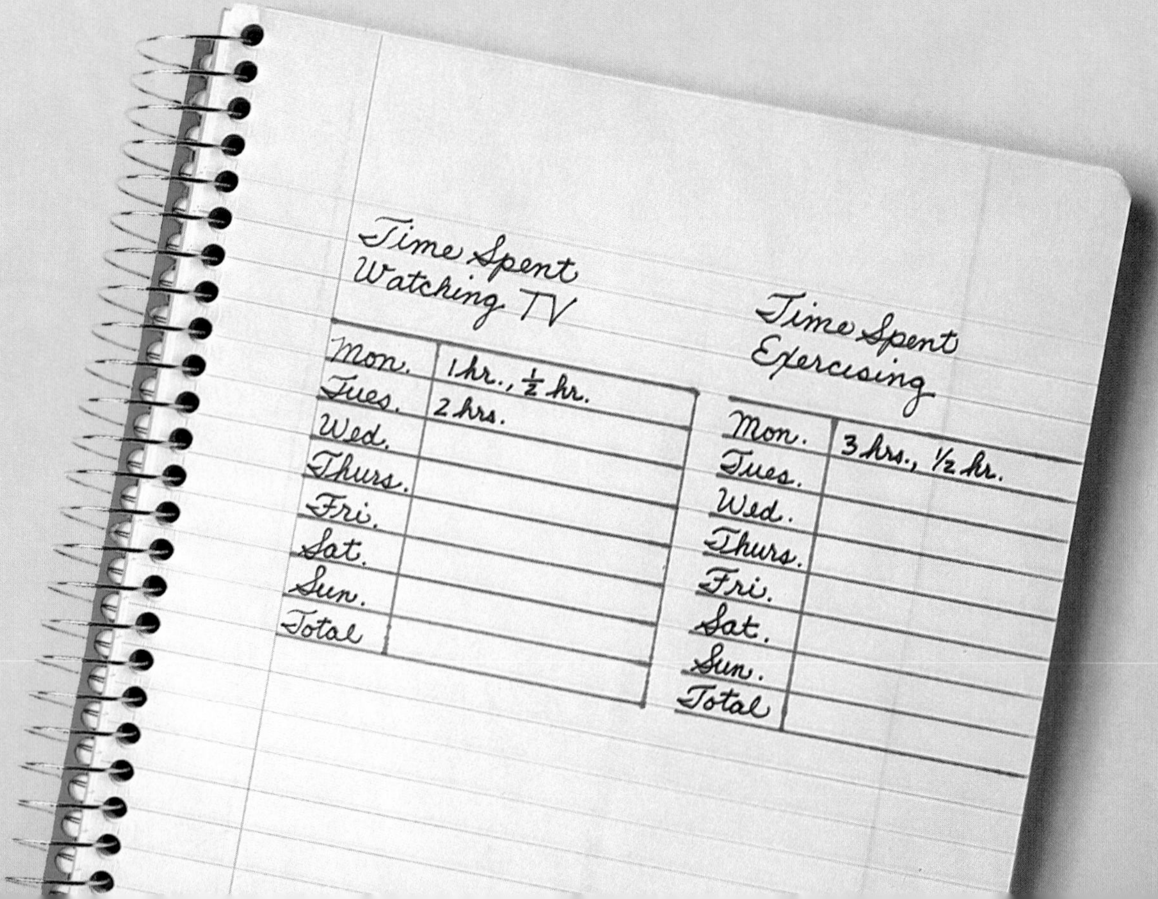

Time Spent Watching TV
Mon. 1 hr., ½ hr.
Tues. 2 hrs.
Wed.
Thurs.
Fri.
Sat.
Sun.
Total
Time Spent Exercising
Mon. 3 hrs., ½ hr.
Tues.
Wed.
Thurs.
Fri.
Sat.
Sun.
Total

3. Look at ads and stories about physical fitness on TV and in newspapers. Notice ways fitness helps people. Then make up your own ad for fitness. Draw a picture and write a fitness message to go with your ad.

4. Make a poster that shows how one kind of muscle fitness helps you. Include a slogan such as the one shown below. What kind of muscle fitness do you think the slogan suggests?

Reach up and out for fitness

Looking at Careers

5. Many schools have a **physical education teacher.** This person helps students learn about physical fitness. A physical education teacher must go to college to learn about how the body works. He or she also learns many sports, games, and exercises that build fitness. The physical education teacher in the picture leads students in bending and stretching exercises for flexibility. Draw a picture of an activity a physical education teacher might show to build muscle strength.

3 How Can You Build Physical Fitness?

Suppose you decide you want to improve your own fitness. What might you do?

First, you might decide to spend as much time as you can in active play. You could choose the activity this boy enjoys, play soccer, swim, or ride a bicycle. Such playing makes your heart beat faster and helps keep your heart strong. These activities can also help you lose extra body fat.

Second, you might plan to do certain exercises regularly at home. You could do the exercises shown on pages 80–85. These exercises help build the three kinds of muscle fitness as well as fitness of the heart and lungs.

However you choose to build fitness, you need to exercise a little harder than you usually do. You also need to increase the amount of exercise you do. Be sure to start slowly and increase the amount of exercise you do little by little.

Jumping rope helps build a healthy heart. A person who jumps rope regularly also builds muscle strength and endurance.

What Activities Help Build Fitness?

When you choose activities to help build fitness, be sure to choose activities you enjoy doing. Then you will be more likely to do them regularly. The chart shows activities that people can do together or alone. See how an activity you enjoy helps build fitness.

Once you start being active regularly, you might not want to stop. Many people exercise regularly to relax and feel good.

Think Back • *Study on your own with Study Guide page 255.*

1. What are two ways of building physical fitness?
2. What activities help build a strong heart?
3. How must you make your muscles work to build muscle fitness?

Activities That Build Physical Fitness

Activity	Builds Healthy Heart	Builds Strength	Builds Endurance	Builds Flexibility
Badminton	Good		Fair	Fair
Basketball	Excellent		Fair	
Ballet Dance	Good	Good	Good	Excellent
Gymnastics	Fair	Excellent	Excellent	Excellent
Hiking	Good	Fair	Excellent	
Jogging	Excellent		Good	
Ice Skating	Good		Good	
Roller Skating	Fair		Fair	
Cross-Country Skiing	Excellent	Fair	Good	
Downhill Skiing	Fair	Fair	Good	
Soccer	Excellent	Fair	Good	
Swimming	Excellent	Fair	Excellent	Fair
Tennis	Good		Fair	
Volleyball	Fair	Fair		
Walking	Good	Fair	Good	

project keep fit

Project Keep-Fit helps you get fit. You begin with warm-up exercises to stretch your muscles and get them ready for more active exercise. The workout exercises help build strength, endurance, and a healthy heart and lungs. The cool-down exercises help your muscles recover after activity. Ask your teacher to help you learn the Keep-Fit exercises. Also, check with your parent or guardian to find out if there is any health reason why you should not do some of these exercises.

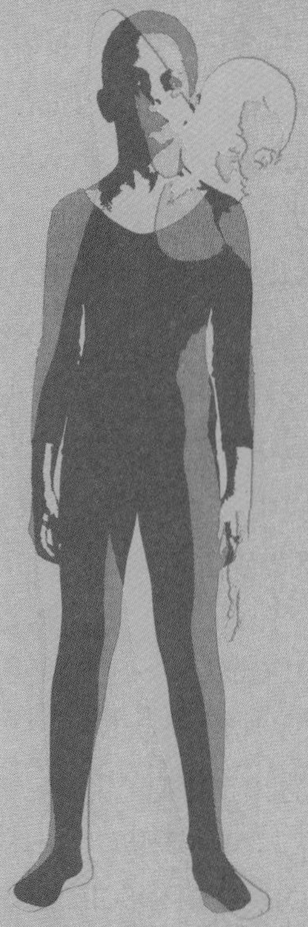

Warm-Up

Toe Reach

Sit on the floor. Spread your legs wide. Reach forward with both hands and grab your right ankle. Keep your legs straight and pull forward with your arms. Try to touch your head to your leg. Hold while you count to ten. Repeat with your left leg. Do up to three times.

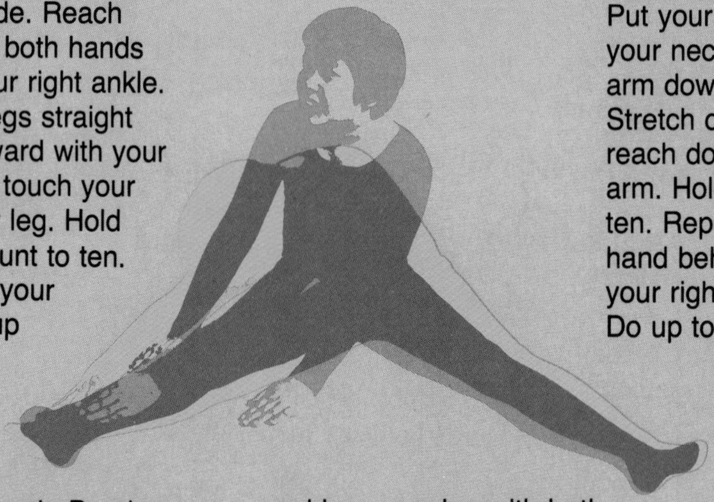

Side Stretcher

Stand with your feet apart. Put your right hand behind your neck. Keep your left arm down at your side. Stretch over to the left and reach down with your left arm. Hold while you count to ten. Repeat with your left hand behind your neck and your right arm at your side. Do up to three times.

Leg Hug

Lie on your back. Bend your right leg and bring it to your chest. Bring your head and shoulders up off the floor and hug your leg with both arms. Hold while you count to ten. Repeat with your left leg. Do up to three times.

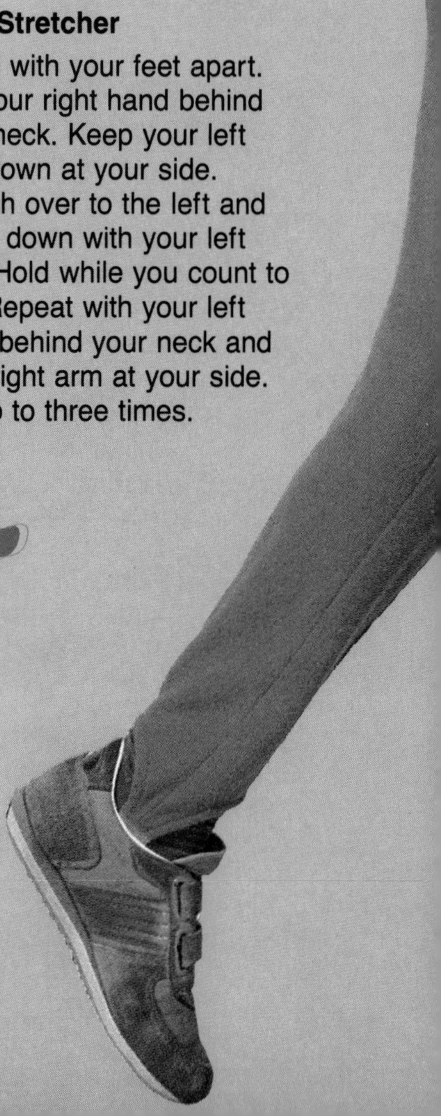

Workout

1. Jog in Place

Jog, or run slowly, in place. Do not move from your place on the floor. Start slowly. Try to jog for one minute.

2. Pogo Hop

Stand with your knees slightly bent. Put your right leg forward and your left leg back. Put your hands behind your head. Jump up straight and move your left leg forward and your right leg back. Keep jumping and moving your legs back and forth. Do this exercise as long as you can up to one minute.

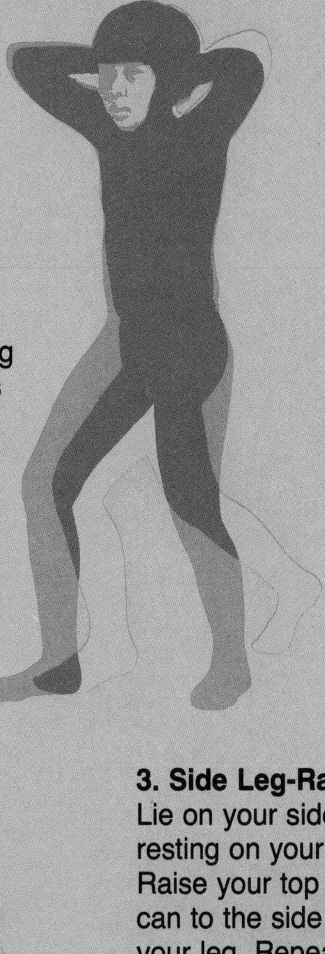

3. Side Leg-Raise

Lie on your side with your head resting on your arm as shown. Raise your top leg as high as you can to the side of your body. Lower your leg. Repeat on the other side. Start with three raises on each side. Do as many as you can up to ten on each side.

4. Bent-Knee Push-Up

Lie on the floor with your hands next to your shoulders. Push the upper part of your body off the floor. Keep your body as straight as you can and your knees touching the floor. Then keep your back straight and lower yourself to the floor. Try to touch your nose to the floor. Start with three push-ups and do as many as you can up to ten.

5. Leg Change

Put your hands on the floor and your right knee up under your chest. Change legs by pulling your left leg forward and moving your right leg back. Keep changing legs. Do this exercise as long as you can up to one minute without stopping.

6. Reverse Sit-Up

Lie on your back on the floor with your knees bent. Place your arms at your sides flat on the floor. Lift your knees toward your chest until your hips are off the floor. Return slowly to the floor. Do as many as you can up to ten.

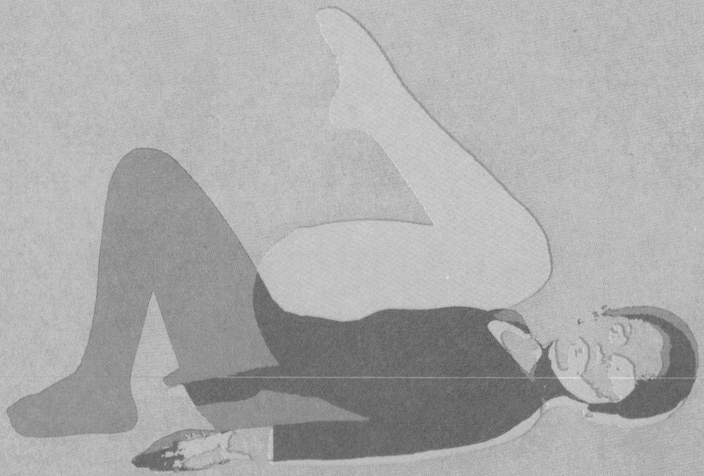

7. Cat Back

Kneel on your hands and knees. Lower your head and arch your back as high as you can. Hold for ten seconds. Next, lift your head up and let your back slowly return to the beginning position. Do whole exercise ten times.

8. Jump Rope

Use a jump rope you can turn easily. Jump rope in place for fifteen seconds. Work up to jumping rope as long as you can up to one minute.

Cool-Down

Now that you have exercised, you need to help your muscles recover. Go back and do the exercises in the warm-up on page 80.

Keep Fit While You Play

Keep Fit While You Sit

You can do these exercises to help yourself keep fit even if you are seated most of the time.

The Swim

Reach forward and pull back with one arm. Then reach forward and pull back with the other arm, just as if you were pulling yourself through water. Try to pull with each arm up to twenty times.

The Fish

Reach forward with both arms as far as you can. Pull your arms back and around and forward again as though you were pulling yourself through water. Do as many as you can up to twenty.

4 How Do Sports Skills Help You?

You and your friends probably play many games together. Some of these games are sports, such as soccer, baseball, or kickball. Any sport involves a certain amount of exercise and has a set of rules to follow. Many sports are competitive, which means one team or one person plays against another team or person.

You need to be somewhat fit to play most sports. You also need sports skills to help you play your best. Running, throwing, catching, and jumping are sports skills. Hitting or bouncing a ball are sports skills. What sports use these skills?

You learn most skills by practice. The boy and girl in the picture practice shooting baskets, passing, and bouncing the basketball. They have more chances to improve these skills during practice than during a game.

Learning an activity, such as swimming, while you are young means you will have a way to stay fit as you grow older.

Learning sports skills now can help you stay fit as you grow older. If you learn to swim and ride a bicycle when you are young, you can continue to do these activities throughout your life.

Lifetime sports are sports that you can do all your life. Most lifetime sports can be played alone or with a few other people. Tennis, golf, and bowling are examples of lifetime sports. The older person in the picture learned another lifetime sport many years ago. What is it? How can this sport help a person stay fit?

Think Back • *Study on your own with Study Guide page 255.*

1. What are three or four sports skills?
2. How does a person build sports skills?
3. How is having sports skills helpful?

5 How Can You Enjoy Playing Sports and Games?

The students in the picture enjoy playing active games. Here they try to keep the ball bouncing among them. If everyone works together, the game lasts a long time.

Just playing a game is fun. You do not always have to win to enjoy the game. Sports and games are often most enjoyable when people play in certain ways. For example, playing sports and games is better when everyone is included. Each person has different sports skills and different amounts of fitness. If you play a certain sport better than someone else, you can try to help that person. You can also be kind to someone who does not play very well.

Games are most fun when everyone is included.

People who enjoy playing sports and games share equipment. Such play is more fun when everyone plays by the rules. Following the rules gives each player or team a chance to win. However, the players enjoy playing whether they win or lose.

Players have the most fun when they enjoy each other and follow the rules. They will also have a good chance to improve their fitness. Being active is an important part of being physically fit. What active games do you and your friends play? What makes playing the games so much fun?

On Your Own
Look at the picture on these two pages. Choose one person in the picture. Write a story telling why that person is joining in the activity and how the activity will improve his or her fitness.

Think Back • *Study on your own with Study Guide page 255.*

1. What are some ways to enjoy playing sports and games?
2. What can people improve by enjoying playing games and sports?

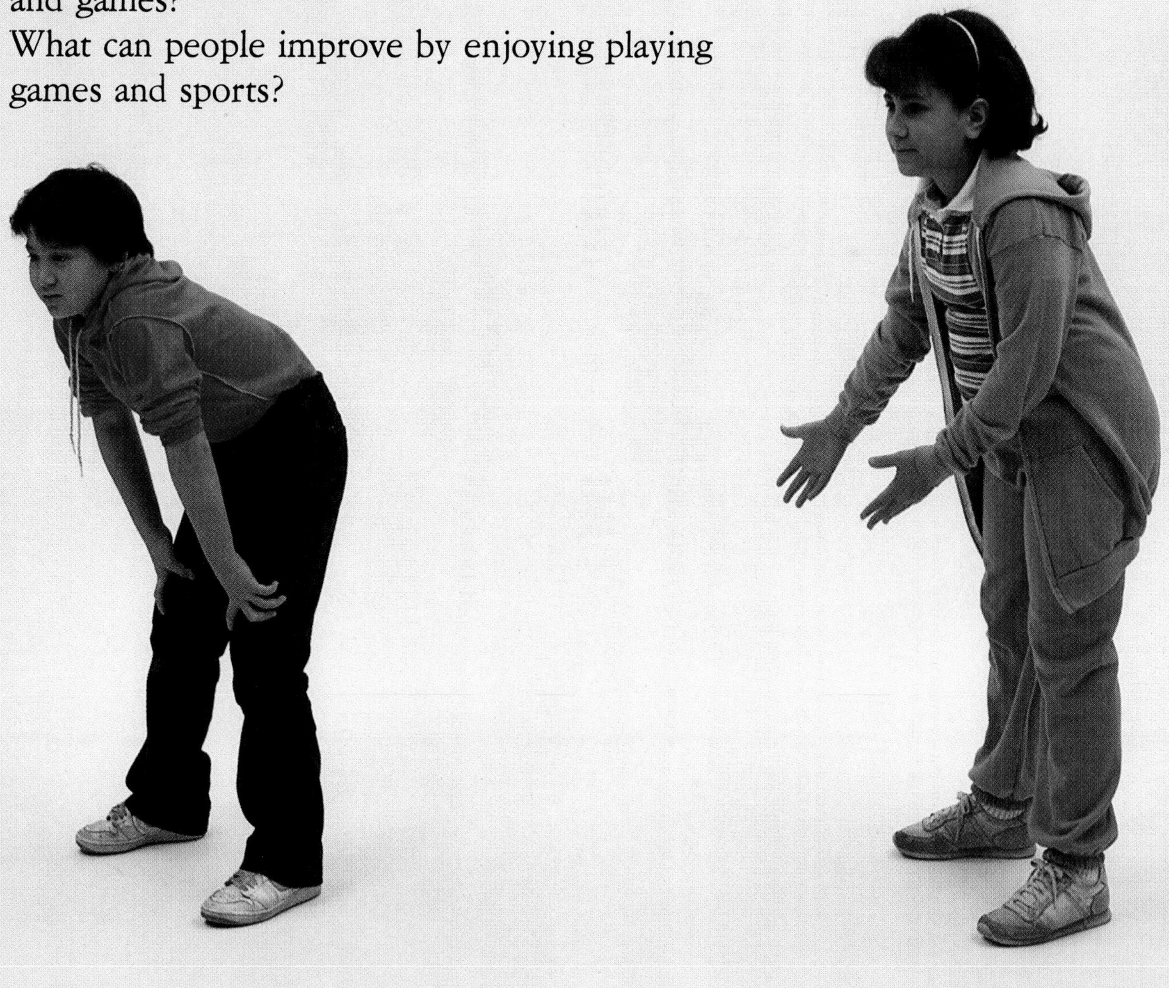

Anita DeFrantz Rows Her Way to Fitness

Swimming, jogging, and playing tennis are lifetime sports most people know about. Did you know that rowing is another lifetime sport? When it is a sport, rowing is usually called crew.

Rowing is also an Olympic sport. The Olympic games are contests of sports and games held every four years in different countries. Anita DeFrantz, the middle person in the picture, was one of the first women to ever row in the Olympics, in 1976. She and her seven teammates won the bronze medal that year. To become winners, they practiced many hours.

Anita DeFrantz has not always been so serious about crew. She joined her first rowing team just to exercise outside in the fresh air. She enjoyed working together with her teammates. After four years of rowing, she started training to try out for the 1976 Olympics.

Anita DeFrantz kept rowing after the Olympics. She says that practicing is as much fun as racing. She plans to keep rowing as a lifetime activity.

Talk About It

1. Why did Anita DeFrantz start rowing?
2. How do you think rowing could help build fitness?

Sharing Information About Fitness

You have learned many ideas about building and improving physical fitness. Your family might be interested in what you have learned. For example, you might show them how much fun it is to do the exercises in Project Keep-Fit.

Maybe some family members will want to exercise with you. If so, be a good leader. Encourage everyone to exercise regularly. However, it is a good idea for any adult over thirty-five to check with a doctor before starting any exercise program.

Reading at Home

Exercise: What It Is, What It Does by Carola S. Trier. Greenwillow, 1982. Discover more exercises you can do for fitness.

Keeping Your Body Alive and Well by Joy Wilt. Word, 1978. Find out what exercises you can do to keep yourself healthy.

Chapter 3 Review

Reviewing Lesson Objectives

1. State ways physical fitness helps people stay active and healthy. (pages 70–71)
2. Tell what flexibility, strength, and endurance are and how each kind of muscle fitness helps people work and play. Explain how muscle fitness helps improve posture. (pages 72–75)
3. Give two ways to build physical fitness and tell how each way helps the body. (pages 78–79)
4. List some sports skills. Tell how to build sports skills and why they can be helpful. (pages 86–87)
5. Describe ways to enjoy playing sports and games. Tell what this kind of playing helps people improve. (pages 88–89)

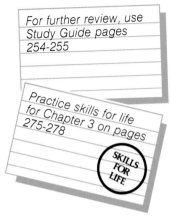

For further review, use Study Guide pages 254-255

Practice skills for life for Chapter 3 on pages 275-278

SKILLS FOR LIFE

Checking Health Vocabulary

Number your paper from 1–5. Match each definition in Column I with the correct word or words in Column II.

Column I

1. the way you hold your body when you sit, walk, or stand
2. the ability to use muscles a long time without getting tired
3. the ability to exercise, work, or play without getting tired or injured easily
4. the ability of muscles to produce force
5. the ability of muscles to move freely and easily

Column II

a. muscle endurance
b. flexibility
c. muscle strength
d. physical fitness
e. posture

Number your paper from 6–11. Next to each number write the word that completes the sentences in the paragraph.

endurance	flexibility	muscles
fitness	heart	strength

Everyone needs to have physical __6__ in order to work and play without getting tired easily. Exercising regularly helps your __7__ and __8__ become stronger. You can stand for a long time without getting tired if you have muscle __9__. You can stretch and reach easily if you have __10__. You can carry a load of books home from school without feeling sore if you have muscle __11__.

Reviewing Health Ideas

Number your paper from 1–12. Next to each number write the word or words that best complete the sentence. Choose the words from the list.

catching	heart
endurance	jogging
body fat	sit-ups
fit	stretching
flexibility	strong
health	weak

1. Physical fitness is needed for good ____.
2. The fitness of the ____ improves when a person plays actively.
3. A person builds flexibility by ____ muscles.
4. If you can bend, twist, and turn easily, you have ____.
5. ____ muscles help people lift and carry easily.
6. Doing ____ helps make muscles over the stomach strong.
7. A person with muscle ____ can row a boat for a long time without getting tired.
8. Muscles get ____ when they are not used.
9. ____ builds fitness of the heart.
10. ____ is an example of a sports skill used in baseball.
11. Exercising regularly might help a person get rid of extra ____.
12. A lifetime sport helps a person stay ____ throughout life.

Understanding Health Ideas

Number your paper from 13–23. Next to each number write the word or words that best answer the question.

13. What two body organs are helped by being physically fit?
14. What are the three parts of muscle fitness?
15. What exercise helps a person test for flexible muscles?
16. What do you need to be able to lift, carry, push, and pull?
17. What do you need to be able to ride a bicycle for a long time without tiring?
18. Which part of muscle fitness helps you have good posture?
19. To build fitness, how should you increase the amount of exercise you do?
20. What kind of sport has one team or person playing against another team or person?
21. What is the best way to learn sports skills?
22. What is a sport called that you can do all your life?
23. What do players need to follow to enjoy playing a game?

Thinking Critically

Write the answers on your paper. Use complete sentences.

1. What are some ways to make getting fit fun?
2. What would you say to a person who thinks that getting fit is hard and takes up too much time?

Chapter 4

Knowing How To Be Safe

How does the person in the picture help others stay safe? What good safety habits might she help people make? This chapter will describe some important safety habits that can help prevent accidents. You will learn about being safe as you walk and drive a bicycle. You will learn how to avoid some kinds of accidents. These habits can help you stay safe now and in the future.

Health Watch Notebook

Collect articles from a newspaper about traffic accidents in your community. Put them in your notebook. After each article, write down how the accident might have been prevented.

pedestrian
(pə des/trē ən), a person who travels by walking.

Did You Know?
By law, a car or bus driver must stop for a pedestrian in a crosswalk, even if the crossing has no traffic light. However, a careful pedestrian must always check that no cars are coming before crossing any street.

1 What Should Careful Pedestrians Do?

The children in the picture walk to school. They are **pedestrians,** people who walk on a street or sidewalk. At times you are a pedestrian too. If you follow the safety rules on page 97, you will be a safe pedestrian.

Some pedestrians are not safe. Maybe you have heard the word *jaywalker.* A person who is a jaywalker is not a careful pedestrian. Jaywalkers often walk or cross streets without paying attention to safety rules. They might not look carefully for cars before crossing a street. Jaywalkers often have or cause accidents.

When the sign for walk lights up, what should you do before you cross?

How Can You Walk Safely?

The rules below describe ways to walk safely. Which of these rules are the students in the picture following?

- Before you cross a street, look to the left, then right, and left again. Look for cars that might turn in front of you. Cross only when no cars are coming toward you.
- Obey traffic lights and signs. Know and follow signs for pedestrians.
- Always stop at the curb or outside edge of a parked car before entering the street. Wait on the sidewalk, not in the street, for cars that are turning to pass.
- Be careful whenever you cross a street, even when you cross at a corner or in a marked crosswalk. Be sure the driver of any oncoming car sees you.
- Walk on the left side of the street or road if the road or street has no sidewalk. You will face the traffic and can see oncoming cars. Walk one behind the other if you walk with others.
- Wear light-colored clothing and carry a light if you walk at night.

Think Back • *Study on your own with Study Guide page 256.*

1. What are five rules for crossing streets safely?
2. Where and how should a person walk if a road or street has no sidewalk?
3. What should a pedestrian do when walking on a street or road at night?

Did You Know?
You might wonder why bicycle riders are called drivers. Bicycles, cars, buses, trucks, and motorcycles are vehicles, or machines that move people. Anyone who operates a vehicle is called a driver.

2 What Should Careful Bicycle Drivers Do?

Look closely at the picture below. See if you can figure out whether the drivers are on the right or left side of the street.

Did you notice that the drivers were on the right side of the street, close to the curb? Driving in this way is one important safety rule for bicycle drivers. Other safety rules are listed on the next page. Think about how each rule can help keep a bicycle driver safe.

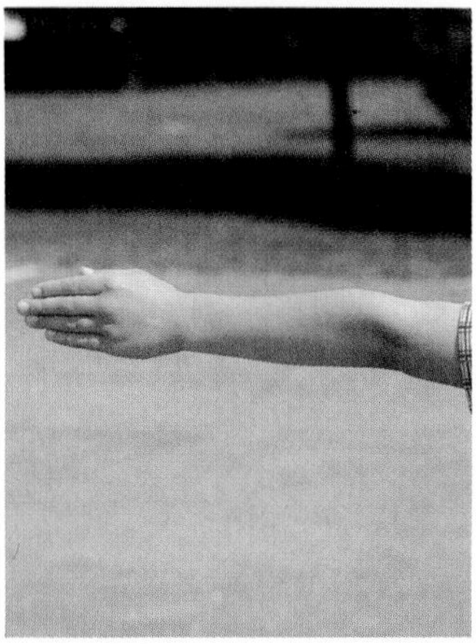

Left turn

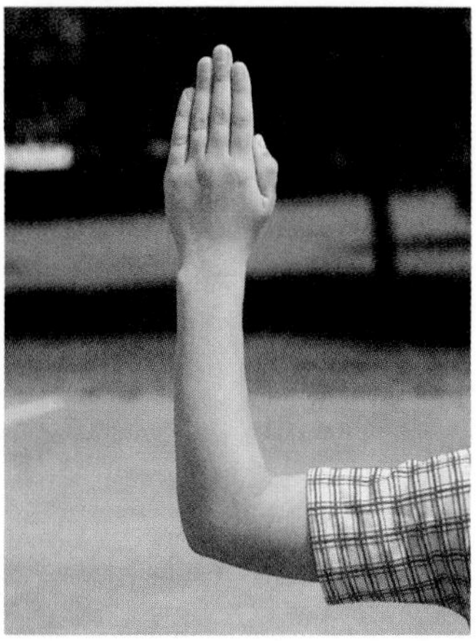

Right turn

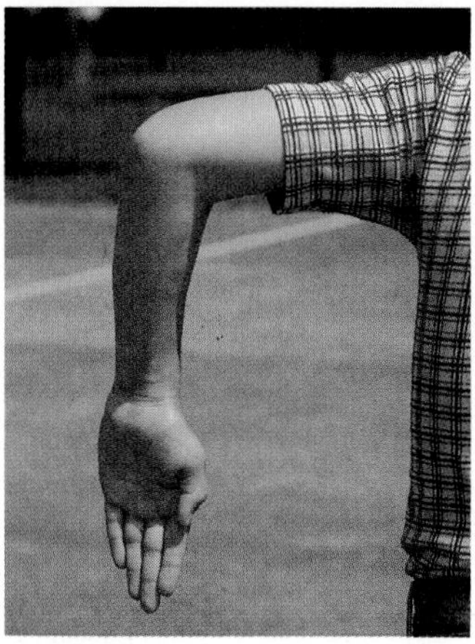

Stop

How Can You Stay Safe on a Bicycle?

If you drive a bicycle, you should follow these rules to drive safely. Which rules do you follow now?

- Learn the laws your community has about driving bicycles. For example, find out if bicycle drivers can drive on the sidewalks where you live. Use sidewalks if you can.

- If you drive in the street, always keep to the right and drive with traffic.

- Obey all traffic rules and all signs, signals, and markings on the street.

- Drive one behind the other on streets, roads, or sidewalks when you are with others.

- Walk your bicycle across busy streets.

- Use hand signals when turning or stopping. You can see the correct hand signals for turning left, turning right, and slowing or stopping in the pictures to the left.

- Try to drive in a straight line. When you drive on a street, drive as close as you can to the right-hand side of the road. Watch out for cars coming into or out of driveways. Watch out for people getting into or out of cars.

- Carry books or packages in a basket or on a carrier.

- Do not drive with another person on your bicycle. Carrying a person makes it harder to see where you are going and to steer and stop your bicycle.

- Slow down on wet, slippery, or rough roads. Be very careful driving over wet leaves and metal, such as railroad tracks. Both can be very slippery.

What Makes a Bicycle Safe to Drive?

You need a bicycle that is safe to drive. A safe bicycle is one you can ride easily. A safe bicycle has all needed safety equipment in good working order.

A safe bicycle is also the right size for you. Your feet should touch the ground when you sit on the seat. Your hands should reach the handlebars without stretching. The picture shows Tad's father making his bicycle safer for him. He fixes the seat so Tad can reach the ground easily. He will also move the handlebars so Tad can lean forward a little as he rides. Then Tad can push down on the pedals easily. He also can turn and stop safely.

The seat and the handlebars of a bicycle can be raised to fit you as you grow taller.

The bicycle on this page has needed safety equipment. Keep your bicycle safe by checking it often. Get help to keep the parts of your bicycle working as they should.

Think Back • *Study on your own with Study Guide page 256.*

1. What are three safety rules for bicycle drivers?
2. What makes a bicycle safe to drive?

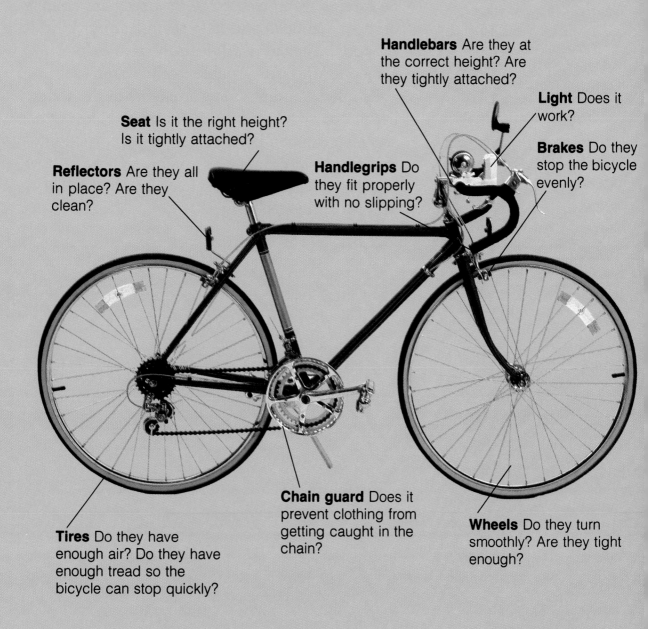

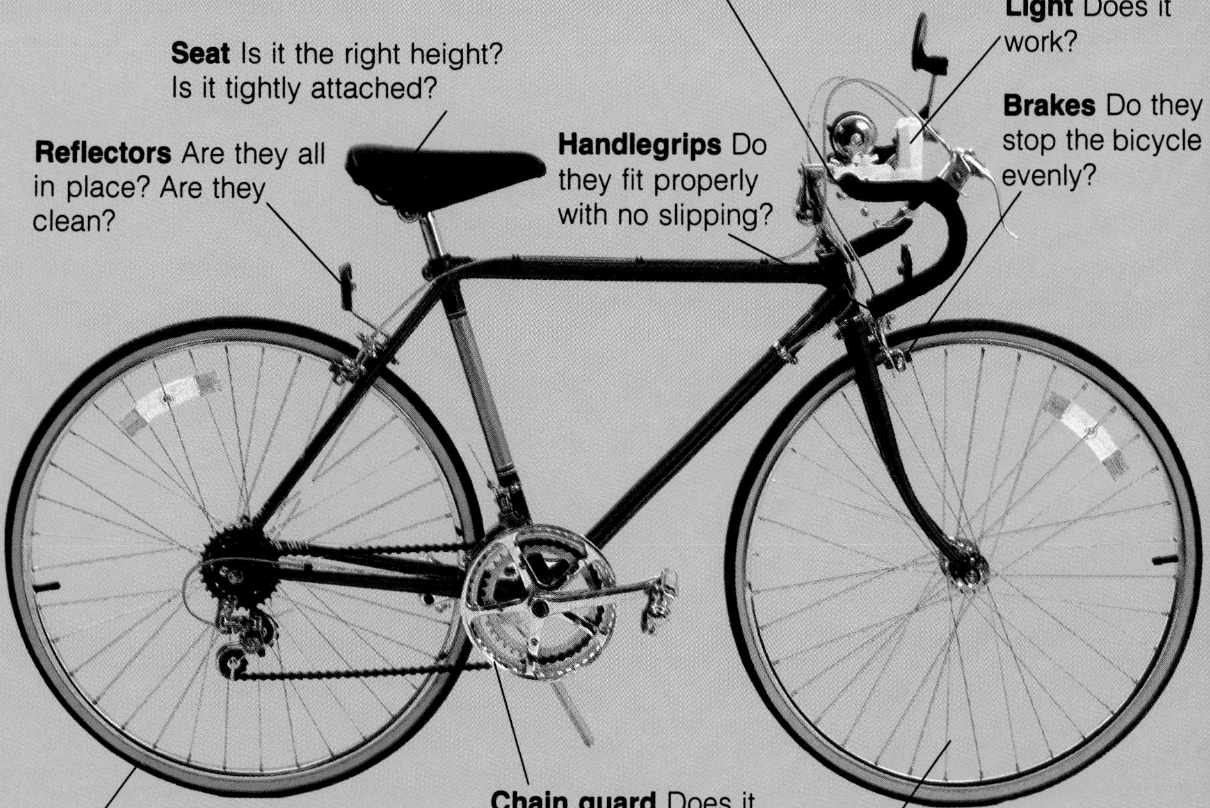
Handlebars Are they at the correct height? Are they tightly attached?
Light Does it work?
Seat Is it the right height? Is it tightly attached?
Brakes Do they stop the bicycle evenly?
Reflectors Are they all in place? Are they clean?
Handlegrips Do they fit properly with no slipping?
Chain guard Does it prevent clothing from getting caught in the chain?
Wheels Do they turn smoothly? Are they tight enough?
Tires Do they have enough air? Do they have enough tread so the bicycle can stop quickly?

3 What Should Careful Swimmers Know?

On Your Own
Two children played a game at a beach. They pretended to be in trouble. They called for help. A lifeguard rushed to help the children and found they did not need help. The lifeguard told the children to leave the beach for the day. Pretend you are the lifeguard in this situation. Write several paragraphs telling what you would say to the children to help them understand why their game was unsafe.

The young people in the picture are learning how to be safe in the water. What do you think they are learning?

You are right if you said they are learning to swim. Knowing how to swim is the most important first step to being safe in the water. The children in the picture are learning ways to be careful swimmers. Note how they are holding onto special boards to help them learn to kick properly. They also will learn how to help someone who is in trouble in the water.

People sometimes have accidents in the water because they take chances and break rules. Other accidents happen because people slip or fall into the water and cannot reach safety. Knowing how to swim safely and be careful near water helps prevent accidents.

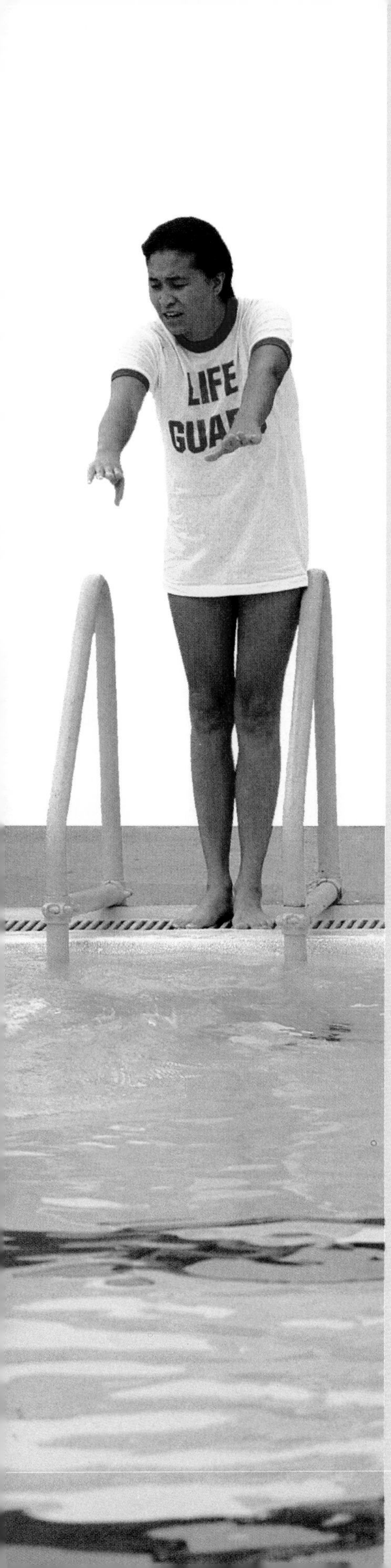

How Can You Be Safe in the Water?

A safe swimmer knows many safety rules for playing and swimming in the water. If you want to be safe in the water, you should know the rules listed here. Think about the reason for each rule.

Rules for swimmers are usually posted near a pool or beach. Wherever you swim, check the rules for that place and follow them.

Read the rules shown below. Where might they be posted? How does each rule help keep swimmers safe?

- Swim only where and when it is safe to swim.
- Swim only in a place where a parent or lifeguard can watch you.
- Come out of the water if you feel tired or chilly.
- Come out of the water if you hear thunder or see lightning. It is not safe to swim outdoors during a storm.
- Swim in water that is over your head only if you can swim well.
- Never push anyone into the water or hold anyone's head under water.
- Do not push or shove people around a swimming pool.
- Do not run when you are near a swimming pool. The deck can be slippery.
- Do not bring anything made of glass near a swimming pool.

The children in the picture are following the rule about swimming only where someone can watch them. Who is watching them?

rescue (res′kyü), to save or free a person from danger or harm.

How Can You Help Someone in the Water?

Suppose you see a person fall into a lake off a boat dock. The person does not seem to know how to swim. What could you do to help?

First, call loudly for help. If you can, send someone to get help from a grown-up. Do not jump in the water to try to get the person. You would risk your own life. If you are the only person available to help, give help in a safe way. The students on these two pages are practicing two safe ways to **rescue** a person. In a water rescue, you save a person from drowning. In each way, one student holds or throws something out to the person in the water.

Hold a pole, belt, shirt, oar, stick, or rope out to the person. Be sure you hold on to something so you do not fall in the water yourself. Then pull the person to safety.

Suppose you do not find anything to hold out to a person in the water. If the person is your size or smaller, lie down and reach out to the person. Be sure to hold on tightly to something so you do not fall in the water. Grab the person's hand or clothes and pull the person to safety.

Throw or push out anything that will float to a person in trouble in the water. Use a ring buoy attached to a rope and pull the person to safety. An inner tube, a cooler, or a piece of wood can also keep the person afloat until help arrives.

Think Back • *Study on your own with Study Guide page 257.*

1. What is the first thing to know to be safe in the water?
2. What are four safety rules for swimmers?
3. How might a fishing pole be used to rescue someone in the water?

Health Activities Workshop

Thinking About Safety

1. Two very important safety rules for swimmers are in code below. See if you can break the code and figure out the safety rules. Here is a hint: The first word in Rule 1 is *never*.

Rule 1

14 5 22 5 18
19 23 9 13
1 12 15 14 5.

Rule 2

19 23 9 13 15 14 12 25
23 8 5 18 5
20 8 5 18 5 9 19 1
12 9 6 5 7 21 18 4.

2. Make a safety study of your neighborhood. Look for safety aids such as crosswalks, safety signs, and overpasses. Look also for places that could be dangerous, such as construction sites and dumps. Draw a map of your neighborhood that includes the information you find.

3. Look at the poster and tell what safety message it gives. Then plan and make a poster yourself. Put a safety message on your poster telling another way to be safe.

4. Find out where you can learn to swim. You might talk to a swimming teacher. What might you learn besides how to swim? Share what you find out with your class.

Looking at Careers

5. A **lifeguard** watches swimmers in pools and on beaches. A lifeguard's job is to keep swimmers safe. He or she knows how to rescue people in trouble.

A lifeguard receives special training. He or she passes swimming tests and lifesaving tests. The tests show if a person can do the work of a lifeguard. Draw a picture of what a lifeguard might need to know how to do on the job.

first aid, the first help given to a person who has been hurt or has become suddenly ill.

4 What Should You Do in an Emergency?

Suppose you are watching a younger brother or sister. Your mother has just gone next door for a minute. The child falls and gets hurt. What would you do?

Suppose you and an uncle are home alone. Your uncle suddenly feels very ill. What would you do?

Falls or sudden illnesses are emergencies. They do not happen often. However, you need to be prepared and know what to do in case of an emergency.

1. Stay calm. If you stay calm, you can do what you need to do.
2. Get help from a grown-up. Call a close neighbor on the telephone. Run to the neighbor's house or apartment if you have no telephone.
3. Suppose the person seems badly hurt and you cannot reach a neighbor. In some communities, you can dial 911 to get help in an emergency. Otherwise, dial 0 for operator. Tell the person who answers your name and address. Tell what has happened. Listen to what the person tells you to do before you hang up.

An accident, such as a fall, can cause an injury. An injury might be a cut, a nosebleed, a burn, or a blister. If you or someone else has a small injury, you can help with simple **first aid.** The first help a person gets in an emergency is first aid. Sometimes you may need to give yourself first aid if you are alone. Look at the pictures on the next two pages and read how to give some kinds of first aid. Remember to always tell a grown-up if you hurt yourself. Report your injury as soon as you can.

The First Aid for Cuts and Nosebleeds

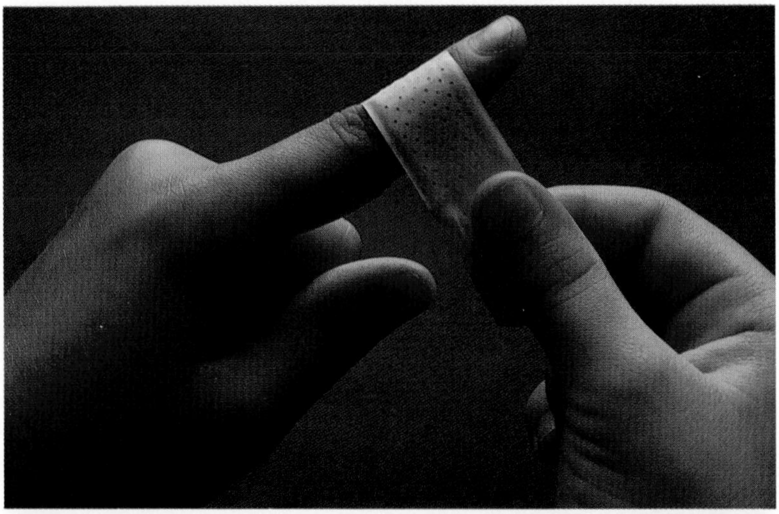

A cut is a break in the skin. Wash any cut with soap and water. Dry the cut gently and cover with a clean small bandage. The bandage helps keep the cut clean while it heals.

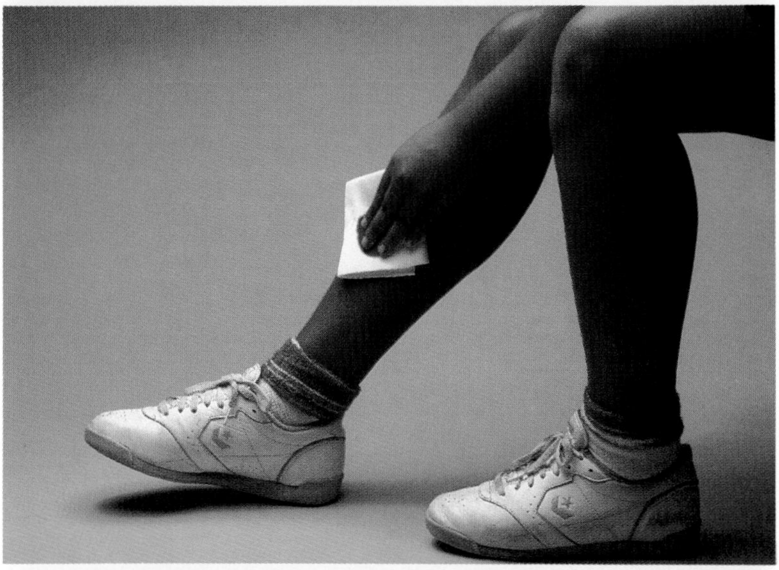

Get help from a grown-up right away for a deep cut. Try to stop the bleeding while you wait for help. Hold a clean cloth on the cut. Push down firmly. If blood comes through the cloth, do not remove it. Instead, place another cloth on top and keep pressing.

If you get a nosebleed, sit down and lean forward. Pinch your nostrils shut for five to ten minutes. Breathe through your mouth and sit quietly. If your nose is bleeding after ten minutes, get help from a grown-up.

blister (blis′tər), a small swelling in the skin that is filled with a watery substance.

Tell a grown-up if you get burned. Treat only a mild burn yourself. Mild burns redden the skin but do not blister or break it. Hold the burn under cold running water, or put a cold, wet cloth or ice wrapped in a cloth on it. Do not put anything else on a mild burn. These burns usually do not need bandages.

A **blister** is an injury on the skin caused by rubbing or burns. You might get a blister by wearing shoes without socks. A watery substance under the top layers of skin causes the skin to swell up. Show a blister to a grown-up. Do not break a blister. Instead, cover it with a bandage. If a blister does break, wash the area with soap and water. Dry gently. Cover the area with a clean bandage.

The First Aid for Burns and Blisters

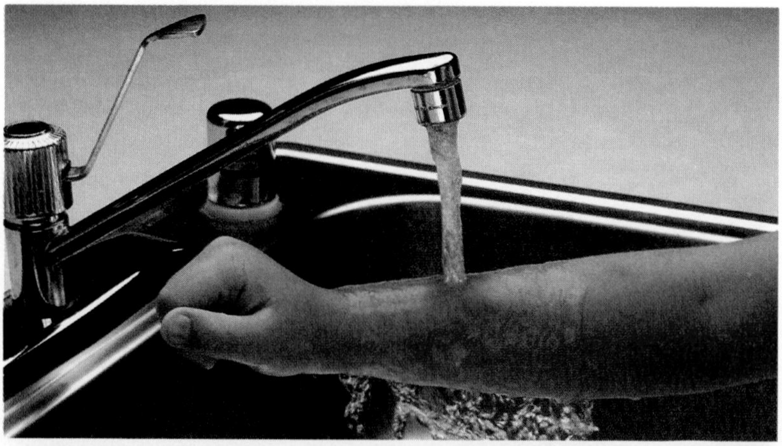

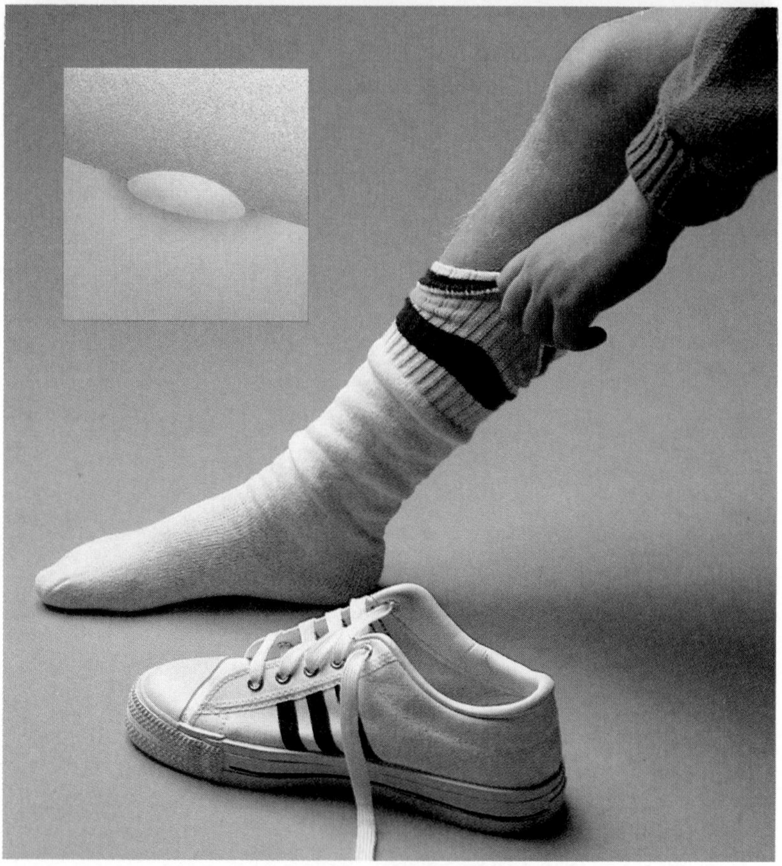

Think Back • *Study on your own with Study Guide page 257.*

1. What should be done when an emergency happens?
2. What is the first aid for cuts and nosebleeds?
3. What two things should be done for a mild burn?
4. What is the first aid for a blister?

Health Activities Workshop

Thinking About Emergencies

1. Look in the front of the telephone book for your community. What information can you find about what to do in an emergency? What phone number do you call in an emergency?

2. Find an important action in an emergency. Use your own paper and copy the sentence below. Then fill in the vowels.

G__t h__lp fr__m __ gr__wn-__p

__t __nc__ __f

y__ __ c__n.

3. Make up some short plays about emergencies. Act out what to do if you are alone with a grown-up who gets sick. Act out what to do if you fall and cut your knee. Act out what to do if a player on your baseball team gets a nosebleed.

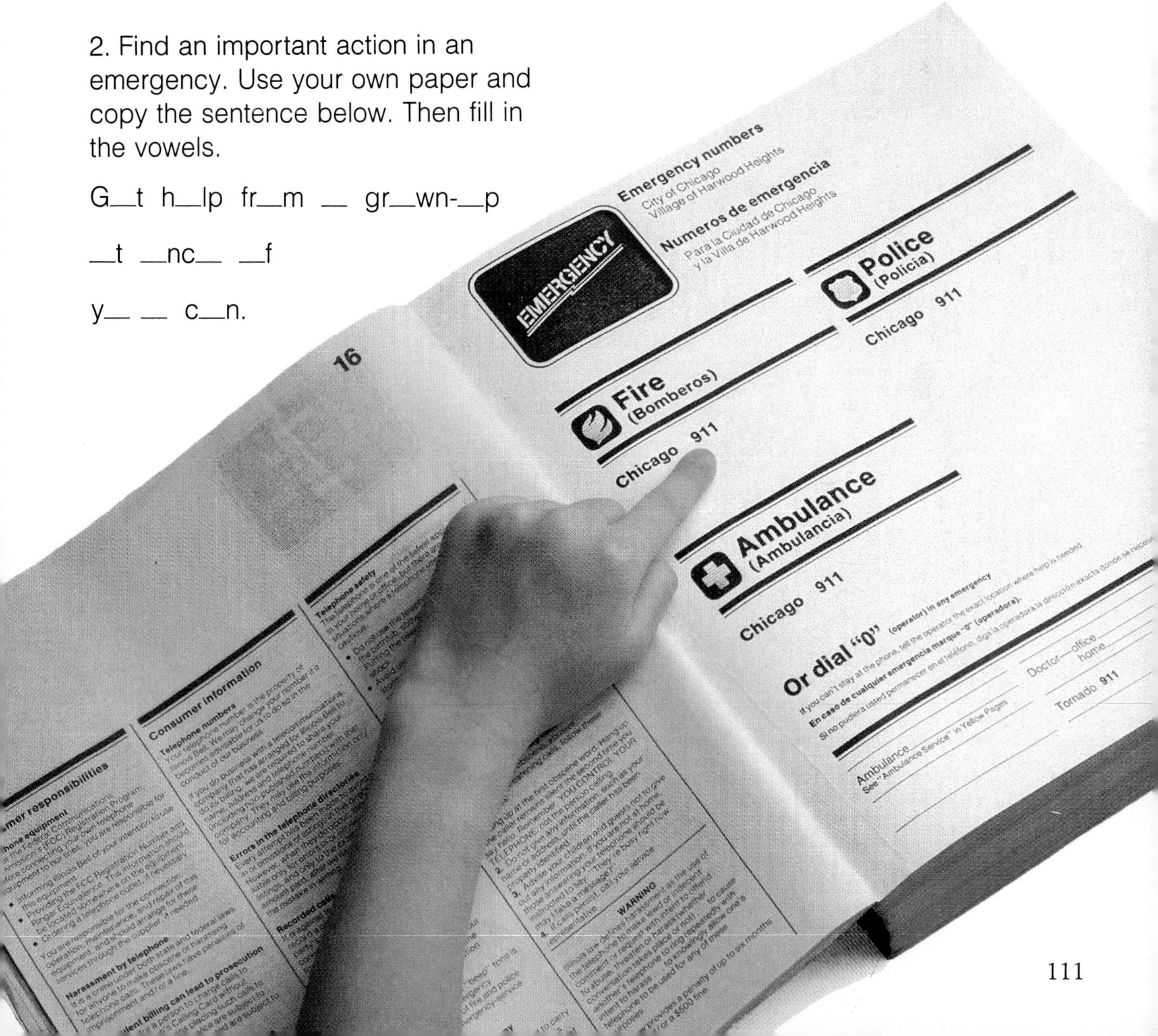

5 How Can You Be Safe If You Are Alone?

Suppose you will be the only person at home after school today. How will you keep safe? When you are alone, you are in charge. You need to make sure you do not get hurt.

Be sure to keep the doors locked. Do not let any strangers into your home. Never open a door to a stranger no matter what the stranger tells you. Do not tell the stranger you are alone. Say that your mother or father is busy and cannot come to the door. Maybe the stranger will not go away. Then call a family member on the telephone. If that is not possible, call a neighbor or the police and tell what has happened.

Suppose the telephone rings while you are home alone. A person you do not know asks for a family member. What will you do? The girl in the picture helps keep herself safe. She does not say over the telephone that she is alone. What does she say?

You and your family should make a plan about whether you can have friends visit when you are alone. Do not invite friends to visit you without family permission. Also, do not leave home unless your family has given permission.

The telephone can be useful in an emergency. You should keep a list of important numbers near the telephone. The list might include the numbers at work of grown-ups in your family. The list should also include safety helpers in your community. What safety helpers are shown in the list on the next page? How could each help in an emergency?

Knowing how to be safe while you are home alone is important. It is part of learning to grow up safely.

Think Back • *Study on your own with Study Guide page 257.*

1. What should be done if an uninvited person comes to the door when a young person is home alone?
2. What should a young person who is home alone tell someone who calls for a grown-up?
3. When is it safe to have friends visit when a young person is home alone?
4. What safety helpers could a person call in an emergency?

Health Focus

A Bicycle Safety Roadeo

The boy in the picture is testing his bicycle safety skills in a bicycle safety roadeo. The roadeo was held at Loyola School in Los Altos, California.

On the day of the roadeo, six stations were set up around the playground. A bicycle driver got points for completing each part correctly.

Any child who wanted to test his or her bicycling skills could take part in the roadeo. At the first station bicycles were checked for safety. A driver got points for having a bike with good brakes, smooth fenders, safe tires, and other safety equipment.

At the second station each bicycle driver drove inside a figure eight drawn with double lines. To get a high score, the driver had to drive without touching the lines.

At the third station the bicycle drivers drove in and out between a row of small, rubber cones. This part showed how well a driver could steer a bicycle.

Drivers showed other skills at other stations. For example, a driver had to pedal hard for a distance and then stop quickly without skidding. Finally, each driver rode through a maze. To get a high score, each driver had to use the correct hand signals, look both ways at corners, stop at stop signs, and stay on the right side of the road.

Talk About It

1. What did students do at the bicycle roadeo?
2. How could the roadeo help keep bicycle drivers safe?

Health at Home

Sharing Safety Rules

You have learned many safety rules and ideas in this chapter. You might want to share some of them at home. For example, you might talk with your family about telephone numbers. What important numbers should be kept by your telephone? Together, you and your family members could make a list of the numbers.

You and your family might also talk about ways to be safe around the home. You might talk about how to use certain equipment safely. What kitchen equipment do you think you might talk about? What workshop equipment could you talk about? What do you think some of the safety ideas for using equipment around the house might be?

Reading at Home

All Alone After School by Muriel Stanck. Albert Whitman, 1985. Read about a boy who learns to be safe when he must be alone after school.

Swimming Is for Me by Lowell A. Dickmeyer. Lerner, 1980. Follow Lisa as she learns about water safety.

This family reads the directions to help them use a new toaster safely.

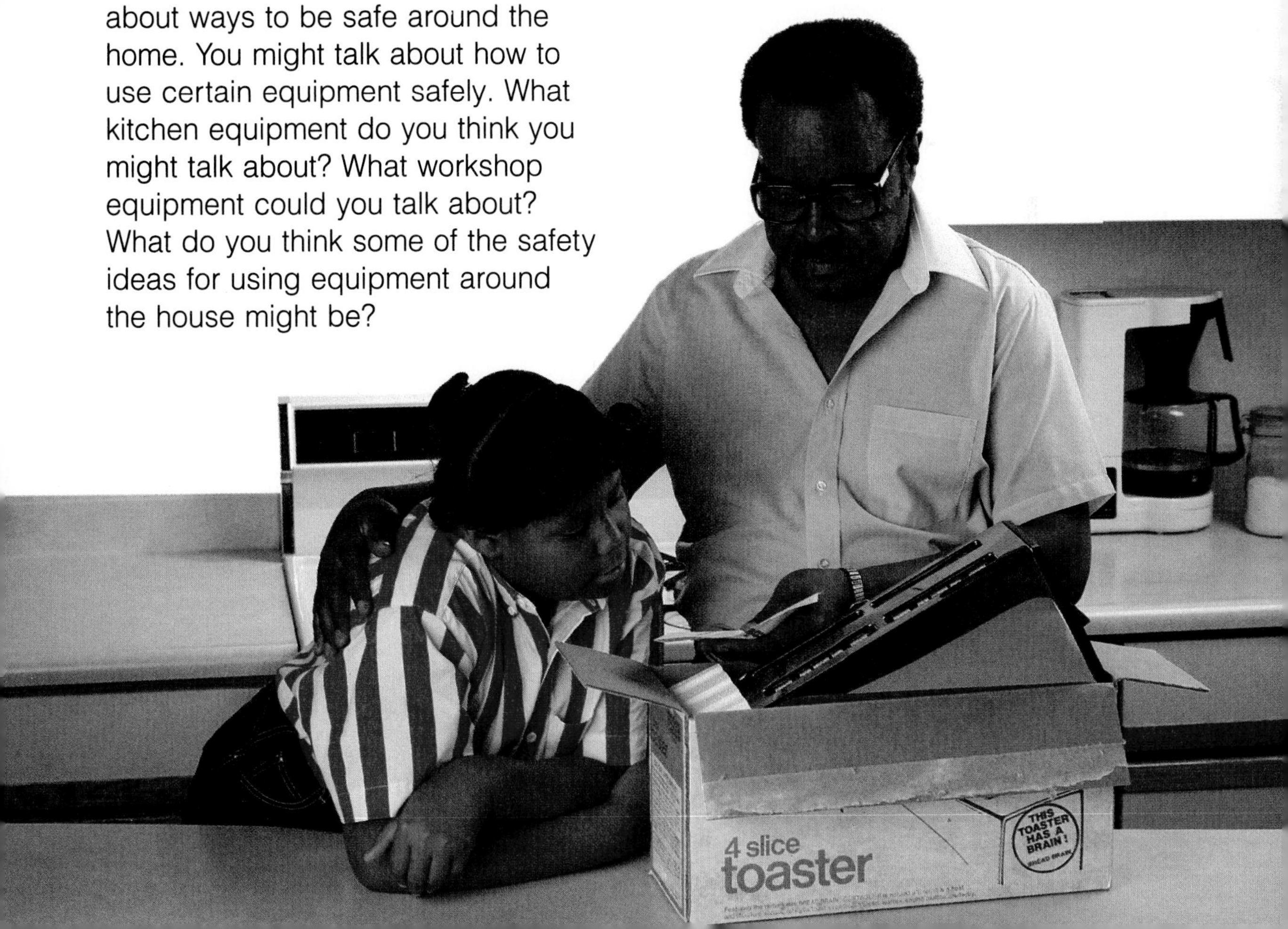

Chapter 4 Review

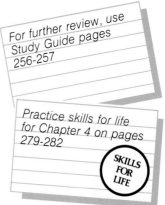

For further review, use Study Guide pages 256-257

Practice skills for life for Chapter 4 on pages 279-282

Reviewing Lesson Objectives

1. Explain how to cross streets safely, and tell where to walk if the road has no sidewalk. (pages 96–97)
2. List safety rules for driving a bicycle. Describe a safe bicycle. (pages 98–101)
3. List rules for safe swimming. Describe a safe way to help someone who is in trouble in the water. (pages 102–105)
4. Explain what to do in an emergency. Tell the first aid for small cuts, nosebleeds, mild burns, and blisters. (pages 108–110)
5. Explain what to do if a stranger comes to the door or calls when you are home alone. List whose telephone numbers can be used in an emergency. (pages 112–113)

Checking Health Vocabulary

Number your paper from 1–4. Match each meaning in Column I with the correct word or words in Column II.

Column I

1. a person who travels by walking
2. the first help given to a person who has just had an accident or has become suddenly ill
3. a skin injury caused by rubbing or by burns
4. to save a person from danger or harm

Column II

a. blister
b. first aid
c. pedestrian
d. rescue

Number your paper from 5–9. Next to each number write the word or words that best complete the sentence. Choose the words from the list below.

jaywalker	first aid
emergency	lifeguard
hand signals	

5. A person who does not obey safety rules when walking is a ____.
6. A person who has fallen might need ____.
7. Use ____ when you drive a bicycle.
8. People can swim safely where there is a ____.
9. Everyone should know how to act in an ____.

Reviewing Health Ideas

Number your paper from 1–14. Next to each number write the word or words that best complete the sentence. Choose words from the list.

bicycle driver	mild burn
deep cut	pedestrian
emergency	right
first aid	stranger
forward	swim
left	telephone
lifeguard	walk

1. A safe ____ looks left, right, left before stepping into the street.
2. A ____ follows the same traffic signs as a car driver.
3. A pedestrian walks on the ____ if there is no sidewalk.
4. Holding the arm pointing up is the signal for turning ____.
5. A person cannot ____ safely outdoors during a storm.
6. A person should ____ a bicycle across busy streets.
7. At a beach or pool, a ____ helps keep people safe.
8. In an ____ you can dial 0.
9. Putting a bandage over a cut is an example of ____.
10. Pressing on a ____ helps stop bleeding.
11. Lean ____ and pinch the nostrils shut for a nosebleed.
12. Cold running water is used to treat a ____.
13. A young person alone should never open a door to a ____.
14. Keep needed numbers by the ____.

Understanding Health Ideas

Number your paper from 15–24. Next to each number write the word or words that best answer the question.

15. What kind of clothing should a pedestrian wear when walking at night?
16. In traffic, which direction should bicycle drivers ride?
17. How is the arm held when giving the correct hand signal for stopping?
18. For safety, what should cover a bicycle's chain?
19. What is the most important first step in being safe in the water?
20. What should a person do first in any emergency?
21. What kind of object should you throw to someone you cannot reach who is in trouble in the water?
22. Who should a young person tell if he or she is injured?
23. What should be used to cover a blister?
24. What safety helper would a person call if a fire starts?

Thinking Critically

Write the answers on your paper. Use complete sentences.

1. Suppose you are swimming at a backyard pool. What safety rules should you follow?
2. How could keeping yourself safe help other people stay safe?

Chapter 5

Taking Care of Your Body

You can care for your teeth better when you learn about them, as the girl in the picture is doing. Taking care of your teeth is just one way to take care of your body. Your ears, eyes, and skin also need good care. You need to get enough sleep. When you use health products, you need to know how to choose them wisely.

This chapter describes ways you can take care of some parts of your body. Knowing how to take care of your body can help keep you healthy now and as you grow older.

Health Watch Notebook

Cut out ads for different types of health products from magazines and newspapers. Make a collage of these ads in your notebook.

1 Why Do You Need Sleep?
2 What Kinds of Teeth Do You Have?
3 How Can You Keep Your Teeth and Gums Healthy?
4 Why Is Your Skin Important?
5 How Can You Take Care of Your Eyes and Ears?
6 What Information Helps You Choose Health Products Wisely?

> ***Did You Know?***
> You might make as many as forty different movements in one night's sleep. As you sleep, you kick, twitch, turn over, move your lips, roll your head, and move your arms.

1 Why Do You Need Sleep?

All day Bruce has been busy. Nerves in all his sense organs sent messages to his brain. What are some of the messages the sense organs might have sent to his brain? In answer to messages from sense organs, Bruce's brain sent messages to muscles. These messages told muscles to move bones so he could walk, bend, turn, and sit. Bruce's brain also worked to help him remember how to do his schoolwork.

Now many parts of Bruce's body are tired. He gives them a chance to rest as he sleeps.

What Happens During Sleep?

While you sleep, your body does many of its jobs more slowly. Your sense organs send fewer messages to your brain. The brain sends fewer messages to muscles. During sleep sense organs and muscles get a chance to rest. The part of your brain that helps you think and remember also rests.

Your body does not just shut down as you sleep. A few muscles move from time to time. Your heart continues to pump blood. You continue to breathe. However, your heart beats slower at times and your lungs breathe slower. At such times, your heart and lungs get a chance for some rest.

How Does Enough Sleep Help You?

Most young people your age need about eleven hours of sleep. However, some of you need more and some need less. You have had enough sleep when you feel rested after being up in the morning for a while.

When you have had enough sleep, your brain is alert. It can get messages from your sense organs and act on them correctly. You can think clearly when you are rested. You are less likely to make mistakes in your schoolwork.

Getting enough sleep also helps you to get along with others. You are less likely to be grouchy when you have had enough sleep.

Missing an hour or two of sleep once in a while is not serious. However, not sleeping enough night after night can harm your health. You need enough sleep to grow and learn as you should.

On Your Own

Write a paragraph that describes how you feel and act on a day when you have had enough sleep. Try to remember an event that happened. Tell how feeling rested helped you enjoy or deal with the event.

Think Back • *Study on your own with Study Guide page 258.*

1. What changes take place in the body during sleep?
2. How can sleep and rest affect the way a person learns?
3. How can sleep change the way a person gets along with others?

Body parts, such as the muscles and the brain, rest during sleep.

2 What Kinds of Teeth Do You Have?

Have you ever noticed that you have different kinds of teeth in your mouth? You might have noticed different primary teeth, or first teeth. You also saw different new, or permanent, teeth.

You will have four kinds of permanent teeth. They are called incisors, cuspids, bicuspids, and molars. You can see a full set of permanent teeth on page 123. Notice that teeth of the upper jaw match teeth of the same kind in the lower jaw. Find each kind of teeth in the picture. Which kinds of permanent teeth do you have now? Which ones have yet to grow in?

Roots hold your teeth in your jaw. The picture on this page shows the way teeth are held in your mouth. You can see the roots of the teeth in the picture, but you cannot see the roots in your mouth. Soft tissue called gum covers the roots. The part of a tooth you can see is the crown. A hard white covering called enamel protects teeth.

What can you tell about the number of roots these teeth have?

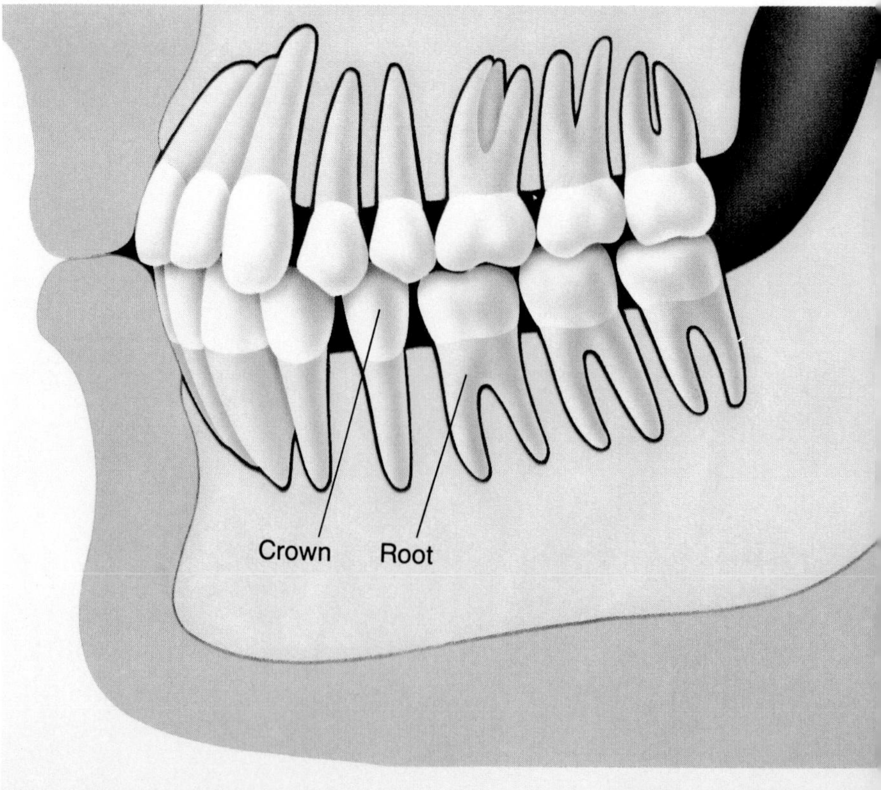

Your Permanent Teeth

Here is a complete set of thirty-two permanent teeth. Which teeth do you have right now? Which ones have yet to grow in?

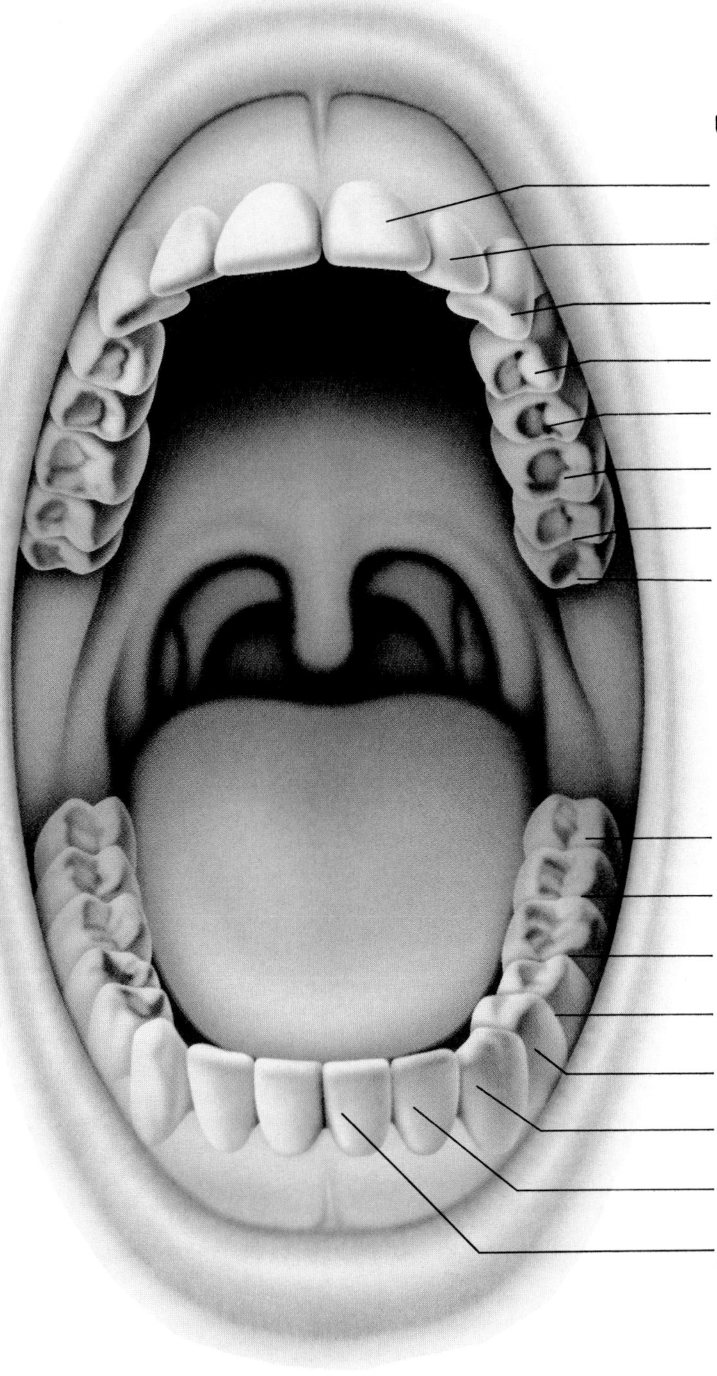

Upper Teeth	Age Teeth Appear
Front incisor	7-8 years
Side incisor	8-9 years
Cuspid	11-12 years
First bicuspid	10-11 years
Second bicuspid	10-12 years
First molar	6-7 years
Second molar	12-13 years
Third molar	17-21 years

Lower Teeth	Age Teeth Appear
Third molar	17-21 years
Second molar	12-13 years
First molar	6-7 years
Second bicuspid	10-12 years
First bicuspid	10-11 years
Cuspid	11-12 years
Side incisor	8-9 years
Front incisor	7-8 years

incisor (in sī′zər), the kind of tooth with flat edges used to cut food. There are eight incisors.

cuspid (kus′pid), the kind of tooth with a sharp point used to tear food. Adults have four cuspids.

bicuspid (bī kus′pid), the kind of tooth with two sharp points used to tear and crush food. Adults have eight bicuspids.

molar (mō′lər), the kind of tooth with a broad top used to grind food. Adults have twelve permanent molars.

How Does Each Kind of Tooth Help You?

You can see a pair of each kind of teeth in the pictures. Your front teeth are **incisors.** Your upper jaw has four incisors and your lower jaw has four. Incisors have sharp, straight edges. They cut food. When you eat an apple, you use incisors to bite off pieces.

Cuspids are the teeth next to the incisors. You have four cuspids. Each has one point. The sharp points tear apart foods.

Right now you probably have primary molars next to the cuspids. You will probably lose your primary molars between ages nine and twelve or so. Teeth called **bicuspids** grow in to replace primary molars. You will have eight bicuspids when all your permanent teeth come in. Each bicuspid has two points. These teeth break up food into small bits. Bicuspids usually have one or two roots.

Molars are the teeth at the back of your mouth. You will have twelve molars when all your permanent teeth come in. Molars have broad tops with four or five points. They grind food into very tiny bits. Some molars have two roots. Other molars have three or four roots.

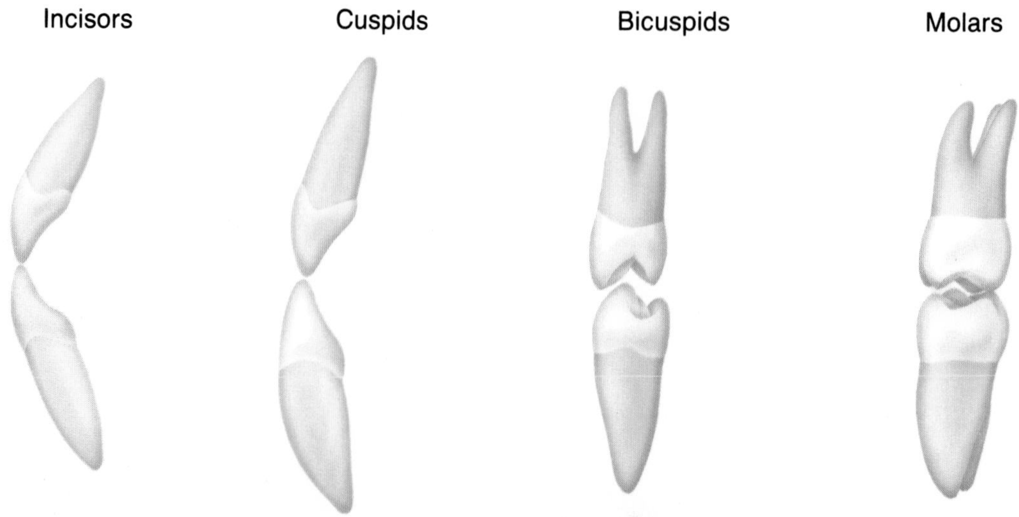

Why Might Teeth Come in Crooked?

Sometimes primary teeth come out too soon. Teeth nearby might tip to fill part of the empty space. If that happens, the permanent teeth can grow into the wrong position. The teeth might come in crooked.

An orthodontist is a dentist who can help make crooked teeth straight. An orthodontist might use braces like the ones the girl in the picture wears. The braces slowly and gently shift teeth into the right position. Moving the teeth might take several years.

Once people thought an orthodontist could change the position of teeth only in childhood years. Now people know that teeth can be straightened later in life too.

Think Back

1. What are four kinds of teeth, and what does each kind do?
2. Why might permanent teeth come in crooked?

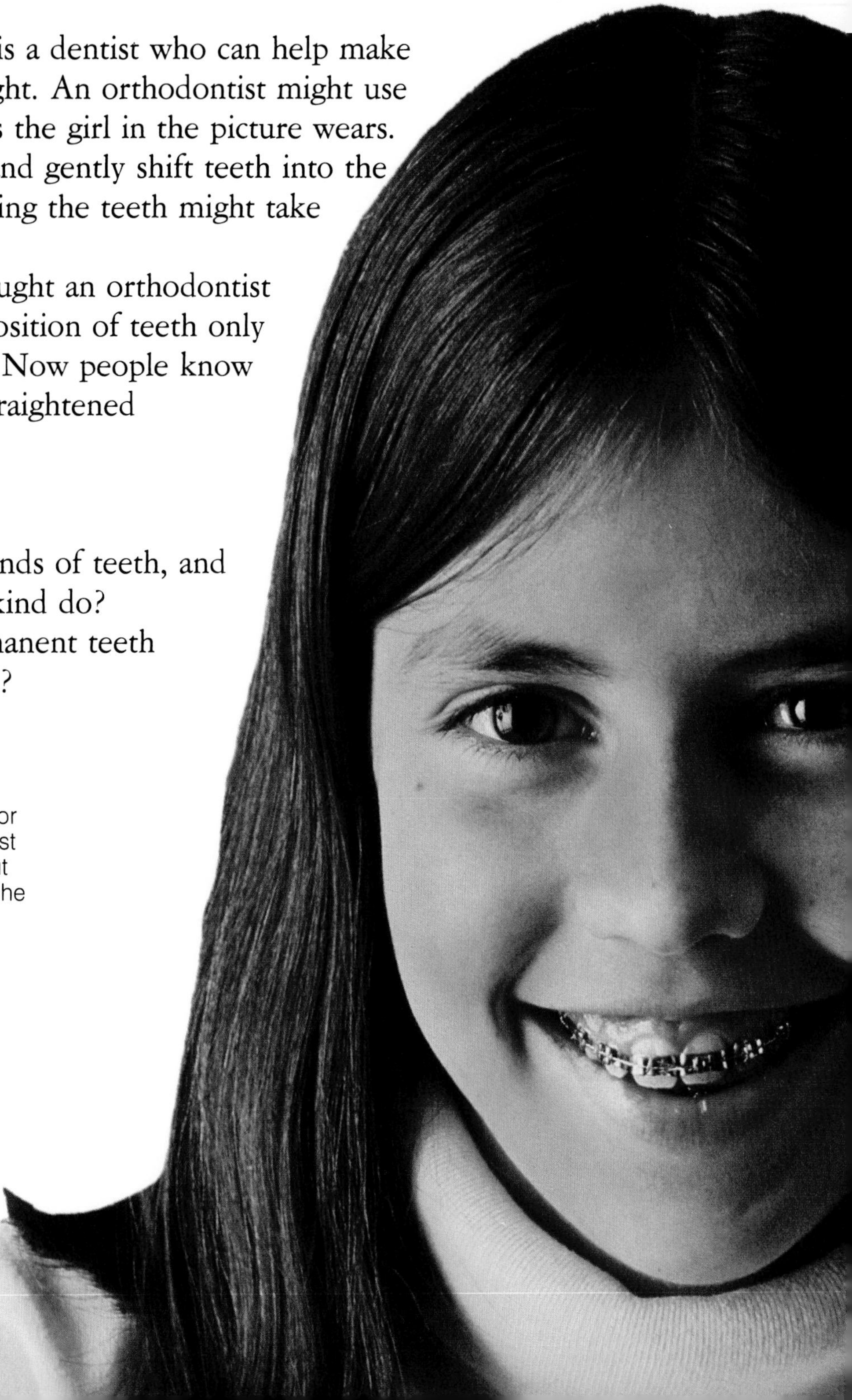

Sharon will wear braces for about two years. Why must she be extra careful about cleaning her teeth while she wears braces?

3 How Can You Keep Your Teeth and Gums Healthy?

Long ago people did not take good care of their teeth the way you do today. They did not take care of their gums. People cleaned their teeth with toothbrushes they made. Instead of toothpaste, they used materials such as chalk, eggshells, or spices.

Today people know more about how to keep teeth and gums healthy. What can you do to keep your teeth and gums healthy? You can eat fewer sweet foods that stick to your teeth. You can use a toothpaste that contains fluoride, a mineral that helps prevent tooth decay. You can visit a dentist to have your teeth checked. You can also brush and floss your teeth every day, especially after you eat. The pictures on these two pages show good ways to brush and floss your teeth.

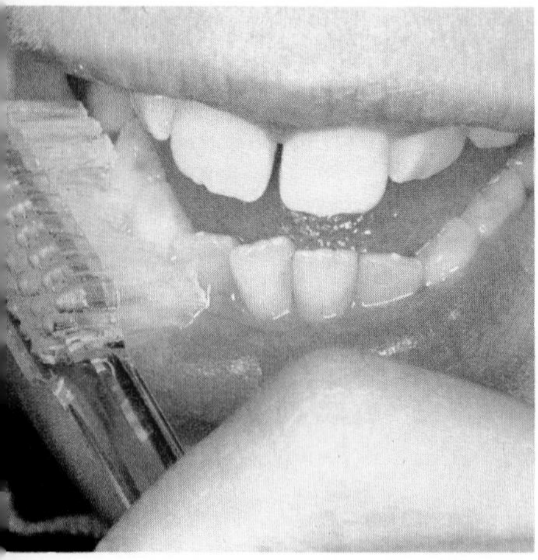

Tip your toothbrush against your gum line. Brush the outsides of all your upper and lower teeth. Use short strokes.

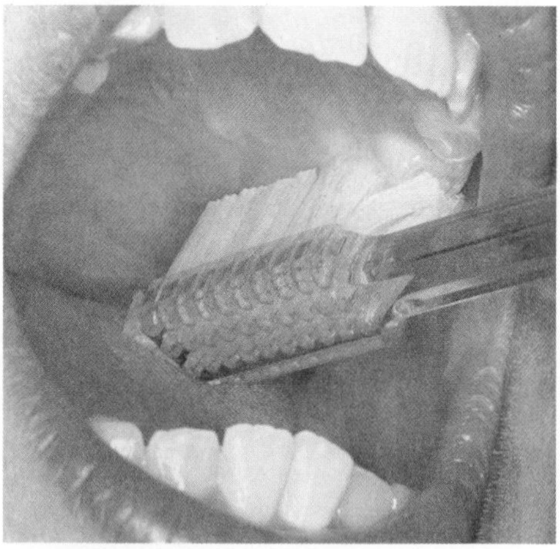

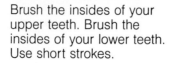

Brush the insides of your upper teeth. Brush the insides of your lower teeth. Use short strokes.

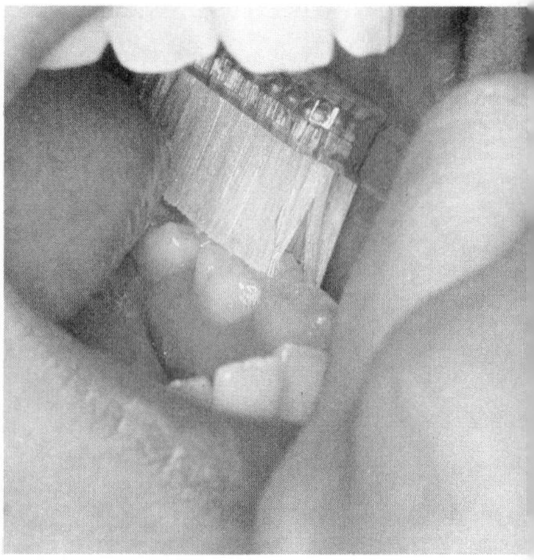

Brush the tops of your upper and lower teeth. Plaque and food can collect in the grooves on the tops of teeth.

Brushing and flossing help remove bits of food on and between your teeth and from under the gum line. Brushing and flossing also help remove **plaque** from your teeth. Plaque is a sticky, colorless layer of harmful bacteria. Plaque is always forming on your teeth.

Bacteria in plaque use sugars in the foods you eat and form acids. Such acids can destroy the enamel of a tooth. A hole called a cavity forms in the tooth when part of the enamel is gone. A small cavity might become very large if it is not filled. The tooth might be destroyed.

You help keep **calculus** from forming when you brush and floss. Calculus is plaque that has hardened. This hard material builds up between teeth and at the gum line, causing gums to pull away from teeth. Gum disease might result, which might cause teeth to loosen or fall out later in life.

plaque (plak), a sticky, colorless layer of harmful bacteria that is always forming on a person's teeth.

calculus (kal′kyə ləs), hardened plaque that forms at the gum line, causing gums to pull away from teeth.

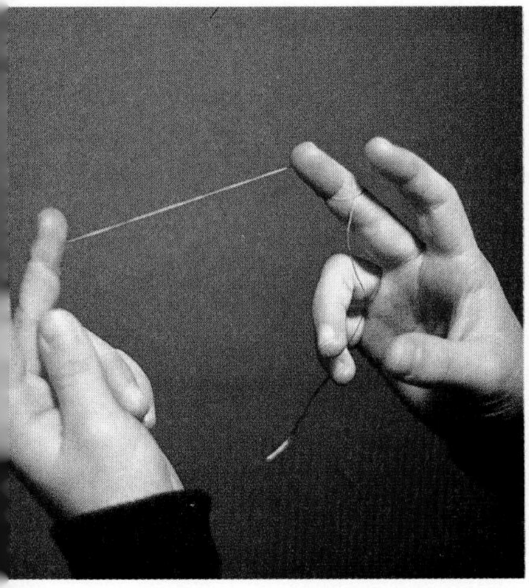

Wind some dental floss around each of your middle fingers. Hold the floss between each thumb and forefinger.

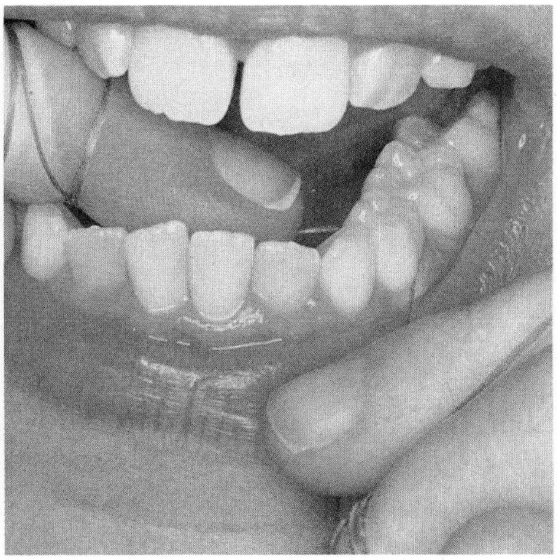

Work with about an inch of floss. Hold the floss tightly and move it back and forth gently until it reaches your gum line.

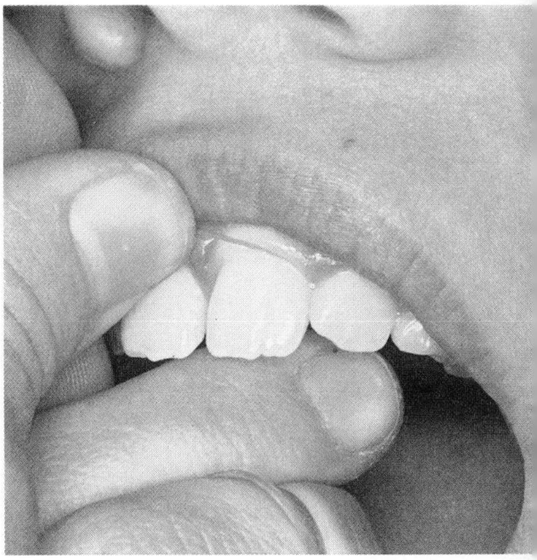

Gently scrape the floss up and down against the side of each tooth. Use a clean part of floss for each tooth.

What Happens at a Dental Checkup?

A dentist looks at your teeth and gums during a checkup. He or she checks for tooth problems.

The dentist first looks for cavities. He or she uses special tools like those shown on the tray. The dentist uses a small mirror to help look for cavities. The dentist will clean and then fill any cavity with some hard material. The filling keeps germs from causing the cavity to get bigger.

The dentist might take X-ray pictures if needed. Such pictures will help the dentist find cavities between the teeth or cavities too small to be seen with the mirror. An X-ray picture of your teeth will also show permanent teeth still forming in your jaw.

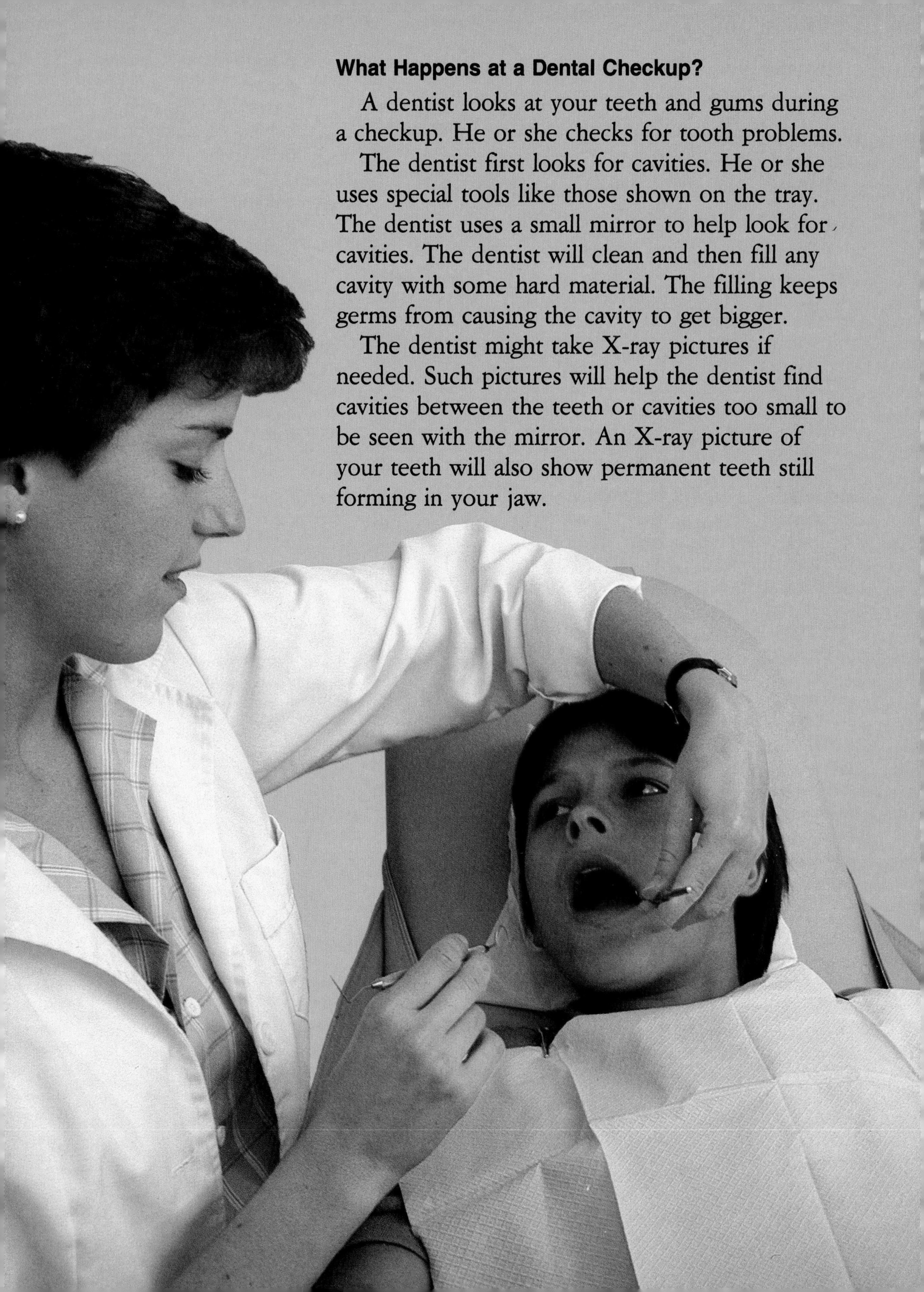

At the checkup or during another visit, the teeth are cleaned. Either the dentist or a dental hygienist cleans your teeth. The cleaning removes all the calculus on your teeth. Then special electric brushes clean and polish your teeth. These electric brushes do a better job of cleaning than toothbrushes.

Think Back • *Study on your own with Study Guide page 258.*

1. How do brushing and flossing help keep teeth and gums healthy?
2. How does fluoride help protect teeth?
3. How can teeth be harmed by eating sweet foods that contain a lot of sugar?
4. How does a dentist help keep a person's teeth and gums healthy?

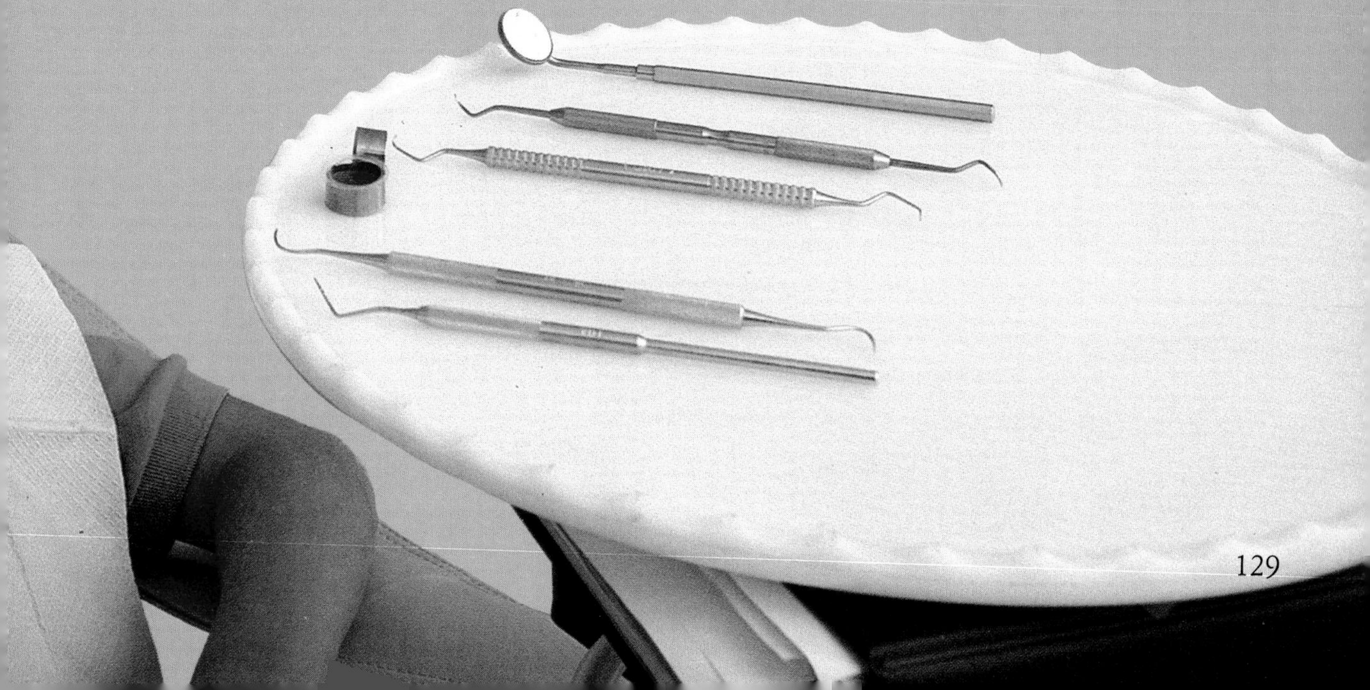

The dentist uses a mirror to check for cavities and a scaler to scrape off bits of calculus.

Learning More About Teeth and Sleep

1. Make a poster that shows one good way to take care of your teeth.

2. If you can, use a small, rounded mirror to look inside your mouth. Draw a picture of the teeth in your mouth. How many teeth do you have? What kinds of teeth do you have?

3. Keep a sleep diary for a week. Each night, write the time you go to bed. The next morning, write the time you get up. Figure out how many hours of sleep you got. Write down the number.

Next, write down how you feel each morning. Write down how you feel when you first wake up. Then, write down how you feel in an hour or so.

Before you go to bed, write a sentence or two about your day. Did you finish your schoolwork? Did you get along with friends and family?

After a week, look over your sleep diary. Notice how you felt the day after you got about eleven hours of sleep. Notice how you felt if you got less than that amount of sleep. How many hours of sleep seem the best for you?

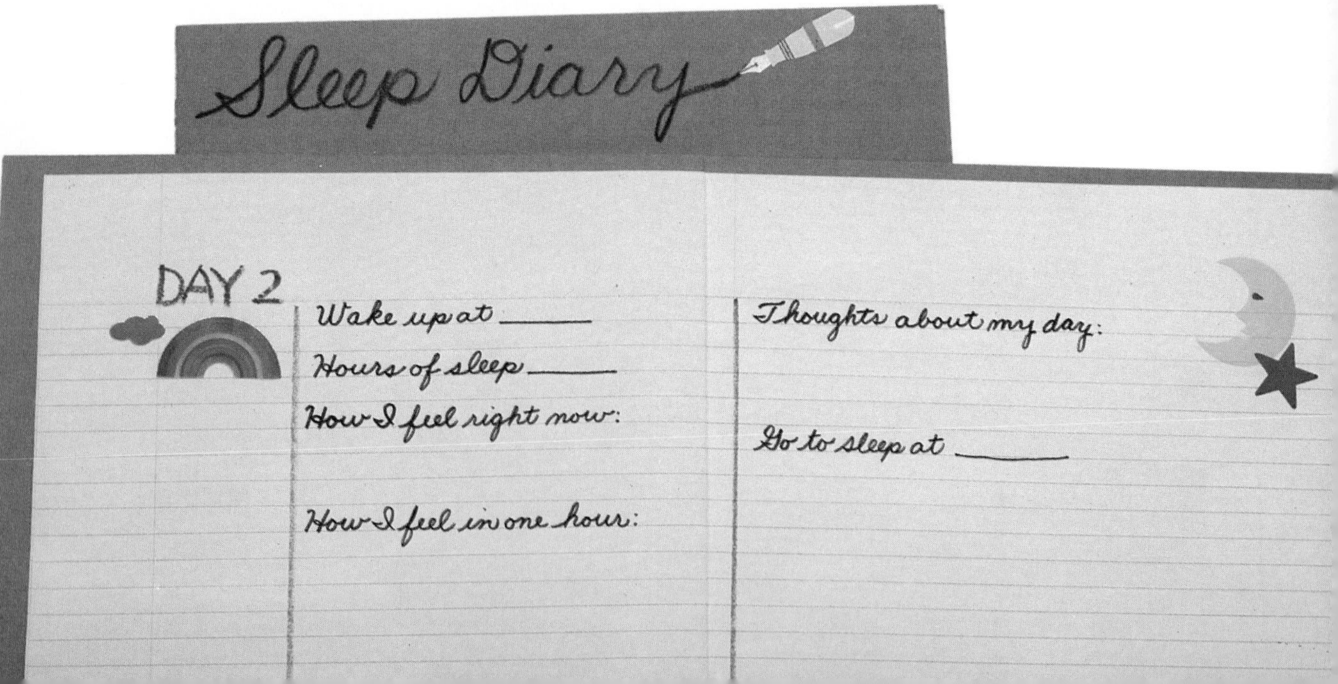

4. Unscramble the letters below. Figure out the names of four kinds of teeth.

cusdips
larsmo
sucdipsbi
cisorsin

5. Make up a short play about a person who has not had the right amount of sleep. How could sleep affect the way a person sits? walks? plays a fast game of kickball? How could sleep affect the way a person takes a test in school?

Looking at Careers

6. Most dentists have one or more **dental assistants** who work in their offices with them. A dental assistant keeps records for the dentist. For example, the dental assistant writes down all treatments each patient receives. The dental assistant answers the telephone and makes appointments. He or she might also order supplies the dentist needs.

A dental assistant often hands tools to the dentist. The assistant might also mix material for a tooth filling.

A person must graduate from high school to be a dental assistant. The person then takes a training course that might last from nine months to two years.

Write a short story about why a person might choose to be a dental assistant. Draw a picture that shows one of the duties of a dental assistant.

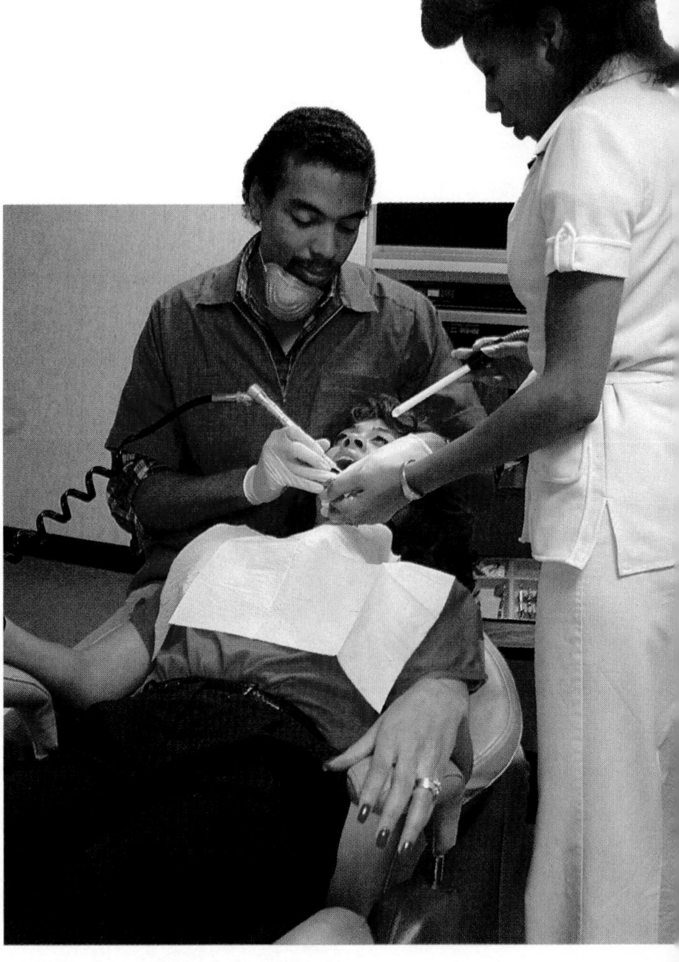

pore (pôr), a very small opening in the skin through which sweat leaves the body.

Did You Know?
Each hair in your skin has tiny muscles around the bottom of it. These muscles get shorter when you are cold. This causes hairs to stand straight up. Little bumps on your skin appear. People call these bumps goose pimples or goose bumps.

4 Why Is Your Skin Important?

Do you know that your skin does more than cover you from head to toe? Your skin protects you and helps you stay healthy. Skin helps keep germs out of your body. Germs cannot get in unless skin is cut or broken. Your skin also can stretch and fold. It grows as you grow.

Your skin helps keep your body cool in hot weather. Sweat comes out of tiny **pores,** or openings, in the skin. Sweat then evaporates into the air. When sweat leaves your skin, you feel cooler. Also, tiny blood vessels under your skin get larger when you are warm. More blood comes near the skin surface. Heat from blood leaves your body and you feel cooler.

When you feel too cool, the blood vessels under your skin get smaller. Less blood comes to the skin surface. Less heat is lost from your body.

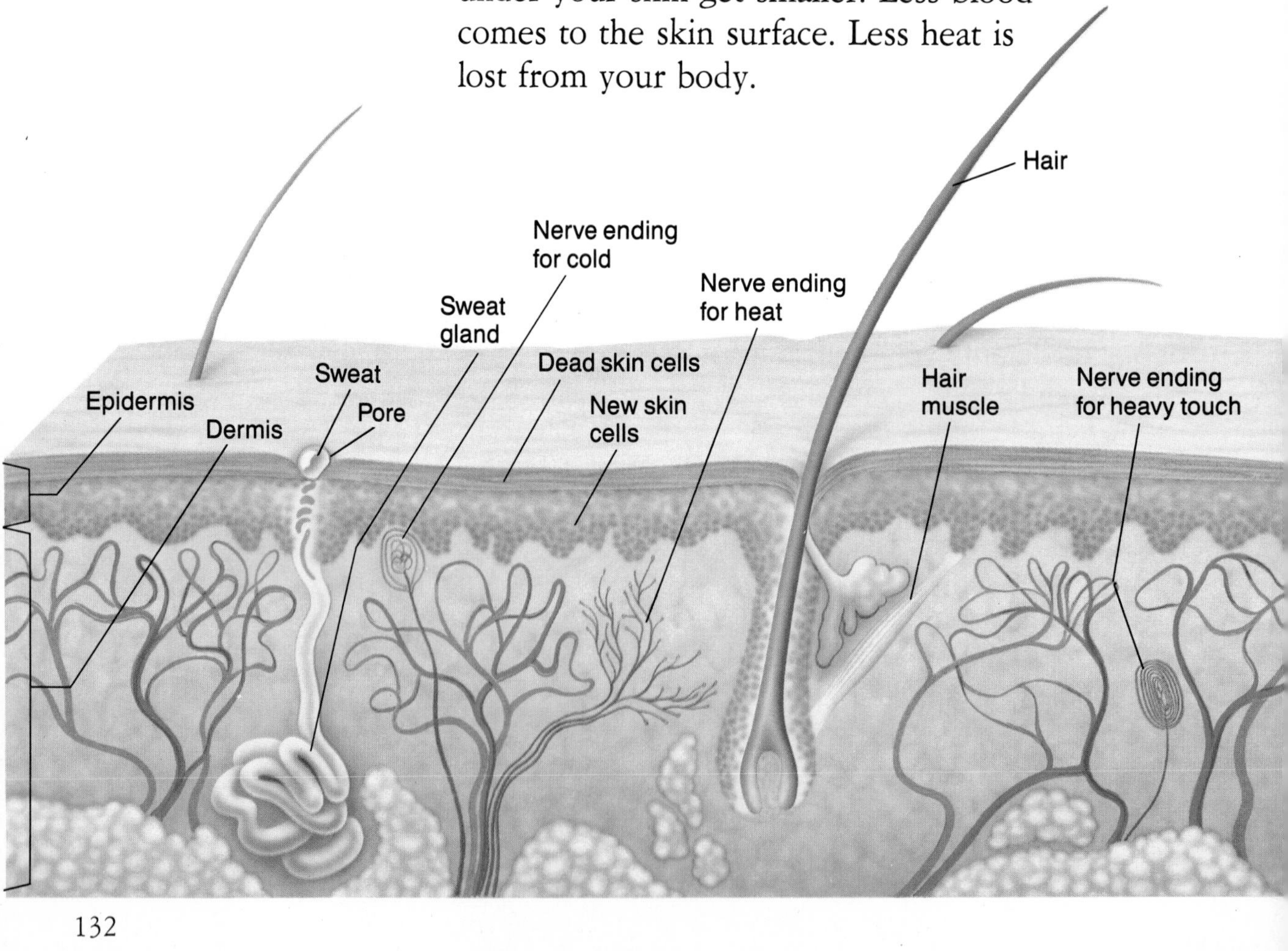

Notice in the picture that skin has two main parts. The outer part is the **epidermis.** This part is made of many layers of skin cells. The top layer is mostly dead skin cells. These dead skin cells are being rubbed off constantly.

New skin cells form in the lower layers of the epidermis. As these cells grow, they push up to the top part of the epidermis. New skin cells take the place of the older, dead cells.

The **dermis** is under the epidermis. Blood vessels and nerves are in the dermis. Oil glands in the dermis make a special kind of oil. The oil helps keep your skin soft, smooth, and waterproof.

Hair grows from pits in the dermis. Notice that each tiny hair has a nerve ending near it. These nerve endings and other nerve endings in the dermis send messages to the brain. The messages tell whether the skin has been touched by something cold, hot, hard, soft, or something that causes pain. Some nerve endings react just to hot temperatures. Some nerve endings react just to cold temperatures. Still others react to light or heavy touch or to pain.

epidermis
(ep′ə dėr′mis), the outer layers of skin.

dermis (dėr′mis), the part of skin below the epidermis.

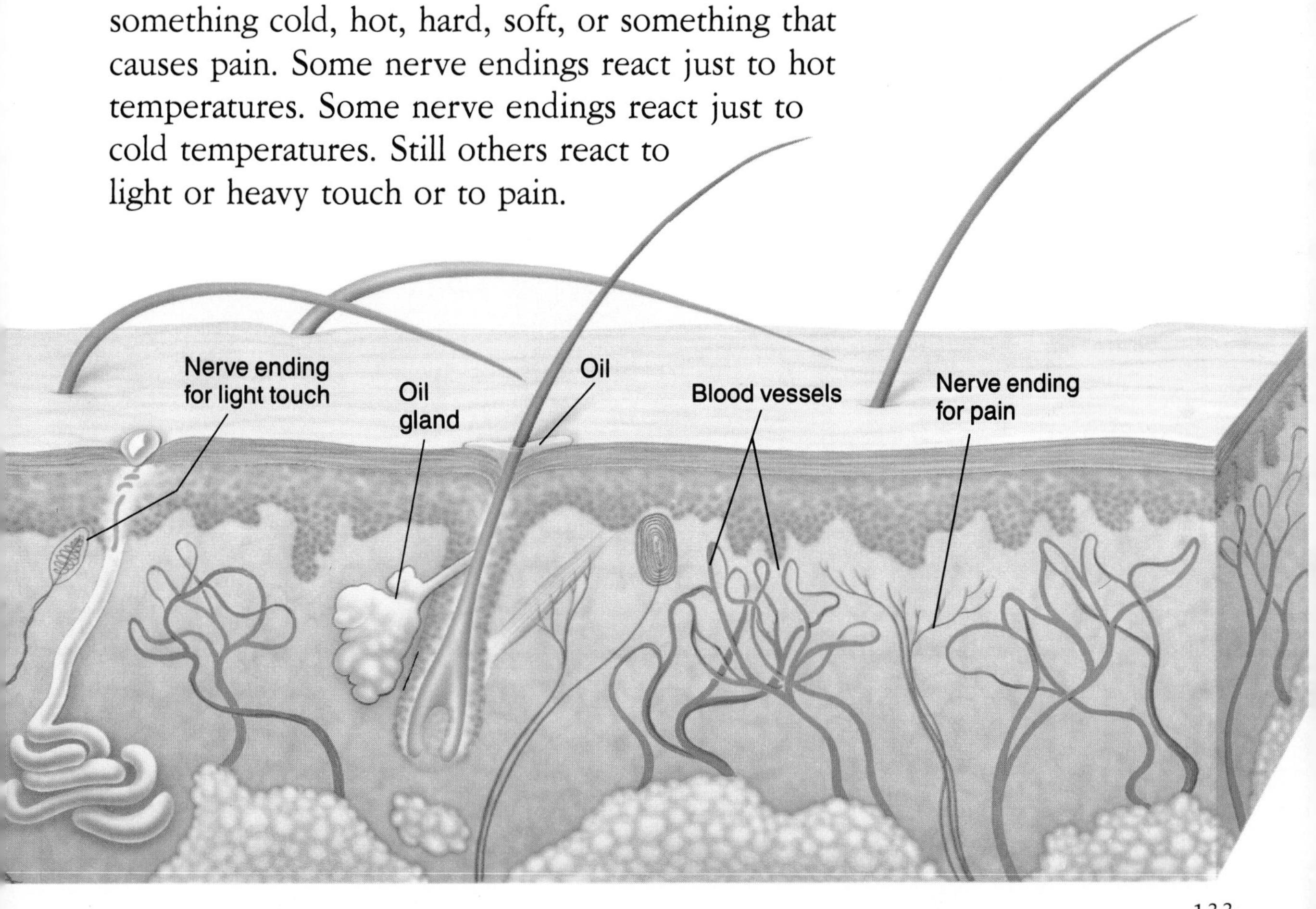

How Can You Take Care of Your Skin?

You take care of your skin by washing it. You also take care of your skin by protecting it.

When you wash, you get rid of dirt, germs, and extra oil from your skin. Wash your face with soap and water at least once a day. Wash your hands before eating and after using the toilet. Keep the rest of your body clean by taking baths or showers.

Your skin should not feel scratchy. It should not be cracked or chapped. Tell a family member if your skin is very scratchy, cracked, or chapped.

A little sunshine is good for most people. However, too much sunshine over a long time harms the skin. Protect your skin from sunburn by limiting how long you stay in the sun. Ask a family member about using a special lotion to protect your skin against sunburn. How is the girl shown here caring for her skin?

Dress warmly on cold, windy days. Very cold air can harm your skin.

Think Back • *See Study Guide on page 259.*

1. How does skin protect you?
2. How does skin help cool the body?
3. What are two ways to take care of the skin?

Learning More About Skin

1. Find out about your sense of touch. Work with a partner. Cut a file card in half and put one piece on top of the other. Slide one piece down and to the left until you have two points 1/2 cm apart, as shown in picture a. Staple the two pieces together.

Have your partner hold out a hand and close his or her eyes. Touch the palm of the hand very gently with 1 or 2 points of the card, as shown in picture b. Ask your partner if he or she felt 1 or 2 points. Repeat the procedure with 1 or 2 points on different parts of the hand. Where did your partner feel 1 point with the 1-point card? 2 points with the 2-point card? Are the nerve endings closer together where you can feel one point or where you can feel two points?

2. Think about the way the weather changes where you live. Then draw a picture that shows how you need to protect your skin during one or more different times of the year. Write a sentence or two about your picture so a person looking at the picture will learn how to protect the skin.

3. Make prints of each of your fingers. Use an inked stamp pad and drawing paper. First, press each fingertip into the stamp pad. Then press each fingertip onto the paper. Ask your classmates to do the same. How are your fingerprints alike or different from those of your classmates?

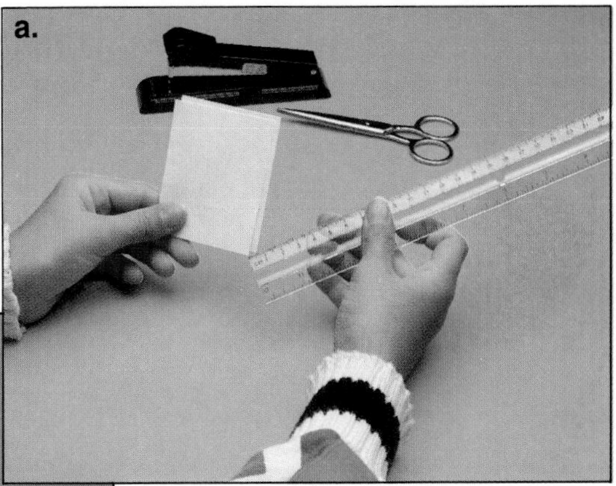

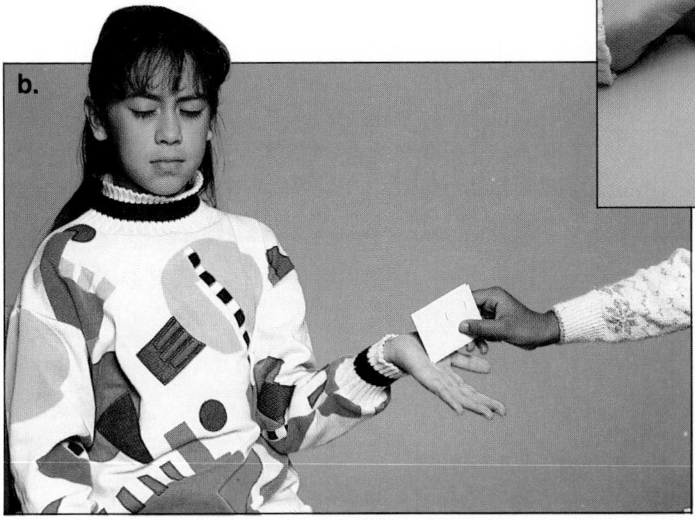

5 How Can You Take Care of Your Eyes and Ears?

Can you imagine what your life would be like if you could not see or hear? Your ears and eyes help you learn about the world around you. They also help you do many things. Your eyes and ears are very sensitive organs that need to be cared for to keep you healthy. The charts below show some other ways to keep your eyes and ears healthy.

Knowing some signs of possible eye problems can help you care for your eyes and protect them from damage. Your eyes might itch or burn, or become red and watery. These can be signs of an infection or some kind of allergy. You might have trouble seeing objects clearly unless you are close to them, like the person in the picture. You might also get headaches after reading or using your eyes for a long period of time. These might be signs that you need to wear glasses.

How To Take Care of Your Eyes

- If something is in your eyes, do not rub them. Let your natural tears wash it away. Tears can kill germs that may be in your eyes.
- Make sure you always work in a room with bright lights that do not shine directly in your eyes.
- Rest your eyes often when you are reading, watching television, or doing other close work.
- Never look directly into the sun. The rays of the sun can damage your eyes.
- Use your own towel and washcloth to avoid spreading germs that can get in your eyes.

Signs of ear problems include ringing or buzzing in your ears, dizziness, or having an earache. Another problem is fluid draining from your ears. These might be due to infections or problems with the inside parts of your ear. Some ear problems can be treated. The boy in the picture is getting drops of medicine to help treat an ear problem.

You might have a hearing problem if you cannot hear things clearly. If you need to ask many questions or sit very close to a person to hear properly, you might have a hearing problem.

If you have any of these signs, be sure to tell your parent or school nurse right away. Because your ears and eyes are so important, you should have them checked often when you are young.

Think Back • *Study on your own with Study Guide page 259.*

1. What are some signs of vision problems?
2. What are some signs of hearing problems?
3. How can you take care of your eyes? your ears?

How To Take Care of Your Ears

- Do not use small objects, such as cotton-tipped sticks, to clean your ears. A small object can damage the ear if it gets too far inside.
- Wear safety helmets to protect your ears when you play certain sports. Getting hit on the outside of the ear can damage the inside of your ears.
- Do not listen to very loud sounds, such as loud rock music, for a long period of time. Small nerve cells in the ear can be damaged by loud sounds. Nerve damage can lead to hearing loss. Sudden, loud noises can also harm nerve cells.

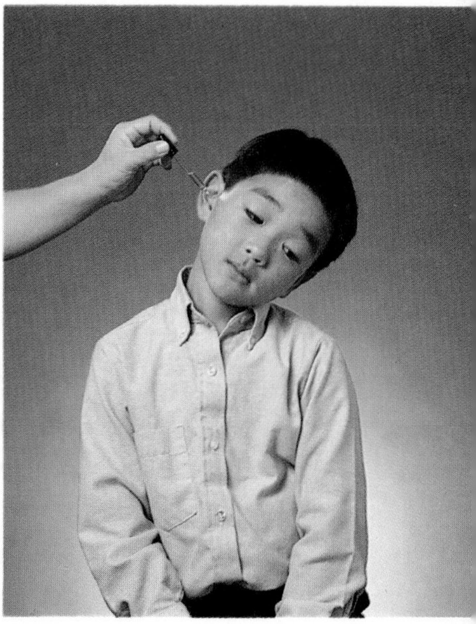

6 What Information Helps You Choose Health Products Wisely?

Imagine you are in a drugstore. You have to choose a shampoo. Which will you choose?

Shampoo is one of many health products you can buy. Such a product changes the way a person looks or feels. People buy health products for their skin, nails, hair, and teeth.

You have already read in Chapter 1 about how to make a decision. Recall the five steps.

1. Realize that a decision is needed.
2. List the possible choices.
3. List the possible results of each choice.
4. Decide which choice is best.
5. Judge the decision.

How do you think you could follow these five steps and choose a good shampoo for yourself? First, you need to get information. You can get information about health products from labels, such as the ones you see here. Ads, certain magazines, and other materials have information about health products. People who know about health can also give you information. Once you get more information about a health product, you could use the steps to decide about it.

What Can You Learn from a Label?

Anything you buy that comes in a package has a label. The label gives information about the product. Find the following on the label of the product shown on these two pages:

- the name of the health product
- what the health product is
- the weight of the health product
- the ingredients—what the product is made of
- the directions for using the product
- warnings or cautions for using the product

Information on the label of a health product can help you choose wisely. Suppose you want a shampoo for normal hair. You can look on the label for the words *for normal hair.* You would not buy those shampoos that have the words *for dry hair* or *for oily hair.*

You may need to try a product to see if it is right for you. You might choose the small size of a new product to try.

What other information might be helpful for a person choosing a shampoo?

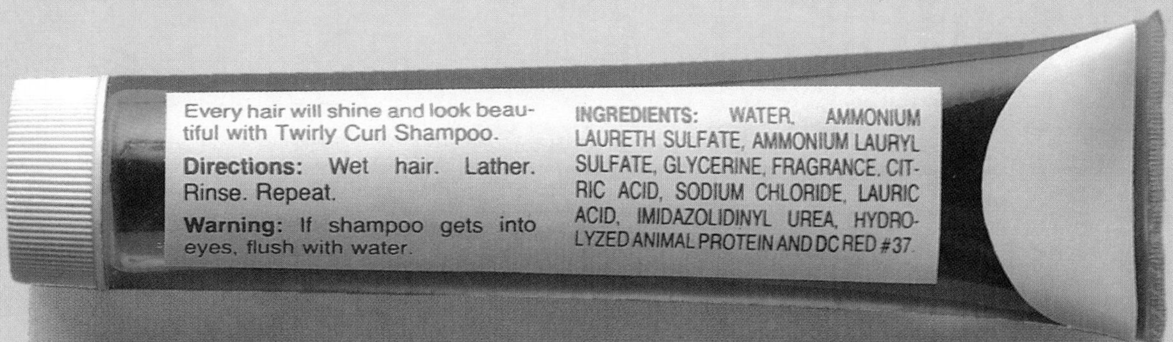
Every hair will shine and look beautiful with Twirly Curl Shampoo.
Directions: Wet hair. Lather. Rinse. Repeat.
Warning: If shampoo gets into eyes, flush with water.
INGREDIENTS: WATER, AMMONIUM LAURETH SULFATE, AMMONIUM LAURYL SULFATE, GLYCERINE, FRAGRANCE, CITRIC ACID, SODIUM CHLORIDE, LAURIC ACID, IMIDAZOLIDINYL UREA, HYDROLYZED ANIMAL PROTEIN AND DC RED #37.

On Your Own

A person must choose between two kinds of soap that are the same size. One soap comes in a brightly colored box. This soap smells nice. The other kind has a plain paper covering, no nice smell, and costs less. Write two or three sentences explaining why a person might choose the kind in the brightly colored box. Write two or three sentences explaining why a person might choose the other kind. Then write what choice the person might make and why.

What Should You Know About Ads?

The purpose of any advertisement is to get you to buy a product. Ads provide information about the product. Some information is helpful in choosing a health product. Some information in an ad is not so helpful.

Helpful information states what the product can or cannot do. The ad for one soap states it has no perfume. If you wanted a soap without perfume, then this information would be helpful.

Ads sometimes include a statement by a person or a group of people. Such statements can be helpful or not so helpful.

These ads give information about two toothpastes. One ad has a statement by a famous tennis player. The other ad has a statement by the American Dental Association (ADA), a group of dentists. Which ad do you think is more helpful in making a choice about toothpaste?

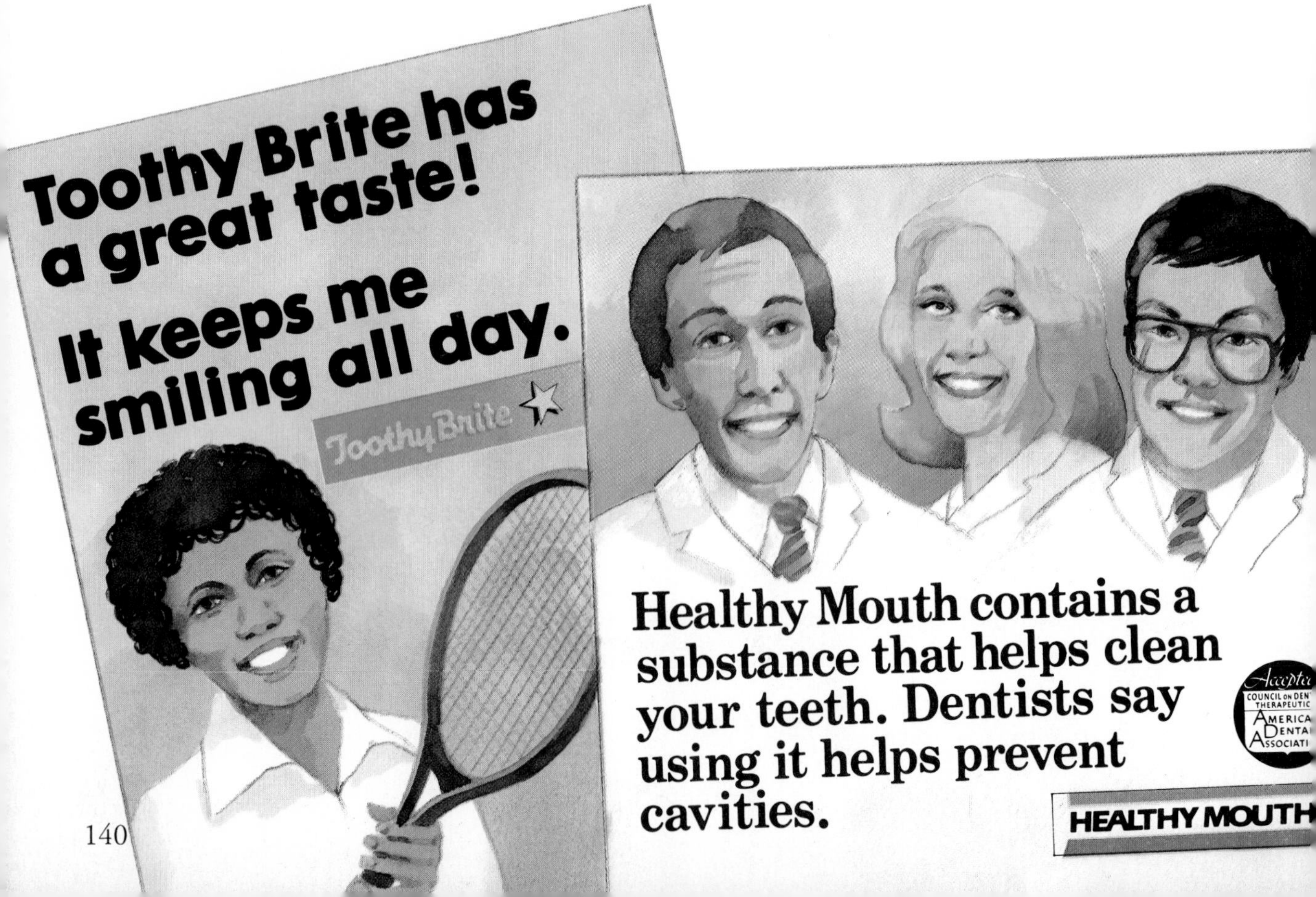

Where Can You Get More Information About Health Products?

Sometimes you need more information to decide about a health product. Labels or ads might not tell all you want to know.

You can get help from people who know about health products. You can ask a doctor, school nurse, pharmacist, or dentist. Ask a member of your family who has used the product, as this girl is doing. Your family might give you helpful information.

You can also find information about health products at a library. Ask a librarian to help you find magazines and materials for young people about health products.

Think Back • *Study on your own with Study Guide page 259.*

1. How can you get helpful information about health products?
2. What kinds of information does a label provide on a health product?
3. What kind of helpful information can be found in an ad?

Growing a New Skin

Playing with matches caused a terrible accident for two brothers. In the accident, almost all the skin of both boys was destroyed. The boys, Jamie and Glen Selby, were not expected to live. Yet both boys are alive today. Doctors grew some new skin for each boy.

The skin covers and protects the body. It helps keep germs out of the body. When badly burned people lose a great amount of skin, they might get diseases the skin would usually protect them from getting.

To help people with bad burns, doctors often try to take unburned skin from the person. They put the unburned skin over a burned part of that person's body. The skin then grows together. Doctors could not help the boys in this way. They did not have enough unburned skin left.

Dr. G. Gregory Gallico led a team of doctors in Boston, Massachusetts, and tried something new to save the boys' lives. The doctors took a piece of unburned skin about the size of a stamp from each boy. They broke the skin down into cells. Then they put the skin cells from each boy into a bottle. They mixed the cells with nutrients to help the cells grow.

After only a few weeks, the skin cells grew into pieces like the one shown. The doctors then put the skin over the burned parts of the boys' bodies. The boys began to get better.

The new way to grow skin was discovered by Dr. Howard Green. Both Dr. Gallico and Dr. Green hope the new treatment can help other people. The doctors hope that people with burns will have a better chance to get well.

Talk About It

1. How did doctors grow new skin for Jamie and Glen Selby?
2. What important job must a new skin be able to do?

Here you can see skin cells growing in a special container in a laboratory.

Being Helpful About Sleep

You have learned that people need sleep for good health. You might want to share with family members reasons why sleep is important. You might do more on your own about getting to bed yourself. You might also want to talk about ways family members can help each other get the sleep they need.

Following are some suggestions. What other ways can you think of?

- Get your homework done well before bedtime. Then you can fall asleep knowing you are ready for school the next day.
- Take a rest or go to bed without being told when you feel tired.
- Be thoughtful when someone is sleeping. Play quietly.

Reading at Home

The Story of Your Mouth by Alvin and Virginia Silverstein. Putnam, 1984. Describes the jobs of different parts of the mouth and some mouth problems.

What's Skin For? by Patricia Blakely. Creative Education Publishers, 1981. Answers many questions about skin.

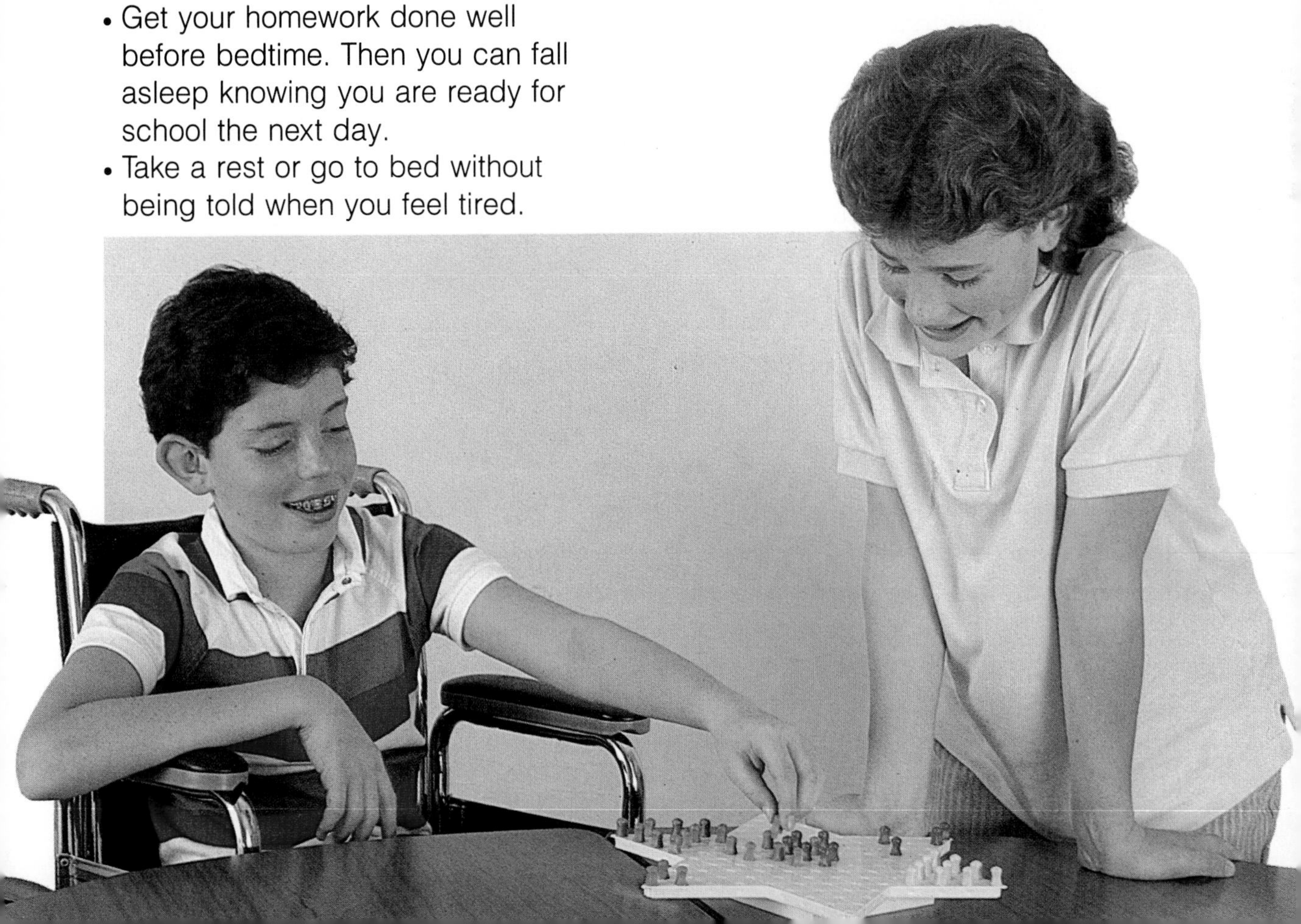

Chapter 5 Review

Reviewing Lesson Objectives

1. Describe body changes during sleep and how sleep and rest affects learning and feelings. (pages 120–121)
2. Name the four kinds of teeth and describe the job of each kind. Explain how teeth might grow in crooked. (pages 122–125)
3. Tell why brushing, flossing, using fluoride, and eating healthy foods are important for healthy teeth and gums. Describe what happens in a dental checkup. (pages 126–129)
4. Explain how skin protects and cools the body. Tell how to take care of the skin. (pages 132–134)
5. Describe signs of vision and hearing problems and how to care for eyes and ears. (pages 136–137)
6. Tell who or what can give information about health products and what the information includes. (pages 138–141)

For further review, use Study Guide pages 258-259

Practice skills for life for Chapter 5 on pages 283-286

SKILLS FOR LIFE

Checking Health Vocabulary

Number your paper from 1–18. Match each meaning in Column I with the correct word or words in Column II.

Column I

1. a tooth used to grind food
2. an opening through which sweat leaves the body
3. information inviting a person to buy a product
4. the part of skin that has nerves and blood vessels
5. a mineral that helps prevent tooth decay
6. harmful bacteria on teeth
7. parts of the body that send messages to the brain
8. a tiny structure that makes oil to keep skin soft
9. the outer part of the skin
10. plaque that has hardened on teeth
11. a front tooth used to cut food
12. the hard white covering of a tooth
13. a sharp tooth used to tear food
14. the tissue that covers the roots of teeth
15. a way to remove plaque and food from between teeth
16. a tooth with two sharp points that tear and crush food
17. where information is found on the outside of a product
18. an item that changes the way a person looks or feels

Column II

a. advertisement
b. bicuspid
c. calculus
d. cuspid
e. dermis
f. enamel
g. epidermis
h. fluoride
i. flossing
j. gums
k. health product
l. label
m. incisor
n. molar
o. oil gland
p. plaque
q. pore
r. sense organs

Reviewing Health Ideas

Number your paper from 1–14. Next to each number write the word or words that best complete the sentence. Choose the words from the list.

muscles	growth
teeth	information
crown	incisors
dental floss	molars
fluoride	roots
germs	skin
gum disease	warning

1. During sleep, the ___ rest.
2. Sleep is needed for ___.
3. Teeth are held in the jaw by ___.
4. People can see the ___ of a tooth in the mouth.
5. ___ are the front teeth that bite and cut food.
6. ___ are the back teeth that grind food.
7. Plaque is always forming on the ___.
8. Hardened plaque can cause ___.
9. Using a toothpaste that contains ___ can help protect teeth.
10. You can use pieces of ___ to remove food from between teeth.
11. Unbroken skin helps keep ___ out of the body.
12. The ___ helps cool the body.
13. A label on a health product might include a ___.
14. An ad for a health product gives ___ about the product.

Understanding Health Ideas

Number your paper from 15–26. Next to each number write the word or words that best answer the question.

15. About how much sleep do people your age need each night?
16. What are new teeth called?
17. What daily activities help keep teeth and gums healthy?
18. What part of a tooth can plaque harm?
19. What does skin make to keep it soft and smooth?
20. What removes germs from skin?
21. What comes out of pores?
22. How can sugary foods harm teeth?
23. What are signs of vision and hearing problems?
24. What should you do if you hear ringing or buzzing in your ears?
25. Where can you find directions for using a health product?
26. What would be an example of an ad that is not helpful?

Thinking Critically

Write the answers on your paper. Use complete sentences.

1. How might healthy teeth and gums help the digestive system work well?
2. Write an answer to a person who says that brushing is the only care teeth ever need.

Chapter 6

Food and Your Body

The boy in the picture often makes the lunch he takes to school. At times he is not sure what food to pack that will taste good and also be good for him. This chapter will explain how to choose good foods for yourself. You will also learn about what harm can come from not eating certain foods. This information can help you develop good eating habits to keep you healthy now and all through your life.

Health Watch Notebook

Each day, write down in your notebook all the different foods you ate. At the end of the day, write down one thing you could add or subtract that would have made your food choices healthier.

1 How Does Your Body Signal It Needs Food?
2 What Can Help You Get the Foods You Need?
3 What Diseases Might a Lack of Nutrients Cause?
4 What Are Some Healthy Eating Habits?
5 How Can You Keep Foods Safe to Eat?

Did You Know?
Food does not just fall down to your stomach. Food you eat is pushed along down the food tube by rings of muscles. This explains why you can swallow food even standing on your head.

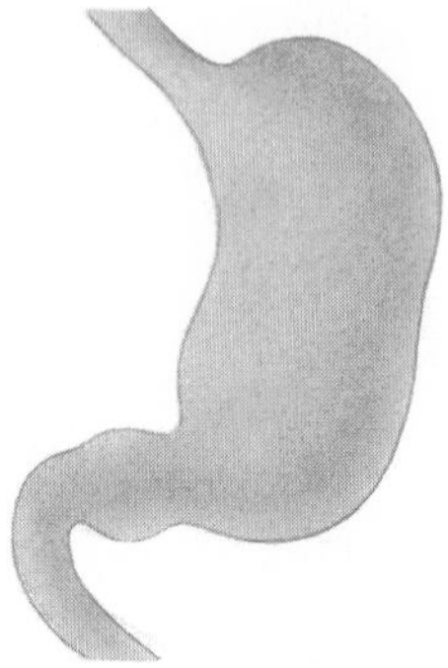

The stomach right after a meal

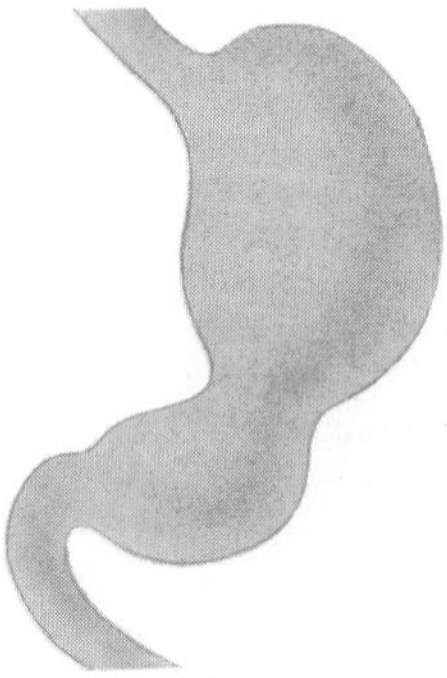

The stomach two hours later

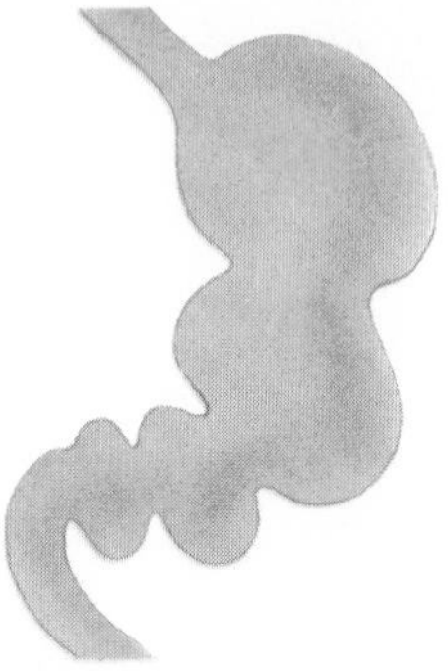

The stomach four hours later

1 How Does Your Body Signal It Needs Food?

Suppose you go to the playground one Saturday morning after breakfast. None of your friends has a watch. Even without knowing the time, you might know when to go home to eat lunch. What could remind you?

Did you decide that your body would help you? If so, you are right. Your body sends some signals that it needs food when your stomach is empty or almost empty.

After you eat, your stomach contains food. Muscles in your stomach walls begin to twist and bend your stomach. These movements mix the food with special liquids in your stomach to help digest the food. The pictures show how the stomach changes as it mixes and digests food.

Some partly digested food is ready to leave your stomach in a short while. Other food stays in your stomach longer. The walls of the stomach keep moving back and forth to mix and help digest the food.

About four hours after you eat a meal, your stomach might be empty or almost empty. When your stomach is empty or almost empty, the walls of your stomach still move back and forth. An empty stomach and the movement of the stomach walls cause messages to go to your brain. Then the brain signals you that you are hungry.

Why Does Your Body Need Food?

You need food to stay healthy. Food also helps you grow by providing what your body needs to build new cells. Food has what your body needs to function as it should. Food also gives you energy for everything you do each day.

Have you ever gone to school without eating breakfast? Starting a day without eating means a person has not had food for a long time. Many people find it hard to keep their minds on their work without enough food. Many people feel tired. They might not have enough energy for work and play.

People need to eat many different kinds of food to stay healthy. Different foods help the body in different ways. For example, some foods provide more energy than other foods. Some foods help build strong muscles. Other foods help keep the parts of your body working together as they should. Read the chart below to learn more jobs food does for you.

On Your Own
Look at the chart of the ways food helps the body. Choose one of the jobs food does. Write a paragraph telling how food does that job for you every day.

How Food Helps Your Body

- Food helps you grow as you should.
- Food helps build strong bones, teeth, and muscles.
- Food builds new body cells and repairs worn-out cells.
- Food gives you energy for work and play.
- Food helps keep your body warm.
- Food helps your body work as it should.
- Food helps you stay healthy.
- Food helps you feel alert and happy.

Think Back • *Study on your own with Study Guide page 260.*

1. How do you know your body needs food?
2. Why does your body need food?

nutrient (nü′trē ənt), a substance in food that the body needs for growth, energy, and good health.

2 What Can Help You Get the Foods You Need?

Suppose you listed all the foods you ate last week. Your list would be a long one. Yet, it would not include all the foods that people can buy in food stores and restaurants. How do you know which of these foods you need to eat to be healthy?

Foods contain substances called **nutrients.** Scientists have discovered more than fifty different nutrients in foods. The six main kinds of nutrients are proteins, carbohydrates, fats, vitamins, minerals, and water. Each kind of nutrient helps your body grow and stay healthy. Some nutrients help make new cells and repair worn-out cells. Other nutrients help provide energy. Still others help your body work as it should. Different foods have different nutrients. Some foods have more than one kind of nutrient. Enough of the different nutrients working together help keep you healthy.

Every day you need foods with enough of the six main kinds of nutrients. One way to get the foods you need is to choose foods from the basic four food groups, shown on pages 151–154. You will get the nutrients you need if you eat the right number of servings from each group. After you read about the four food groups, you will know what the numbers on the boy's balloons mean.

What Foods Are in the Vegetable-Fruit Group?

All fruits and vegetables together make up the vegetable-fruit group. You need four or more servings every day from this group. Every day eat one serving of a fruit or vegetable such as an orange, grapefruit, some green pepper, some broccoli, or a tomato. Every other day eat one serving of a dark green or a deep yellow vegetable. Which dark green or deep yellow vegetable would you choose?

What Foods Are in the Bread-Cereal Group?

Breads, cereals, crackers, and rice are some foods in the bread-cereal group. All foods in this group are grains or are made from grains. You need four or more servings every day from the bread-cereal group. What food from this group have you had today?

What Foods Are in the Milk-Cheese Group?

Milk and foods made from milk make up the milk-cheese group. You need three or more servings every day from the milk-cheese group. Children aged nine to thirteen need two to three cups of milk each day. You can get another serving from the milk group by eating foods made from milk. What foods can you name that are made from milk?

What Foods Are in the Meat-Poultry-Fish-Bean Group?

The foods shown here represent some of the foods in the meat-poultry-fish-bean group. You need two servings from this group every day. What can you eat instead of meat, fish, chicken, or beans for a serving?

What Foods Are Not in One of the Food Groups?

Some foods do not belong in any of the four food groups. These foods include margarine, butter, and salad dressings. People need only small amounts of such foods. Chips, cookies, and candy also do not belong in any of the four food groups. These foods often have large amounts of sugar and fat. They do not have many of the nutrients you need to grow and be healthy. Try not to eat such foods too often or in too large amounts.

The girl in the picture eats a healthy lunch at school. What food groups does her lunch include?

Think Back • *See Study Guide on page 260.*

1. What are the basic four food groups?
2. What are three foods from each food group?
3. What do the numbers 4–4–3–2 tell about food groups?

School lunches, such as the one this girl is eating, might include foods from several food groups.

Health Activities Workshop

Learning More About the Four Food Groups

1. You can make a sandwich that has foods from several food groups. What foods are in the sandwiches in the picture? What food group does each food fit into?

Think up a sandwich you like that has foods from more than one food group. Draw a picture of your sandwich and label the foods in it.

2. Think about the many different kinds of fruits and vegetables. Make a list of all the vegetables you know. Try to make a list of all the fruits you can think of too. Then compare the lists others in your class made. What are the names of some fruits and vegetables that are new to you?

3. Find a recipe you could copy and bring to school. You might choose one your family likes. You might choose a recipe that uses foods from more than one food group. Work with your classmates to make a cookbook with the recipes. What foods do you need to make the recipe shown? What food groups do the foods fit into?

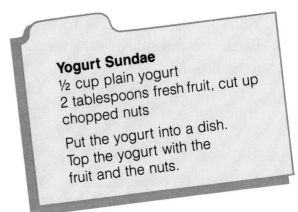

Yogurt Sundae
½ cup plain yogurt
2 tablespoons fresh fruit, cut up
chopped nuts

Put the yogurt into a dish.
Top the yogurt with the fruit and the nuts.

4. Read the list of foods one person ate one day. Copy the chart you see next to the list. Check to see whether this person ate enough foods from the food groups this day. Make a mark for each food. Be sure to check the snacks too. The first box is partly filled in for you. Also write on your paper whether this person ate enough foods from the food groups for the day.

5. Make a list of the foods you ate yesterday. Decide which foods came from plants. Did some foods come from animals that eat plants? If so, which ones?

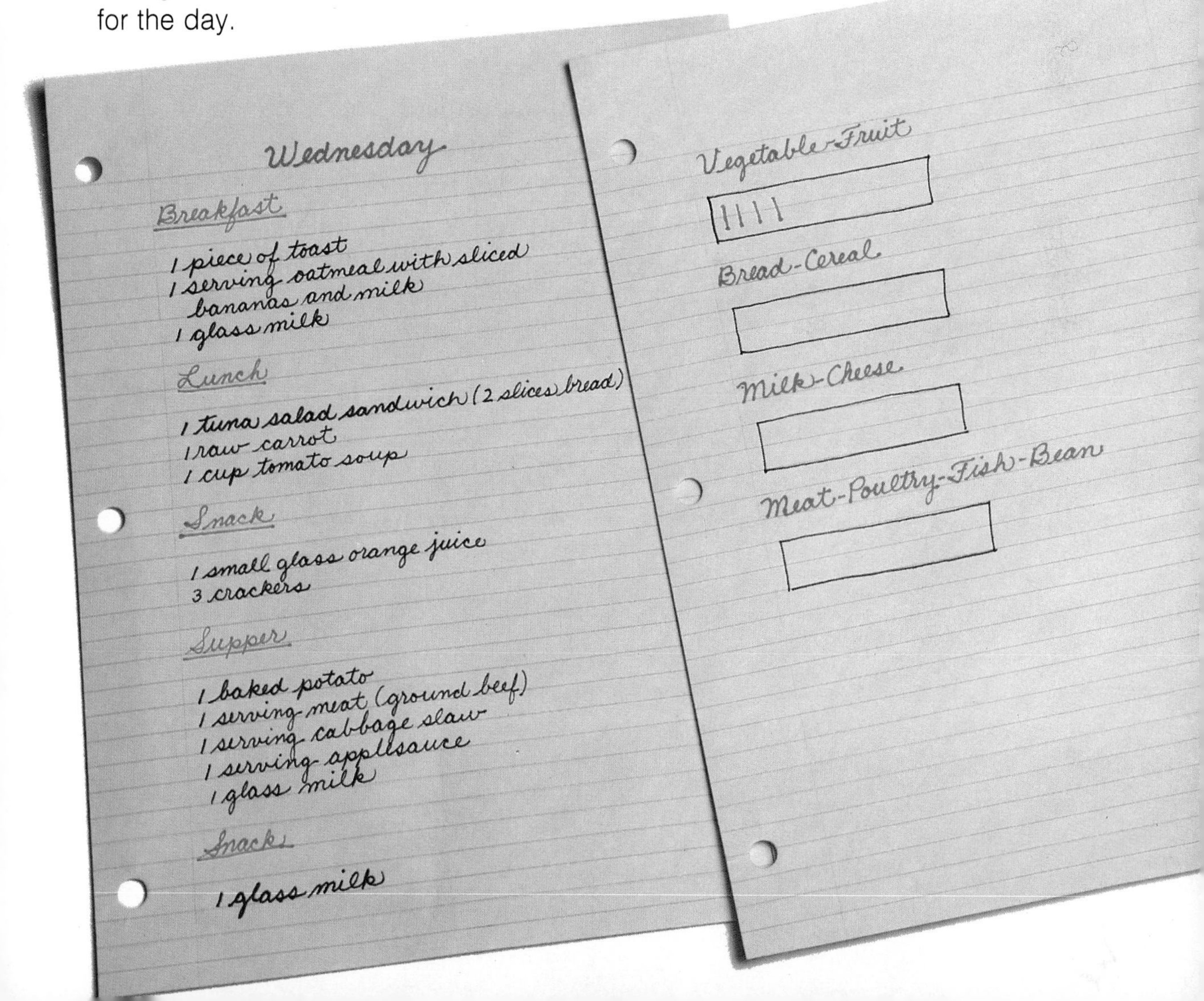

rickets (rik′its), a disease caused by too little vitamin D. The disease causes bones to soften, bend, or become crooked.

3 What Diseases Might a Lack of Nutrients Cause?

You might wonder how what you eat affects your health. Learning about diseases caused by a lack of certain nutrients can give you an answer. Two of these diseases are rickets and scurvy.

Rickets is a disease that causes crooked bones. People with rickets might become crippled. Before 1919 the disease harmed many babies and children in the United States. At that time doctors did not know what caused rickets. Then in 1919 doctors learned that children who had rickets did not get enough of the nutrient vitamin D. The body uses vitamin D to build strong bones and teeth. Without this nutrient, bones become soft.

In the United States not many children get rickets now. Milk and many kinds of cereals have vitamin D added to them. Most people get enough vitamin D from these foods and from natural sunlight. The labels on milk cartons and cereal boxes tell that vitamin D has been added.

Scurvy is a disease that causes bleeding gums, loss of teeth, and bleeding inside the body. For hundreds of years scurvy was a mystery disease. No one knew the cause. Many sailors got scurvy and died.

scurvy (skėr′vē), a disease caused by too little vitamin C. The disease causes bleeding, weakness, and sometimes death.

In 1746 a British Navy doctor made a study of scurvy. He found that sailors on ocean trips had only a few foods to eat. Sailors ate mostly hard biscuits and salted meat. They ate very few fresh fruits or vegetables on their trips. The doctor suggested that sailors drink lemon juice on their ocean trips. As a result, the sailors no longer got scurvy. The doctor did not know why the lemon juice helped, but it did.

About one hundred years later, the cause of scurvy was discovered. A lack of the nutrient vitamin C causes scurvy. British sailors who drank lemon juice did not get scurvy because lemons have vitamin C.

Today very few people get scurvy. People get vitamin C by eating foods such as those shown.

Think Back • *Study on your own with Study Guide page 261.*

1. What is rickets and what causes this disease?
2. What is scurvy and what causes this disease?

Many fruits and fruit juices and certain vegetables have vitamin C.

On Your Own
Two different ways to serve tomatoes are to slice them in a salad and to broil them with bread crumbs. Write down two or three ways to prepare each of these foods: apples, corn, potatoes, and ground beef. Write why you like the foods prepared these ways.

People can buy cereals, salad dressings, canned vegetables and fruits, and other foods that have less salt and sugar in them. What products like these have you tried?

4 What Are Some Healthy Eating Habits?

Martha had supper at her friend June's house. At home Martha told about her favorite part of the meal. "June's father made a beautiful tray of fruit and cheese for dessert. Maybe we can do that soon. I really liked it."

Martha had a good time at June's house. She also learned about a good eating habit June and her family have. What do you think it is?

June's family has started to eat fewer foods made with large amounts of sugar. They choose fruit when they want a dessert or a sweet snack. Eating fewer foods that are made with large amounts of sugar is one healthy eating habit. Such foods as candy, cookies, or soft drinks usually do not have many other useful nutrients. Foods made with large amounts of sugar can also help cause cavities.

Eating fewer foods with large amounts of salt is another healthy eating habit. This habit might help prevent people from getting high blood pressure. Your body needs some salt. However, most foods have all the salt you need. If you taste food before you add salt, you might not want to add it. You might also want to choose foods that are unsalted, for example, unsalted nuts and unsalted chips. Many families are choosing products such as those in the picture that have less salt and less sugar.

Another good eating habit is eating fewer foods with large amounts of fat, such as fried foods. For example, many families often eat baked and broiled chicken, fish, and meat instead of eating these foods fried. Eating many fatty foods over many years might harm your heart and blood vessels.

Trying foods new to you is a way to learn about different kinds of foods you might enjoy. Trying new foods can make meals more interesting. It can also help people eat a wide variety of foods. Notice in the picture that Pete is going to try a new Italian food. Eating many different foods can help you get the nutrients you need.

Think of some of the foods you enjoy most of all. You enjoy them now because you were willing to try them. You might need to try a food several times before you really like it.

Pete and his grandparents often try new foods when they go out to eat.

Think Back • *See Study Guide on page 261.*

1. How might people limit the amount of sugar, salt, and fat they eat?
2. What is one way to make meals more interesting?

Did You Know?
Most bacteria and many yeasts and molds are helpful. For example, certain bacteria are used to make cheese. Certain yeasts help bread dough rise. Certain molds are used to make medicines.

5 How Can You Keep Foods Safe to Eat?

Have you ever seen bread or fruit with spots of black or green mold like those in the picture? Have you ever noticed that some milk has turned sour? All the food pictured is spoiled. Sour milk also is spoiled.

Many foods spoil because of bacteria, yeasts, and molds. These living things can grow in food and spoil it.

You can usually tell if food has spoiled. Often the food has an unpleasant smell. Spoiled food might also look different. It might be covered with green or black mold. Sometimes a scum forms on spoiled food. Eating spoiled food can make you sick. Do not ever even taste a food if it looks or smells spoiled. If you are not sure if a food is spoiled, throw it away to be safe.

Mold growing on these foods means the foods are spoiled.

How Can You Keep Foods from Spoiling?

Storing foods properly helps keep them from spoiling quickly. Bacteria, yeasts, and molds grow best in warm, moist places. They grow very slowly in cold places and hardly at all in icy, freezing places. Most bacteria, yeasts, and molds do not grow in dry places.

Store such foods as bread, milk, cheese, and eggs in the refrigerator. Store meat, fish, and poultry in the refrigerator if they will be used in a few days. For longer storage, put them in the freezer. Most refrigerators also have a special place to store fresh fruits and vegetables.

You can store foods such as dry cereals, crackers, flour, sugar, and mixes outside the refrigerator. They should be kept closed. Some foods in jars, such as most kinds of peanut butter, can be kept on shelves. Many foods in jars need to be stored in the refrigerator only after you open them. Always read the labels on such foods to learn where they can be stored safely after they are opened.

On Your Own
Look at the foods shown on this page. List where each food should be stored to keep it safe to eat.

How Can You Prepare Foods Safely?

You can keep germs from spreading by preparing foods in safe ways. Always wash your hands with soap and water before you prepare foods. Washing helps get rid of harmful bacteria that might be passed from your hands to the food. Harmful bacteria might make you and other people sick or cause the food to spoil.

Wash fresh fruits and vegetables before you eat or serve them. Washing removes harmful bacteria that might be on the food. Washing also removes dirt and chemicals from sprays that might be on foods. Use clean dishes and clean knives, forks, and spoons.

Put leftover food away right after you have finished eating. Cover such foods and put them in the refrigerator. Keeping leftover foods cold helps keep bacteria, molds, and yeasts from growing rapidly in them.

Also be careful about the foods you take from home for a picnic or in your lunch. Some of the foods in the picture need to be kept cold. What other picnic foods can you name that need to be kept cold?

On picnics, carry moist foods, such as salads, and cooked foods, such as baked beans or cooked chicken, in special coolers. Carry milk in vacuum bottles.

How Can You Be Careful When Buying Foods?

You need to be careful when you buy foods in stores. Now and then foods do spoil in stores. Some useful shopping tips are listed below. These tips can help keep you from buying spoiled foods.

- Do not buy any eggs that are cracked. Open the carton and check for broken eggs before you buy them. Cracked eggs might be spoiled.
- Do not buy a can of food that is badly dented. Do not buy a can that is bulging out. These cans might have spoiled food.
- Do not buy any opened package of food that is supposed to be sold in a sealed container.
- Do not buy a box of frozen food if it has started to melt. The food might have started to spoil.
- Check fresh fruits and vegetables for soft places or cuts. Such foods can spoil easily.
- Check to see if a food package has a date for use. If so, do not buy the food after that date.

Why do you think buying the foods shown here might be unsafe?

Think Back • *Study on your own with Study Guide page 261.*

1. What causes foods to spoil?
2. What foods can be stored on shelves?
3. What are three ways to prepare foods safely?
4. What are three shopping tips that can help a person keep from buying spoiled foods?

Health Activities Workshop

Being Safe with Foods

1. Pretend you are returning a badly dented can of food to a store. Act out what you would say to the store manager. Later, talk about what you acted out. Why is it a good idea to return a can that is damaged? Do you think a store manager would be angry at a person who returns such a can? Explain your answers.

2. Find out how milk gets from a farm to a dairy where it is put into bottles or cartons. How is the milk kept from spoiling on the way from a farm to a dairy?

Also find out how harmful bacteria in milk are killed in the dairy. Use an encyclopedia or a book on foods to help you. You could look under *milk*, *pasteurize*, or *dairy*. Be ready to tell or write about what you learned.

3. Talk to a person who works in a restaurant. You might talk to a food server or a cook. Ask the person about ways food is prepared and stored to keep it safe. Make a report about what you learn.

4. Look in an encyclopedia for information about diseases that are caused by a lack of nutrients. Write down how the disease can be prevented by eating enough of certain foods. You might start by looking under *beriberi* or *pellagra*.

Looking at Careers

5. Many people in your community have jobs working with food. A **chef** is a skilled cook. Chefs work in restaurants, hospitals, and schools.

In a hospital, a chef is in charge of the hospital kitchen. Meals are prepared there for patients and for people who work in the hospital. The chef directs all those who do the cooking and those who put together the food. The chef also directs the people who serve food and wash the dishes.

A hospital chef learns his or her work by taking classes in special schools and by working for other chefs. A chef enjoys planning foods that are healthful and tasty. Make a list of some of the foods that a hospital chef might need to include in meal plans for one day in a hospital.

George Washington Carver and the Peanut

What is your favorite food for lunch? If you said a peanut butter sandwich, you should thank George Washington Carver. He helped make the peanut an important food crop in the United States.

George Washington Carver lived from 1864 to 1943. During his life, he developed more than three hundred products from peanuts. Carver is shown with some of his students in a laboratory.

George Washington Carver was born a slave on a farm in Missouri in 1864. When he was eleven years old, Carver moved away from home to go to school. He thought about becoming a painter, but later he decided to study agriculture. Carver earned a college degree in agriculture in 1896.

Carver then went to teach at Tuskegee Institute in Alabama. There he began to study peanuts. Most farmers in the early 1900s thought that peanuts were useless as a crop. Carver showed that peanuts had many nutrients. He also showed that other good foods could be made from ground-up peanuts. These foods included peanut cheese, milk, and flour. Carver also showed how to make such products as ink, dyes, wood stains, and soap from peanuts.

George Washington Carver became famous for his work with peanuts. He also developed products from sweet potatoes and pecans and convinced farmers to plant those crops as well.

Talk About It

1. What new products did George Washington Carver make from peanuts?
2. How did George Washington Carver show that peanuts could be an important addition to healthy meals?

Sharing Information About the Food Groups

You can share what you have learned about foods with your family. You can make some pictures to show your family the four food groups. You might make your pictures like those shown. On your pictures, write the name of the food group that each food comes from.

Hang your pictures where everyone can see them. You might find a place in the kitchen, such as on the refrigerator door.

Reading at Home

The Down to Earth Cookbook by Anita Borghese. Scribner's, 1980. Learn how to make some healthy meals and snacks for you and your family.

Night Markets: Bringing Food to a City by Joshua Horwitz. Crowell, 1984. Learn how different kinds of foods arrive at city markets.

Chapter 6 Review

Reviewing Lesson Objectives

1. Tell what causes feelings of hunger and why the body needs food. (pages 148–149)
2. Name some foods in each of the basic four food groups. Tell how many servings from each group are needed each day. (pages 150–155)
3. Explain what causes rickets and scurvy. (pages 158–159)
4. List some healthy eating habits. (pages 160–161)
5. Explain what might cause food to spoil. List ways to avoid spoiled food. (pages 162–165)

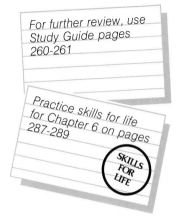

For further review, use Study Guide pages 260-261

Practice skills for life for Chapter 6 on pages 287-289

Checking Health Vocabulary

Number your paper from 1–4. Match each meaning in Column I with the correct word in Column II.

Column I	***Column II***
1. a substance in food that the body needs for health	a. nutrient
2. a disease of soft bones caused by too little vitamin D	b. rickets
3. a disease caused by too little vitamin C	c. scurvy

Number your paper from 4–9. Next to each number write the word that best completes the sentence. Choose the words from the list below.

cells	habits
vitamin D	spoil
rickets	scurvy

4. Food provides nutrients that ____ need to grow.
5. Foods such as oranges, potatoes, green peppers, and tomatoes help prevent the disease ____.
6. Limiting salt and sugar are good food ____.
7. The disease ____ harmed many children in the United States before 1919.
8. Eating cereal and milk with ____ added helps prevent rickets.
9. While some kinds of bacteria cause food to ____, other kinds are useful.

Reviewing Health Ideas

Number your paper from 1–12. Next to each number write the word or words that best complete the sentence. Choose the words from the list.

bacteria	meat-poultry-fish-bean
bones	nutrients
bread-cereal	scurvy
breakfast	vegetable-fruit
energy	vitamin C
fat	vitamin D

1. Without food you would not have ____ for work and play.
2. Eating ____ helps most people do their best work in the morning.
3. Different foods have different ____ needed for health.
4. Two apples, a serving of green beans, and some salad make up the servings you need from the ____ group.
5. Noodles, rice, and cereal are in the ____ group.
6. Nuts are in the ____ group.
7. Milk and cereal have ____ added to them.
8. Rickets harms a person's ____.
9. Long ago, sailors drank lemon juice to get the nutrient ____.
10. Today people avoid the disease ____ by eating fresh fruits and vegetables.
11. One healthy eating habit is to avoid foods with large amounts of ____.
12. ____ can cause food to spoil.

Understanding Health Ideas

Number your paper from 13–22. Next to each number write the word or words that best answer the question.

13. About how many hours does food from a meal stay in your stomach?
14. How do many people feel if they do not eat breakfast?
15. What does food provide to help you work and play?
16. What do all foods have that the body needs for health?
17. How many servings do you need from the vegetable-fruit group?
18. How many servings do you need from the bread-cereal group?
19. What foods other than milk provide servings from the milk-cheese group?
20. How many servings do you need from the meat-poultry-fish-bean group?
21. What did sailors drink on ocean trips long ago to prevent scurvy?
22. What is the first action to take before eating or preparing food?

Thinking Critically

Write the answers on your paper. Use complete sentences.

1. Make up a daily menu with foods you like to eat. Be sure you get the number of servings you need from each food group.
2. How might a family start to use less salt or sugar or begin to try new foods? Tell why starting the new habits might be healthy.

Chapter 7

Medicines and Other Drugs

Look at the buttons the girl wears on her backpack. They show the decision she has made about using drugs. This chapter has important information about medicines and other drugs. You will learn about some kinds of medicines and how people use them. You will learn about some drugs and how they can harm your health. You will be able to use this information to make healthy decisions about medicines and other drugs now and in the future.

Health Watch Notebook

Go to a library or some restaurants in your community and find out their smoking policies. Write the policies in your notebook. Also write down why you think these rules were made.

1 What Are Medicines and How Do People Use Them?
2 How Does Tobacco Affect Health?
3 How Does Alcohol Affect the Body?
4 How Do Marijuana, Cocaine, and Other Substances Affect Health?
5 How Can You Make Healthy Decisions About Drugs and Medicines?

JUST SAY
NO
GET HIGH
ON
LIFE
JUST SAY NO

drug, a substance other than food that causes changes in the body.

This medicine is in the form of drops. It kills the germs that cause the child's ear infection.

1 What Are Medicines and How Do People Use Them?

You know people use medicines. You probably know medicines must be used safely. Did you know that medicines are a kind of drug?

A **drug** is a substance that causes changes in the way the body works. A drug can change the way a person thinks, feels, or acts. Medicines are drugs used for health reasons. Medicines come in different forms. These forms include pills, creams, and liquids.

Used safely, medicines can help people in different ways. Some medicines help a sick person get better by helping cure a disease. The child in the picture is getting medicine from her mother. The medicine helps cure the child's ear infection.

Some medicines help control disease. Many people with the disease diabetes take a certain medicine every day. The medicine does not cure the disease but it helps the person's body work as it should as long as the person keeps taking it.

Some medicines can help keep people from getting sick. For example, a certain medicine called a vaccine works to keep you from getting polio. What other diseases can vaccines prevent?

A person in a hospital is given a medicine before an operation. The medicine makes the person sleep very soundly. Then the person does not feel pain during the operation. Another medicine can stop pain the person might feel after the operation.

What Are Two Kinds of Medicines?

The grown-up in the picture is choosing an **over-the-counter medicine.** A person can buy this kind of medicine without a doctor's order. Many different stores, including food stores and drugstores, sell over-the-counter medicines.

People use over-the-counter medicines for health problems that are not very serious. These problems include a stuffy nose or a mild headache. Most over-the-counter medicines should be used only for a short time. Labels on the packages tell people how to use the medicines. Warnings on the labels tell people to check with a doctor if the health problem does not go away in a short time.

Some medicines can be bought only with a doctor's order called a **prescription.** A doctor considers a person's age, size, and health problem when ordering medicine. A pharmacist carries out the orders for a prescription. He or she types the doctor's directions on the label. Why should a person read and follow these directions?

over-the-counter medicine, any medicine a person can buy without a doctor's order.

prescription (pri skrip′shən), a doctor's order for a medicine.

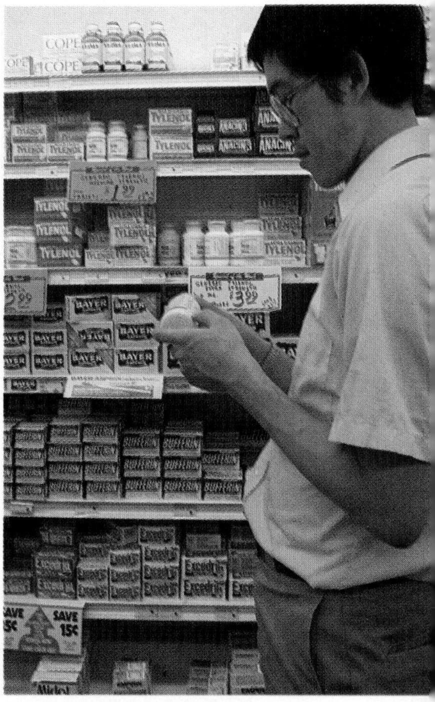

A person needing an over-the-counter medicine should read the label before he or she buys it. When else should the person read the label on the medicine?

side effect, any unwanted change in the body that a medicine causes.

What Are Side Effects?

Many people do not know a very important fact about medicines: A medicine that helps many people might also cause unwanted changes in the bodies of a few people. An unwanted change is a **side effect.** People need to know about side effects to use medicines safely.

Both over-the-counter and prescription medicines can cause side effects. Some side effects are dizziness, upset stomach, headache, or rash. Bleeding or having trouble breathing are more serious side effects.

Some medicines have warnings about certain side effects. A person who has a side effect from taking a medicine should stop taking the medicine at once. If the side effect is caused by a prescription medicine, the doctor who ordered the medicine should be called quickly. Why should the doctor know about a side effect right away?

Report any side effect from a prescription medicine to the doctor who wrote the prescription.

How Can Medicines Be Used Safely?

Jill had a headache one day. She thought about taking some medicine. What should Jill do? She did the right thing. She asked her mother for help. She obeyed the first of the following rules for using medicines safely.

- You should take medicine only with the help of a grown-up you trust.

A grown-up can make sure medicines are used safely. Taking the wrong amount of a medicine can make people very sick. Taking too much of some medicines all at once can kill a person.

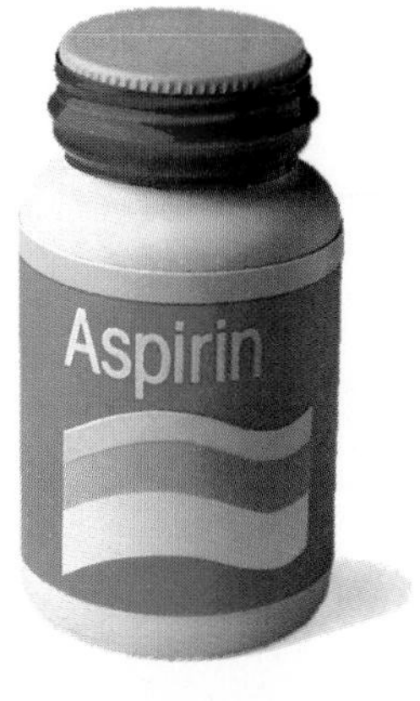

- People need to follow directions to use any medicine safely.

People should read and follow the directions on the package each time the medicine is used. Any medicine should be kept in the jar or bottle it came in.

Do not buy an over-the-counter medicine if the safety seal is broken or missing.

- No one should take a prescription medicine meant for someone else.

The medicine was ordered by a doctor for one person. The medicine could harm someone else.

- Do not buy medicines in opened packages.

Many over-the-counter medicines, like the one in the picture, come in sealed bottles and packages. The seal helps make sure people get a medicine that has not been opened already. Why might this be important?

- All medicines also need to be stored safely.

If medicine containers have safety caps, these caps should be kept on the containers. Medicines should be kept away from small children. A locked cabinet is a safe place for medicines. What other safe places for medicines can you think of?

How Do People Misuse Medicines?

Medicines can be harmful if they are misused, or used in an unsafe way. People can misuse medicines by not following the directions carefully or taking the wrong amount. A person might think if a little medicine helps, more medicine is better. The person might take too much of the medicine at one time. Misusing a medicine in such a way is not safe.

Some people misuse medicines another way. They take medicines when they do not really need them. People need not take medicines for every little ache and pain, such as headaches from feeling tired or hungry. The body often takes care of such health problems without medicines. Sometimes food or rest is all that is needed. A person should take a medicine only when it is really necessary.

Think Back • *See Study Guide on page 262.*

1. What are medicines?
2. How are prescription medicines and over-the-counter medicines different?
3. What are side effects?
4. What are safe ways to use medicines?
5. How can medicines be misused?

Health Activities Workshop

Learning More About Medicines

1. Ask a grown-up in your family to show you the container of an over-the-counter medicine. Read the label together. What kinds of information do you find on the label? Write down the safety information you find.

2. Look for a magazine ad for a medicine. Cut out the ad and paste it on a sheet of paper. Look for answers to these questions about the ad. What is the medicine supposed to do? What are the directions for using the medicines? What advice would you give people before they decide to take the medicine?

Looking at Careers

3. A **food and drug inspector** checks food and medicines for safety. For example, an inspector checks to see that machines that make medicines are clean and work properly. Inspectors also make sure the information on medicine labels is correct. Many medicines have information about the use of the medicine on a paper inside the package. Inspectors check this information.

A person usually needs to go to college for four years to be a food and drug inspector. After school, an inspector might work for the Food and Drug Administration (FDA). Use an encyclopedia to find out what the FDA does.

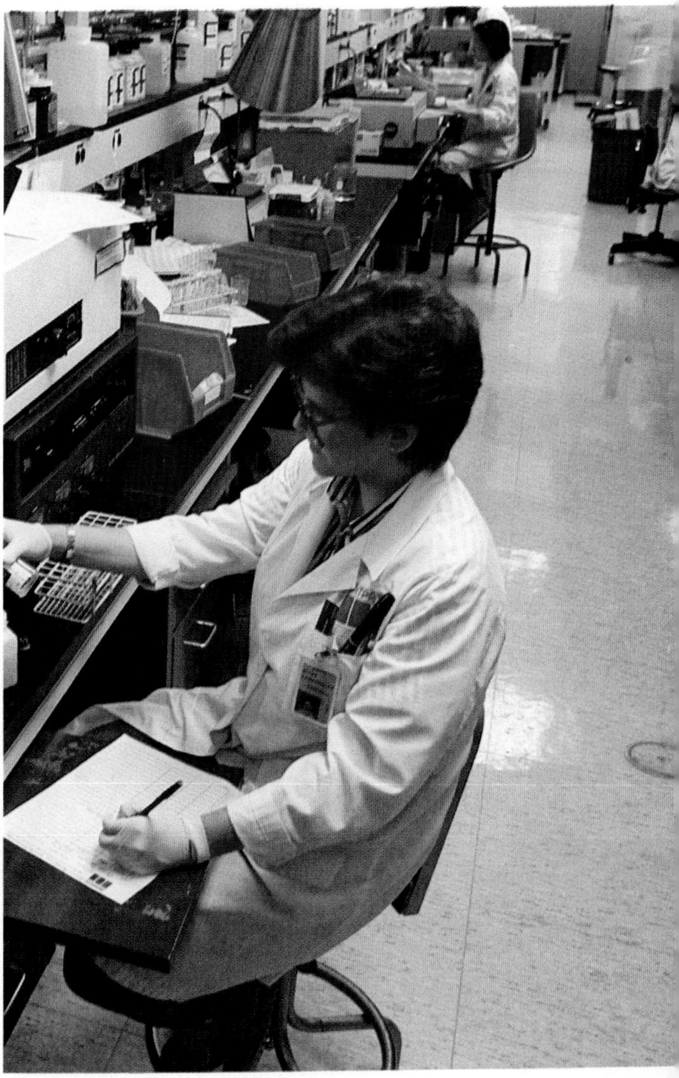

nicotine (nik′ə tēn′), a drug in tobacco that speeds up the heart and causes the blood vessels to become narrow.

2 How Does Tobacco Affect Health?

Have you ever noticed a person smoking a cigarette and coughing? People who smoke or chew tobacco take many harmful substances into their bodies.

How Does Tobacco Harm the Heart and Lungs?

Tobacco is a plant that has a drug in it called **nicotine.** This drug makes the heart beat faster than it should. Nicotine also makes the blood vessels become narrower. Then the heart has to work harder to pump blood through the narrow vessels. A person who smokes cigarettes over many years is more likely to get heart diseases than a person who does not smoke.

Tobacco harms health in other ways. As tobacco burns, a dangerous gas called carbon monoxide forms. This gas causes changes when taken into the body. The gas takes the place of some of the oxygen in the person's blood. Many people who smoke often feel tired because they do not have enough oxygen in their blood.

Healthy lung

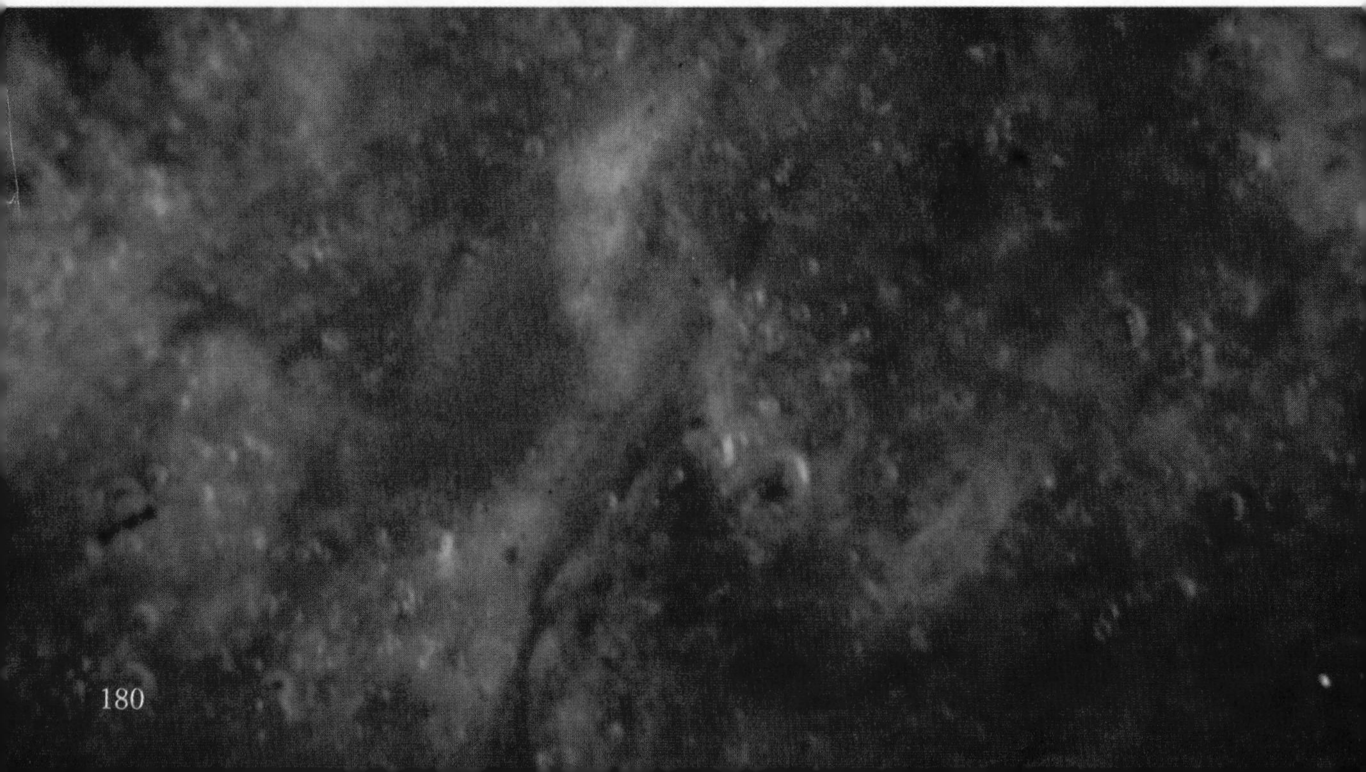

A person who breathes in cigarette smoke harms the lungs and the tubes that lead to the lungs. The pictures show a healthy lung and a smoker's lung. The harmful substances in smoke have damaged the smoker's lung and have turned it black.

People who smoke cigarettes for a long time often get serious lung diseases. Hot smoke makes the walls of the tubes that lead to the lungs red and sore. The soreness causes too much mucus, a wet, sticky substance, to form. The mucus clogs the tubes. These smokers cough hard and for a long time to bring up mucus.

Some of the substances in cigarette smoke harm the air sacs in the lungs. The damaged air sacs cannot take enough oxygen from the air. After years of smoking cigarettes, the smoker might have a hard time breathing.

People who smoke cigarettes year after year are more likely to get lung cancer than people who do not smoke. Lung cancer is hard to cure. Many people die of lung cancer.

Did You Know?
It takes only a few seconds for a cigarette to start making changes in the smoker's body. In just a few seconds, cigarette smoke makes the smoker's heart beat faster, raises blood pressure, and replaces some of the oxygen in the blood with carbon monoxide.

After years of smoking cigarettes, a smoker's lungs will not work as well as the lungs of a person who does not smoke. This picture shows how the walls of air sacs have broken down, making breathing difficult.

Smoker's lung

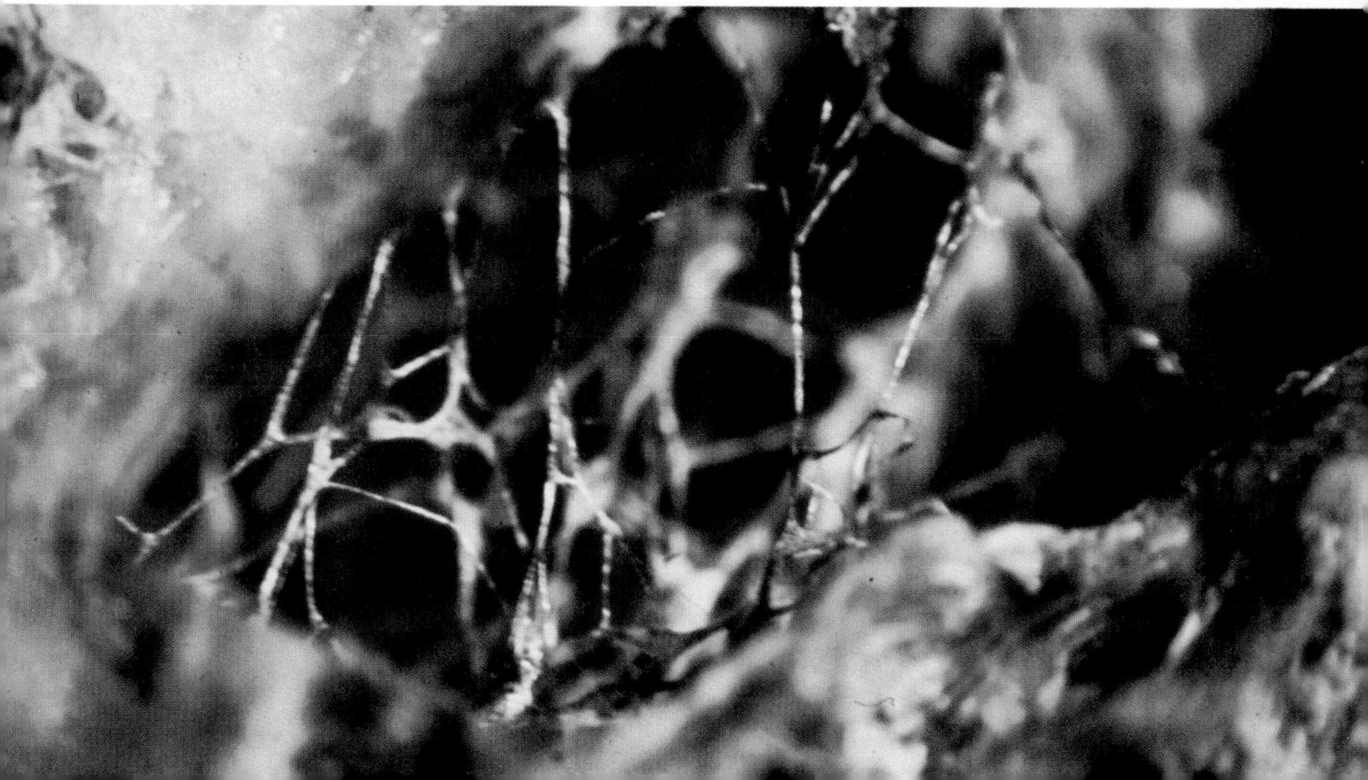

How Does Tobacco Affect Other People?

Tobacco smoke can harm people who do not use tobacco at all. For example, nonsmokers who breathe smoke from other people's cigarettes take the smoke into their lungs just as smokers do. If nonsmokers breathe in enough cigarette smoke for a long time, their lungs can be harmed. Smoke makes some nonsmokers' eyes burn and water. Smoke can also make nonsmokers cough or sneeze.

You have most likely seen signs like the one in the picture below. In order to protect the health of people who do not smoke, many public places have no-smoking sections.

Where have you seen signs about not smoking?

What Are Other Ways Tobacco Affects Health?

Some people chew tobacco instead of smoking it. People who chew tobacco can have serious health problems. The nicotine in chewing tobacco gets into the blood through tiny blood vessels in the mouth. This causes the heart and blood vessels to work harder than they should, just as with cigarettes.

People who chew tobacco are also likely to have white patches in their mouth, as the picture shows. These white patches often turn into mouth cancer. People who use chewing tobacco are more likely to get cancers of the mouth and throat, gum diseases, and heart diseases than people who do not use tobacco. Also, chewing tobacco can cause the color of teeth to change.

People who chew tobacco can get white patches in their mouth that might turn into mouth cancer.

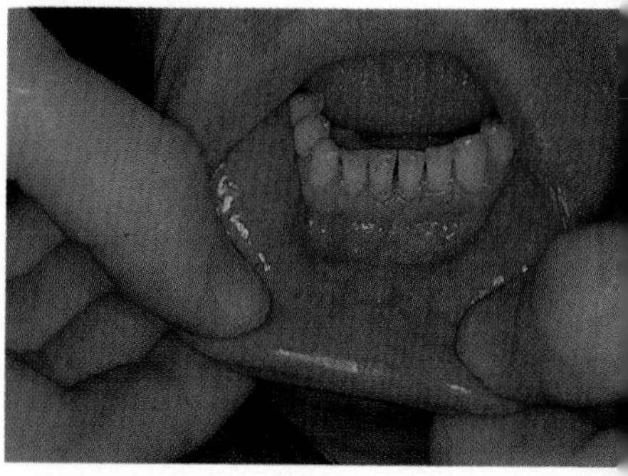

Many smokers know that smoking harms their health. Many want to stop smoking but find it hard to quit. This is because their bodies depend on the drug nicotine. A person who depends on a drug needs it to feel right. It can take a long time to stop depending on nicotine. People who stop smoking or using chewing tobacco often feel quite uncomfortable when they first quit. However, people feel much better when their bodies no longer depend on this harmful drug.

Think Back • *Study on your own with Study Guide page 262.*

1. How does tobacco affect the heart? the blood vessels? the lungs?
2. How might tobacco smoke harm a nonsmoker?
3. How can chewing tobacco affect the body?
4. Why is it hard for a person who is dependent on nicotine to quit smoking?

alcohol (al′kə hol), a drug in beer, wine, and liquor that slows down the nervous system.

3 How Does Alcohol Affect the Body?

Alcohol is a drug that can change the way a person thinks, feels, and acts. This drug can also change the way the body works. Drinks such as beer, liquor, and wine have alcohol in them.

The picture shows what happens when a person takes a drink with alcohol in it. The drug does not need to be digested. It goes right from the stomach and small intestine into the blood. Blood carries the alcohol to the brain. The alcohol reaches the brain very quickly.

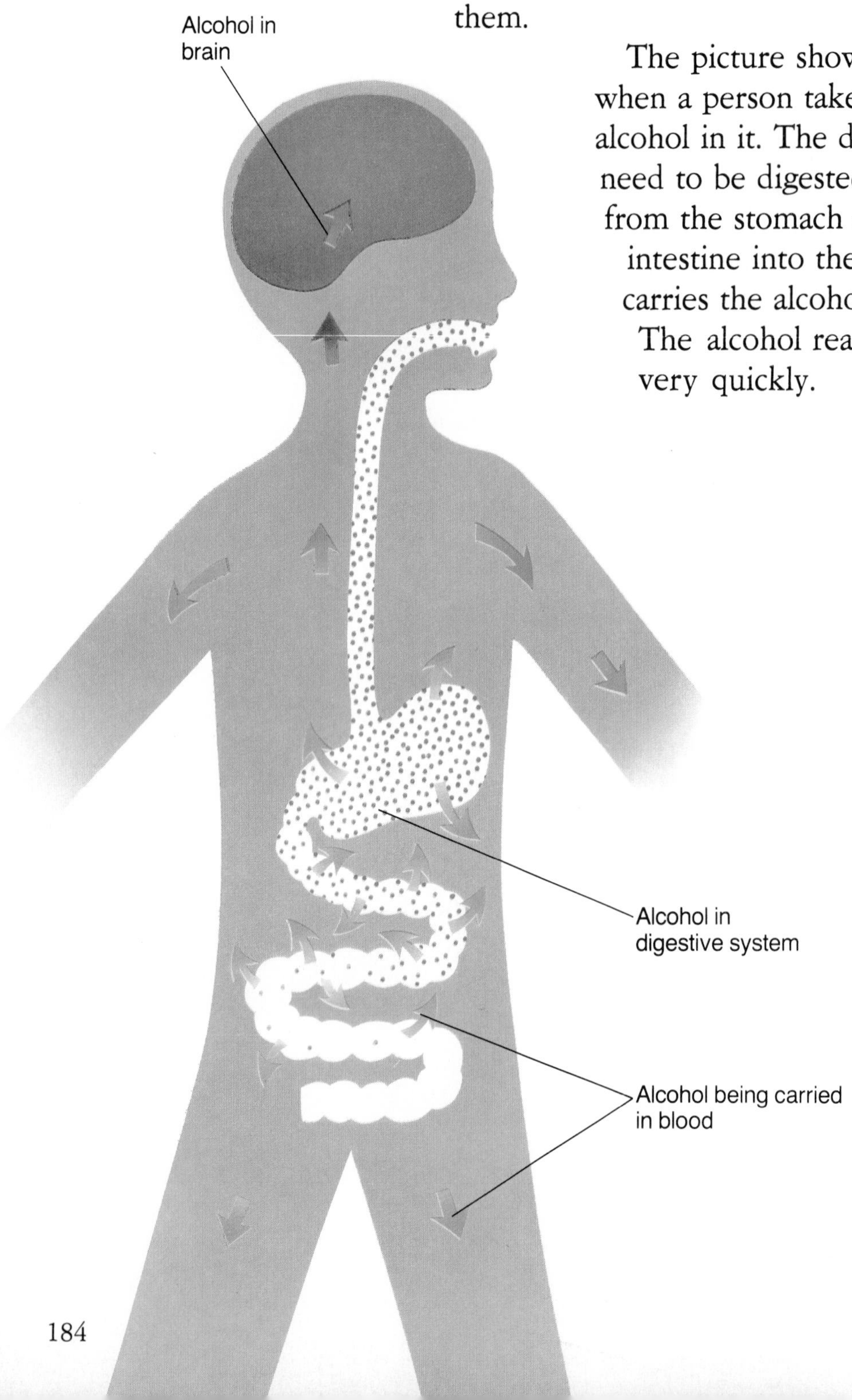

Alcohol slows down the work of the brain. This in turn slows down other parts of the body. Alcohol can keep a person from thinking or speaking as clearly as usual. It might make a person less skillful in using the muscles. The more alcohol a person drinks at one time, the greater its effects will be. Too much alcohol taken at one time can even cause death in a person.

A person who drinks a large amount of alcohol might become sick or very sleepy. He or she might become loud or quarrelsome. The person is more likely to have accidents. For example, a person might cross a street without paying attention to cars going by. He or she might not be able to think fast enough to get out of the way of a car. What might happen then?

A person who drives a car should not drink alcohol. The alcohol can keep a driver from thinking clearly and acting quickly.

Alcohol affects a smaller body more quickly than a larger body. Most young people are smaller than grown-ups. Therefore, alcohol usually affects a young person more than it does a grown-up.

Changes in the Brain from Drinking Alcohol

- change in feelings
- less ability to think, remember, and make decisions
- dizziness
- difficulty walking steadily
- difficulty seeing and speaking clearly

A driver who has taken drinks with alcohol might see the pedestrian as in the picture on the right. Many car accidents happen because people drink alcohol and then try to drive.

How Can Alcohol Affect Others?

A person who drinks alcohol can begin to depend on it. A person who depends on alcohol needs it to feel right. Such a person is likely to drink more and more alcohol and think he or she cannot live without it. A young person can depend on alcohol after drinking it for only a few months.

People who depend upon alcohol are called alcoholics. They usually cannot control their drinking. These people have trouble doing their work and getting along with others. Alcohol causes serious problems for many people. Alcohol can ruin a person's life when the person can no longer control his or her drinking.

Alcohol can also upset other people in a family. If someone in a family is an alcoholic, the lives of each person in the family can become torn apart. The person who drinks might become very mean and selfish. Problems with alcohol can lead to fear, hurt, and anger among the family members. Whether the person who drinks is an adult or a teenager, everyone in the family needs help to recover.

At Al-Anon meetings, family members of an alcoholic can talk about their feelings and problems.

Many communities have groups called Alcoholics Anonymous to help people stop drinking alcohol. People who go to meetings of this group must be willing to say they have a drinking problem. They must promise to work very hard to stop. They learn to talk about their problem and are given help from other people who have stopped drinking. They are also taught that the only cure is to never have another drink.

A group called Al-Anon can help family members of an alcoholic learn to deal with the problems in their lives caused by alcohol. At Al-Anon meetings people can share their feelings of hurt and anger. They can learn that they are not alone with these feelings. Talking about their feelings can help family members deal with their problems. It can take a long time for both the alcoholic and other family members to recover from the effects of alcohol in their lives.

Did You Know?
Every state has a law against selling alcohol to young people. A person has to be a certain age before he or she is allowed by law to buy alcohol. In all states, a person has to be twenty-one years old before he or she can buy or be served alcohol legally.

Think Back • *Study on your own with Study Guide page 263.*

1. How does alcohol affect the body? the way a person thinks and acts?
2. What might happen to a person who depends on alcohol?
3. Why does everyone in a family need help if one person has a drinking problem?

Learning More About Tobacco and Alcohol

1. Become a smoking sign detective. Look for no-smoking signs in the places where you and your friends and family go. Share what you discover with your class.

2. The American Cancer Society is a large group of people who work to help keep people from smoking. One way they try to get their message about not smoking to people is through the use of posters. One of the posters they make is shown here. What is the message on the poster? Make your own poster to tell people about another good reason for not smoking.

3. Look in newspapers for stories about car accidents. Read the stories to learn how many of the accidents happened because someone was drinking alcohol. Work with others in your class to make a bulletin board display with the newspaper stories.

4. Figure out the secret health message. Use the key to the code and write the answer on your own paper.

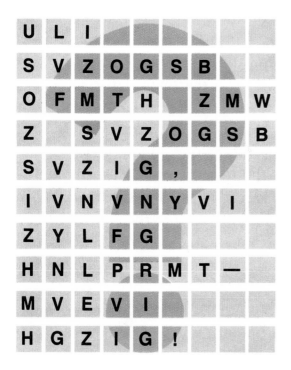

U	L	I						
S	V	Z	O	G	S	B		
O	F	M	T	H		Z	M	W
Z		S	V	Z	O	G	S	B
S	V	Z	I	G	,			
I	V	N	V	N	Y	V	I	
Z	Y	L	F	G				
H	N	L	P	R	M	T	—	
M	V	E	V	I				
H	G	Z	I	G	!			

Key To Code

ABCDEFGHIJKLMNOPQRSTUVWXYZ

z y x w v u t s r q p o n m l k j i h g f e d c b a

5. The pictures show a person deciding to refuse an offer of a drink with alcohol in it. Draw two pictures of your own showing someone refusing a drink with alcohol in it.

marijuana (mar′ə wa′nə); a plant that contains many substances, including drugs, that can cause changes in the body when smoked.

cocaine (kō kān′), a harmful drug made from leaves of the coca plant.

Did You Know?
Marijuana, cocaine, and crack are illegal drugs. It is against the law to buy, sell, or use these drugs.

4 How Do Marijuana, Cocaine, and Other Substances Affect Health?

Marijuana is a plant. Parts of the plant can be made into cigarettes. Marijuana contains many substances, including drugs, that affect people in different ways.

Marijuana makes the heart beat faster than it should. It makes some people feel dizzy or sick. Marijuana also changes the way a person thinks and acts. It makes some people feel very afraid. Other people might act silly or feel sleepy.

Using marijuana can make learning harder. For example, a person who smokes marijuana might have trouble remembering facts or thinking clearly. Marijuana also affects how a person sees. A person may not be able to judge distances properly. How might the changes due to marijuana affect someone who is driving a car?

Scientists have found more than four hundred different substances in marijuana. The substances harm the lungs and the tubes that lead to the lungs. Tests have shown that marijuana smoke can cause some of the same diseases that cigarette smoke causes, including lung cancer.

The machine in the picture measures the amount of air in the lungs. People who smoked marijuana for a long time were tested on this machine. The tests showed that their lungs did not fill up with as much air as they should.

Another drug that harms the body is **cocaine.** Cocaine is made from the leaves of the coca plant. It is usually in the form of a white powder that is sniffed through the nose. Cocaine is a powerful drug that can cause serious damage to the body and mind.

Cocaine causes the heart to beat very fast and the blood vessels to become narrower. This makes the heart work harder to pump blood through the body. Cocaine can make the heart beat in ways that are not normal. It can also cause blood pressure to rise.

Cocaine can cause changes in the brain that lead to seizures. Seizures upset the normal way the brain works. This can cause the heart and lungs to stop working. Young people have died suddenly from heart attacks or brain seizures after using cocaine, even after the first time.

When people first use cocaine, they might feel energetic and happy. However, that feeling only lasts a few minutes. Then people begin to feel sad, tired, and afraid. Then they want to take more of the drug to feel better.

Many people who use cocaine become dependent on the drug. One form of cocaine, called crack, is especially dangerous because it causes dependency very quickly. Recovery from cocaine dependence is very hard and takes a long time.

On Your Own
Suppose a friend asks you to try marijuana. Write down three reasons why you would not do what your friend asks.

The machine in the picture is a plethysmograph. It measures the amount of air in the lungs and how easily a person can breathe in and out. Using this machine, scientists have found out that people who smoke marijuana have a hard time breathing in and out.

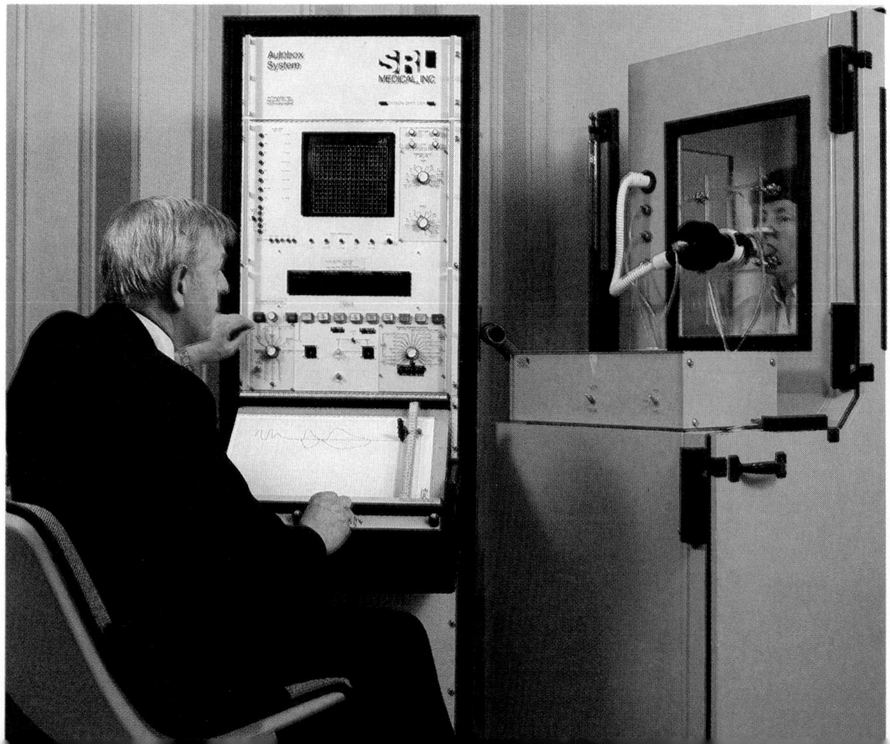

abuse (ə byüz′), using a drug or other substance on purpose in ways that can harm health.

What Other Substances Can Harm Health?

People use the products in the picture to do many different jobs. These products, including paint thinners, certain glues, oven cleaners, spot removers, and gasoline, are not drugs. However, each product gives off harmful fumes. If the fumes are breathed in, they cause changes in the body just as drugs do.

Sometimes people **abuse** these products, or use them in ways that can harm health. They breathe in the fumes from the products on purpose. These people often do not know the danger of doing this. Such fumes can make a person feel dizzy, sleepy, or very sick. The fumes can damage the brain, lungs, liver, and kidneys. Breathing in large amounts of these fumes can cause death.

Always read and follow the directions for using any household product. Store such products away from food and out of the reach of small children.

People should use these products only for the jobs they are meant for, such as cleaning and painting. Careful people can use these products without breathing in large amounts of their fumes. People can use the products safely if they read and follow carefully the directions on the product's package. Most directions tell people to use the products outdoors, as the picture shows, or in rooms with enough fresh air. The products also should be stored safely, away from small children.

This mother and son are following the directions for using a product with harmful fumes safely.

Think Back • *Study on your own with Study Guide page 263*

1. How does marijuana affect a person's thinking?
2. How is the body harmed by marijuana? by cocaine?
3. Why do many people become dependent on cocaine?
4. How might breathing in fumes from certain household products harm the body? how can these products be used safely?

5 How Can You Make Healthy Decisions About Drugs and Medicines?

You know that tobacco, alcohol, marijuana, and other substances can harm health. You might wonder why some people use tobacco or alcohol. Maybe you wonder why a person would want to try smoking marijuana or try breathing in the fumes from a household product.

At times a person might abuse a drug because friends do. The person might not really want to abuse a drug but is afraid to say no to his or her friends. However, saying no about abusing drugs is a way to make a healthy decision.

Have you ever worried about saying no to a friend about something? Sometimes just saying no is hard, but saying no about drugs can protect your health. Saying no sometimes takes courage. You can get that courage by thinking about how badly a drug could harm you.

I don't want the pill you're offering me. I'm just saying **NO!**

A friend might not understand if you refuse to do what he is doing. If your friend gets angry even though you have a good reason to refuse, you might need to look for another friend. Why would that be a wise decision?

Plan what you will do if somebody tries to get you to smoke a cigarette or abuse a drug. Do not make excuses. For example, you can make a healthy decision again by just saying, "No, I don't want to smoke because I want to stay healthy."

Some young people think that smoking cigarettes or drinking alcohol makes them look grown-up. However, most grown-ups do not smoke tobacco or abuse alcohol. Most adults do not wish to harm their health. Many of these grown-ups decided not to smoke tobacco or abuse alcohol when they were young. They did not want to start a bad habit that might be hard to break later.

Here you see the boy from page 194. He feels good and enjoys himself by joining in activities with friends. He and his friends do not misuse medicines or abuse drugs to change the way they feel. They are happy, active, and healthy.

Think Back • *Study on your own with Study Guide page 263.*

1. What might a person say to refuse drugs?
2. Why do some people choose not to smoke cigarettes or abuse alcohol?

You and your friends might enjoy different activities than these young people. Which do you like?

Health Focus

"Smokebusters" in Pewaukee

The fourth-graders at Pewaukee Elementary School in Pewaukee, Wisconsin, became "Smokebusters." They decided to try to help smokers stop smoking. These young people had learned how cigarette smoke harms the lungs. They had seen pictures of the lungs of a healthy person. They also had seen pictures of a smoker's lungs. The smoker's lungs looked dirty compared to the healthy person's lungs.

The students talked to smokers they knew and told them what they had learned. Each "Smokebuster" tried to convince at least one smoker to quit for a day. The class convinced 118 people to stop smoking for a day. Eighty-one smokers were able to stay away from cigarettes all day. Thirty of those people decided to try to give up smoking altogether. The fourth-grade students gave the smokers information about how to break the smoking habit.

With help from this fourth-grade class, many people in Pewaukee took the first step in breaking the smoking habit. This class of "Smokebusters" was proud that they helped some smokers start leading healthier lives.

Talk About It

1. What did the class learn about how smoking affects health?
2. How could you be a "Smokebuster" and help smokers quit smoking?

Sharing Information About Medicines and Drugs

You can share at home what you have learned about alcohol and about smoking. You can also share what you have learned about marijuana and products that give off dangerous fumes. Talking over what you have learned about drugs might make an interesting conversation with family members at home.

Your family might be interested in some of the facts you have learned about safe ways to use and store medicines and certain household products. You and family members might also check the directions on the over-the-counter medicines stored at home. Notice any side effects or warnings listed.

Reading at Home

Breathing by John Gaskin. Watts, 1984. Learn how you breathe and how cigarette smoking harms your lungs.

Pot—What It Is, What It Does by Ann Tobias. Greenwillow, 1979. Learn more about marijuana and how it affects the body.

Harmful products in this home are stored safely so that little children cannot get them.

Chapter 7 Review

Reviewing Lesson Objectives

1. List the safe uses of medicines. Explain the difference between over-the-counter and prescription medicines. (pages 174–178)
2. Tell how tobacco harms health. Describe how tobacco smoke can harm others. (pages 180–183)
3. List ways alcohol harms health. Describe how a person who depends on alcohol can affect others in a family. (pages 184–187)
4. Describe harmful effects of marijuana and cocaine. Explain why breathing fumes from certain household products is dangerous. (pages 190–193)
5. Describe a good way to refuse unneeded medicines or drugs. Explain why some people do not smoke tobacco or abuse alcohol. (pages 194–195)

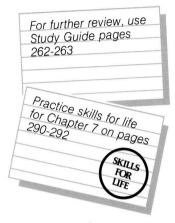

For further review, use Study Guide pages 262-263

Practice skills for life for Chapter 7 on pages 290-292

SKILLS FOR LIFE

Checking Health Vocabulary

Number your paper from 1–9. Match each meaning in Column I with the correct word or words in Column II.

Column I

1. a plant that has drugs that can harm the body
2. a doctor's order for medicine
3. a drug in beer and wine that can affect the way the brain works
4. a drug in tobacco that speeds the heartbeat
5. a medicine a person can buy without a doctor's order
6. a substance in medicine that causes changes in the body
7. to use a drug or substance for purposes other than health
8. an unwanted change caused by a medicine
9. a harmful drug made from leaves of the coca plant

Column II

a. abuse
b. alcohol
c. cocaine
d. drug
e. marijuana
f. nicotine
g. over-the-counter medicine
h. prescription
i. side effect

Number your paper from 10–13. Write a sentence using each of the following words.

10. alcohol
11. dependent
12. marijuana
13. nicotine

Reviewing Health Ideas

Number your paper from 1–12. Next to each number write the word or words that best complete the sentence. Choose the words from the list.

alcohol	label
crack	medicines
decisions	misuses
digested	nonsmoker
family	pharmacist
fumes	smoke

1. Drugs used for health reasons are ____.
2. A ____ carries out the orders on a prescription.
3. You can find directions for using an over-the-counter medicine on the ____.
4. A person who takes an unneeded medicine ____ it.
5. Smoke from the cigarettes of other people might harm the lungs of a ____.
6. Alcohol is not ____.
7. Drinks with ____ affect a person's ability to drive safely.
8. Alanon is the group that helps ____ members of alcoholics.
9. ____ from marijuana might cause lung cancer.
10. ____ is a form of cocaine that causes dependence very quickly.
11. People should use certain glues carefully to keep from breathing in ____ from the glues.
12. A way to make healthy ____ about drugs and cigarettes is to just say no.

Understanding Health Ideas

Number your paper from 13–24. Next to each number write the word or words that best answer the question.

13. What do all medicines contain?
14. Which medicines can people get at a food store?
15. Who writes a prescription?
16. Who should be called if a person gets a side effect from a prescription medicine?
17. Who should give a child medicine?
18. Where should medicines be kept?
19. How can smoking harm the health of other family members?
20. What two parts of the body are most harmed by smoking?
21. How can chewing tobacco harm the mouth?
22. Why does alcohol reach the brain so quickly?
23. How can cocaine damage the heart and brain?
24. Why is the habit of smoking hard to give up?

Thinking Critically

Write the answers on your paper. Use complete sentences.

1. How can people use medicines safely?
2. What advice would you give to someone who is thinking of taking a drink with alcohol?

Chapter 8

Preventing Disease

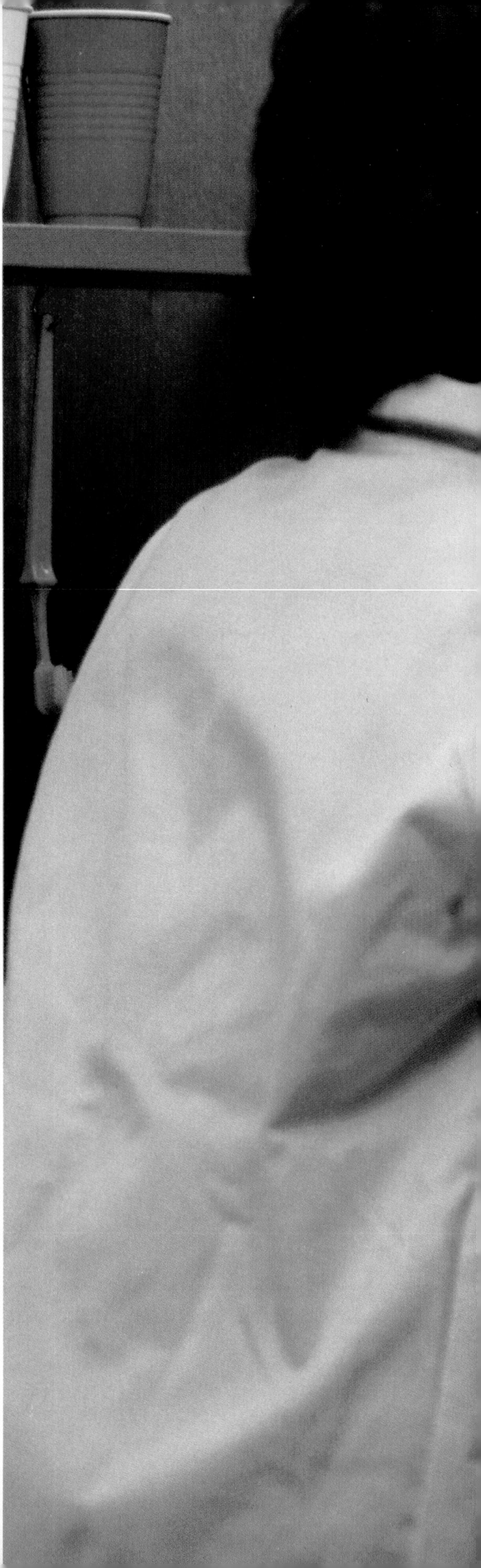

The family members who share the bathroom in the picture want to keep from getting sick. They use their own towels, toothbrushes, and glasses. What has the family done to help themselves know which things are their own?

This chapter will help you understand what causes certain diseases. You will also learn how to protect yourself from getting some diseases. Learning about diseases can help you stay healthy now and as you grow older.

Health Watch Notebook

Collect articles in your notebook about diseases such as cancer, heart disease, diabetes, or high blood pressure. Write down what causes them and how they might be prevented.

1 What Is a Communicable Disease?
2 How Does Your Body Fight Off Disease Germs?
3 How Can You Keep Disease Germs from Spreading?
4 What Is a Noncommunicable Disease?
5 How Can You Build a Healthy Lifestyle?

1 What Is a Communicable Disease?

communicable (kə myü′nə·kə bəl) **disease,** an illness that can spread, usually from one person to another.

bacteria (bak tir′e ə), tiny living things, some of which cause communicable diseases.

A **communicable disease** is one that can spread, usually from one person to another. Communicable diseases include colds, flu, mumps, and measles. Disease germs cause communicable disease.

Germs are found everywhere. Most germs are so tiny that you need a microscope to see them. Most of the germs in the world around you cause no harm or are even helpful. However, certain germs cause diseases. Two kinds of disease germs are bacteria and viruses.

Bacteria are tiny living things all around you. Only certain bacteria can harm you. If harmful bacteria get inside your body, they can cause diseases. Bacteria cause such diseases as strep throat, diphtheria, and whooping cough.

You see these bacteria as they look through a microscope. The bacteria appear many times larger than they really are.

Rod-shaped bacteria

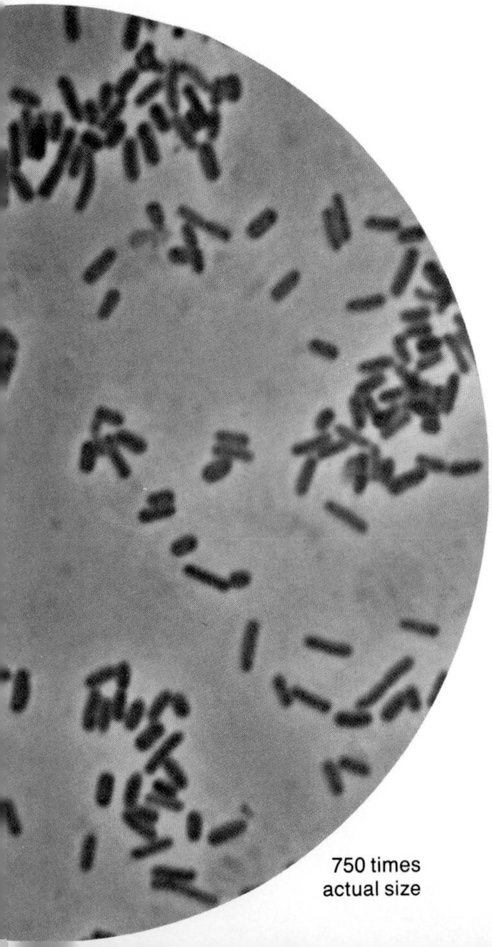

Round-shaped bacteria

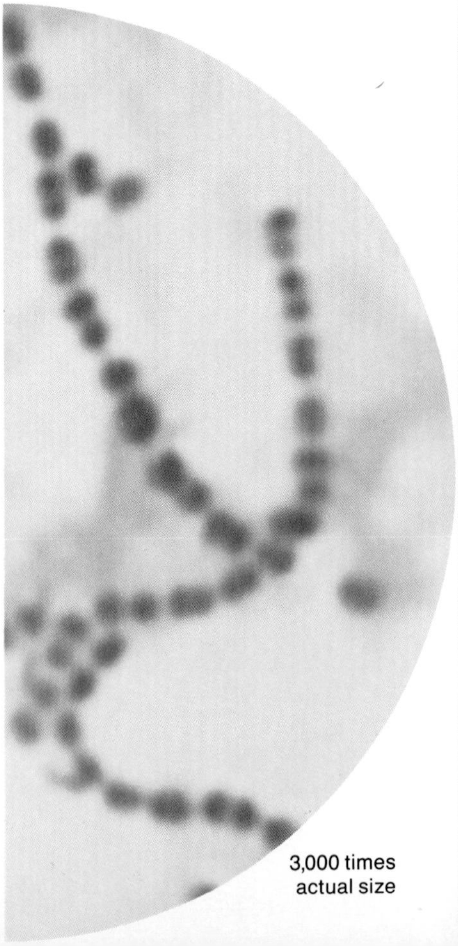

Spiral-shaped bacteria

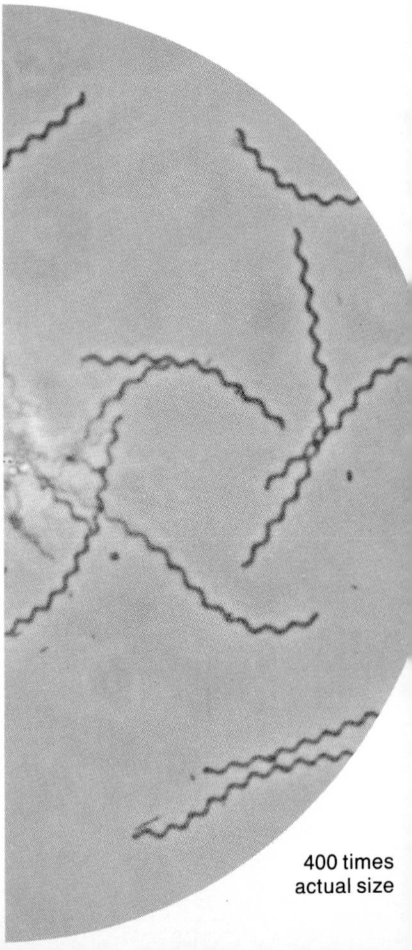

Viruses are the tiniest germs, much smaller than bacteria. A special microscope must be used to see them. It is an electron microscope.

Viruses can be found almost anywhere. Most of the viruses that scientists have learned about can harm you. If viruses get inside your body, they can make you sick. With most viruses, it takes a few days or weeks for you to feel better. Viruses cause colds, flu, polio, mumps, and measles.

The pictures on these two pages show some harmful bacteria and viruses. What shapes do the different bacteria have? How do viruses look different from bacteria?

virus (vī′rəs), a kind of disease germ that causes some communicable diseases, for example, colds and flu.

A special microscope called an electron microscope is used to see viruses. You see viruses here thousands of times larger than they really are.

AIDS virus

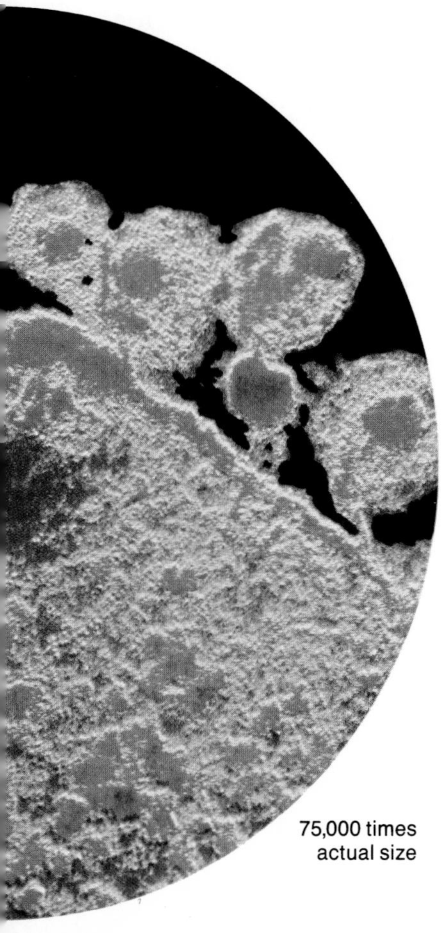

75,000 times actual size

Chicken-pox virus

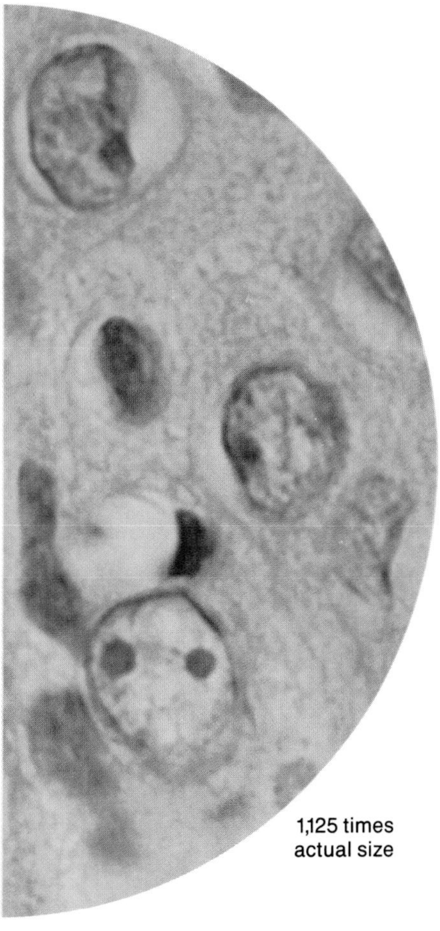

1,125 times actual size

Flu virus

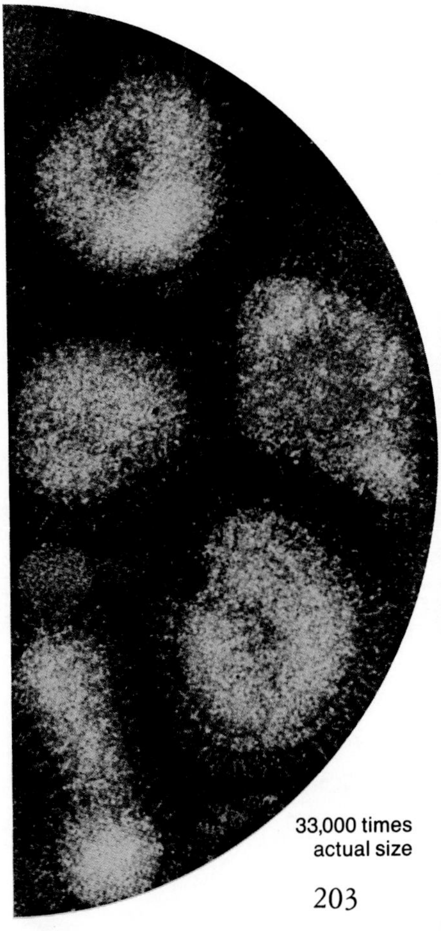

33,000 times actual size

What Happens When Disease Germs Get Inside Your Body?

Germs might enter your body through your nose or mouth. They might enter through cuts in the skin. Once inside the body, how do bacteria and viruses grow?

Bacteria need a warm, damp place to live and grow. They also need food. Certain bacteria get what they need to live and grow inside a person's body. Bacteria start to make more of themselves inside the body. They grow by dividing in half. The picture shows the way they divide. Each half becomes a new living thing. The new germs then divide to make four more. The growing and dividing go on, making many bacteria in the body.

Viruses do not grow and divide the same way that bacteria do. Viruses attach themselves to body cells. They break open a cell and enter it. The viruses make more of themselves in the cell. Then they leave the cell and go on to attack other cells.

When many disease germs of a certain kind are growing in your body, you feel sick. You might have a cough, runny nose, sore throat, upset stomach, or fever. The disease you get depends on the kind of disease germs inside your body.

Bacteria dividing

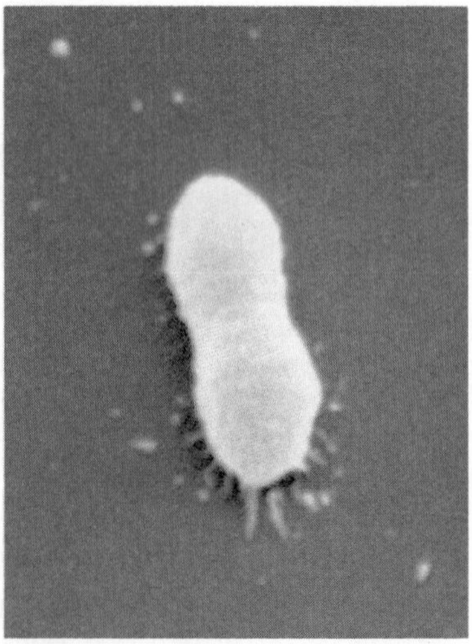

8,800 times actual size

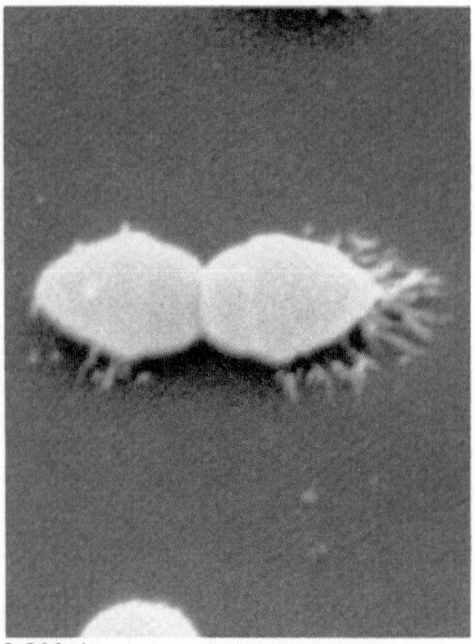

8,800 times actual size

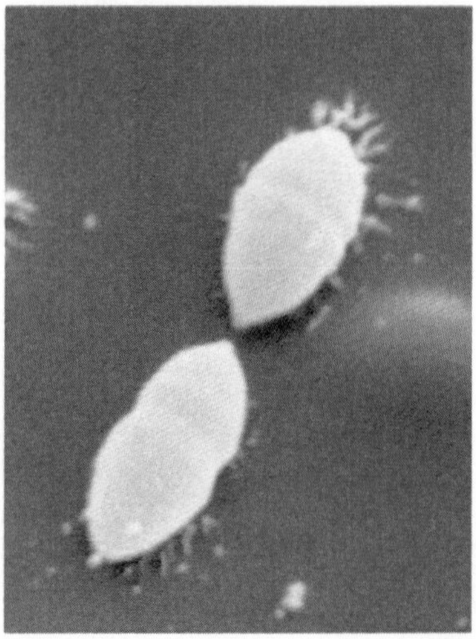

8,800 times actual size

How Do Disease Germs Spread?

Suppose you have disease germs in your body. You can pass them along to others. You can spread germs to others when you cough or talk. How might the girl in the picture spread germs?

Germs can come out of your mouth or nose into the air. Some germs stay in the air. Some germs fall on food, or on such objects as dishes, pencils, or books. The disease germs can then get into other people's bodies.

People might breathe in germs through the air. They might take in the germs with food they eat. They might take in germs if they put pencils or fingers in their mouths. What can happen if disease germs get into a person's body?

Think Back • *See Study Guide on page 264.*

1. What is a communicable disease?
2. What are two kinds of disease germs?
3. How are disease germs spread?

On Your Own

Suppose the girl in the picture was in a group of students at school. Write down several ways she could keep from passing germs to others at school.

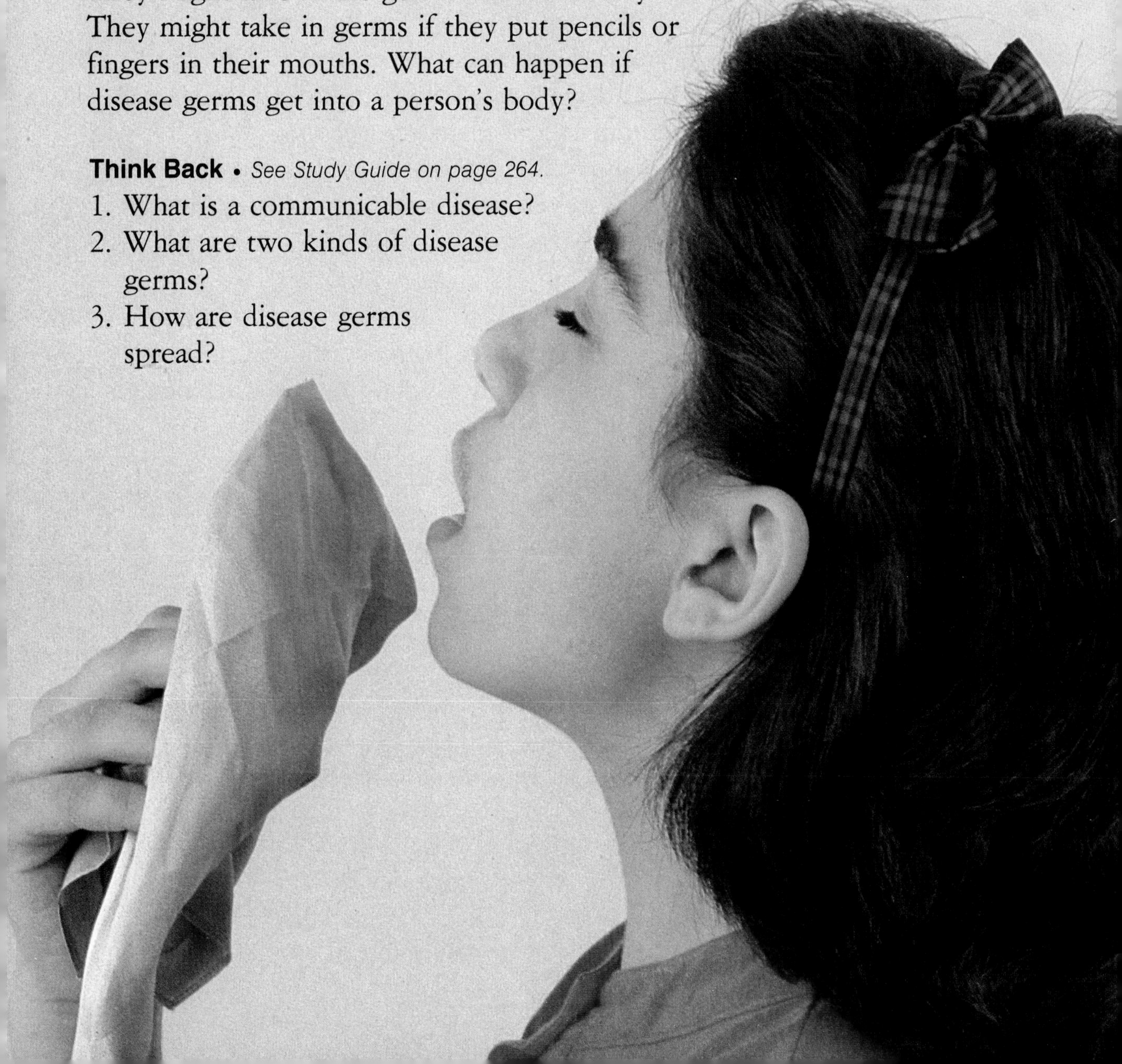

How might using a tissue help prevent germs from spreading?

2 How Does Your Body Fight Off Disease Germs?

Cilia move mucus toward your nose and mouth, away from your lungs.

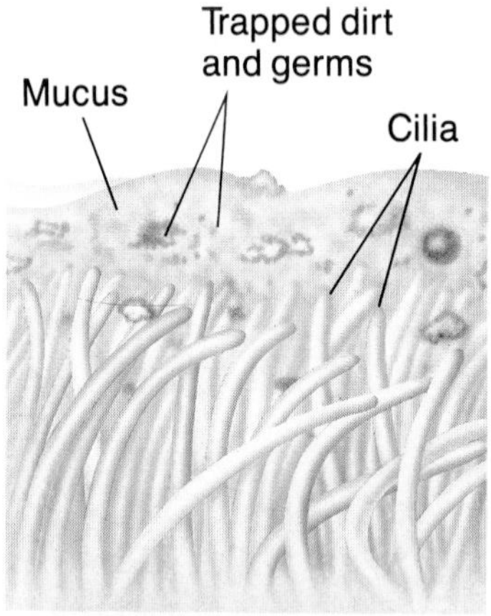

With so many germs all around you, what keeps you from getting sick more often? Your body has several ways of keeping germs out. Your body also has ways to destroy germs that get in.

Your skin covers and protects your body. Unless your skin gets cut or scraped, it keeps many germs from getting inside.

Some germs enter your body with the air you breathe. Tiny hairs in your nose catch many of them. You can then breathe them out. Germs are also trapped and killed another way. The wet, sticky substance inside your nose and throat, called mucus, can kill some germs.

Your body can remove germs trapped in mucus. Places in your nose and throat have cilia—tiny parts that look like hairs. You can see these parts in the picture to the left.

Cilia move back and forth. This movement pushes mucus toward your mouth and nose. Mucus, perhaps with trapped germs, does not go further into the body.

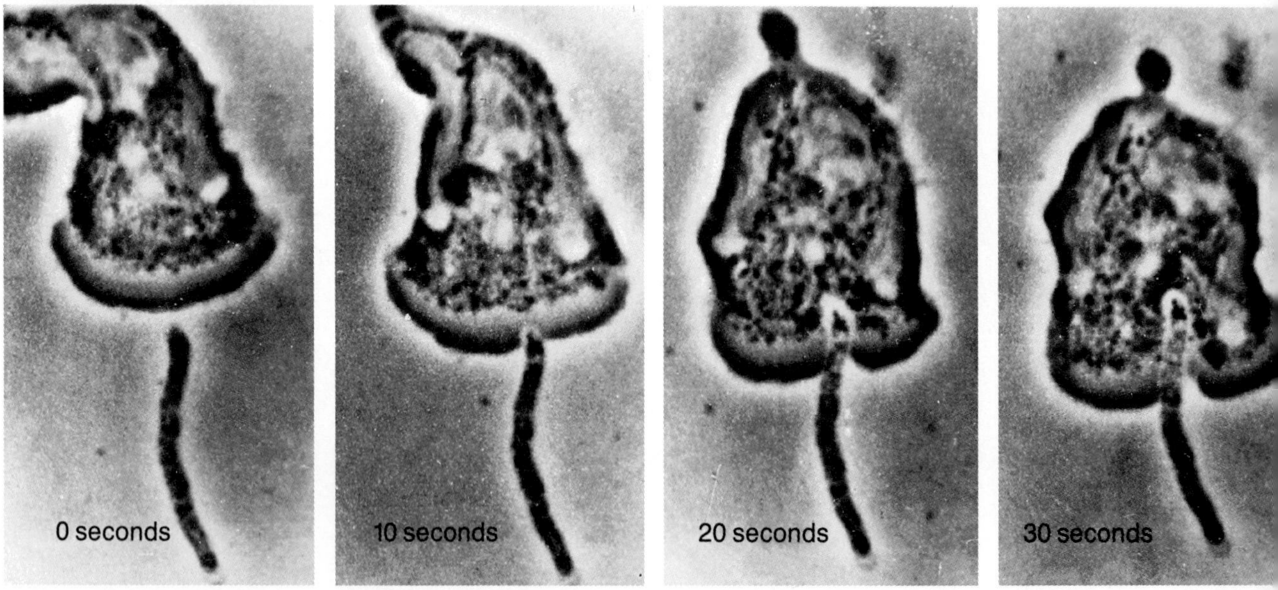

You remove the mucus when you cough, sneeze, blow your nose, or swallow. If mucus goes down your throat, your digestive system gets rid of it.

At times disease germs come into your body with food. Saliva in your mouth can kill the germs. Digestive juices in the stomach can also kill germs.

How Do White Blood Cells Fight Disease Germs?

Some disease germs get past your skin, nose, and throat. Inside your body the number of germs starts to increase. Certain germs give off wastes that are harmful. Other germs get inside cells and harm them. As a result, you feel sick.

When disease germs make you sick, certain cells in your blood help you. White blood cells try to surround disease germs and keep them from spreading. Then the white cells start destroying the germs. As more and more disease germs are destroyed, you feel better.

In the pictures below you can see a white blood cell destroying a disease germ. How long did it take?

What is happening to the disease germ?

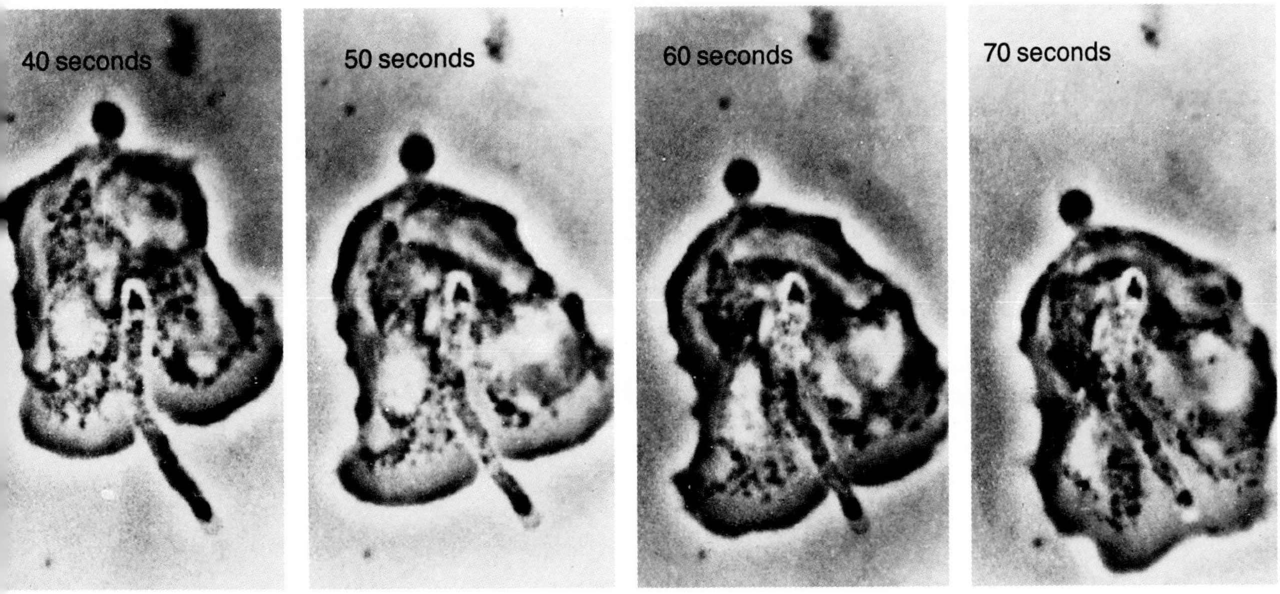

antibody (an′ti bod′ē), a substance made by the body that helps white blood cells destroy disease germs.

immunity (i myü′nə tē), a person's protection from or resistance to disease.

How Do Antibodies Help Fight Disease Germs?

Your body has another way to fight off disease germs. The body makes substances called **antibodies,** which are carried throughout the body by the blood. Antibodies help white blood cells destroy disease germs. Look at the picture to learn more about antibodies.

The body makes a special kind of antibody for each kind of disease germ. Some antibodies can keep you from getting the same disease again soon. Some antibodies can keep you from ever getting the same disease again. These antibodies stay in your blood for a long time. If the same kind of disease germ enters your body again, the antibodies remain to fight them off. You do not get the disease a second time. You have **immunity** to that disease. For example, if you have had chicken pox, you are not likely to get it again. You will have immunity to chicken pox all your life.

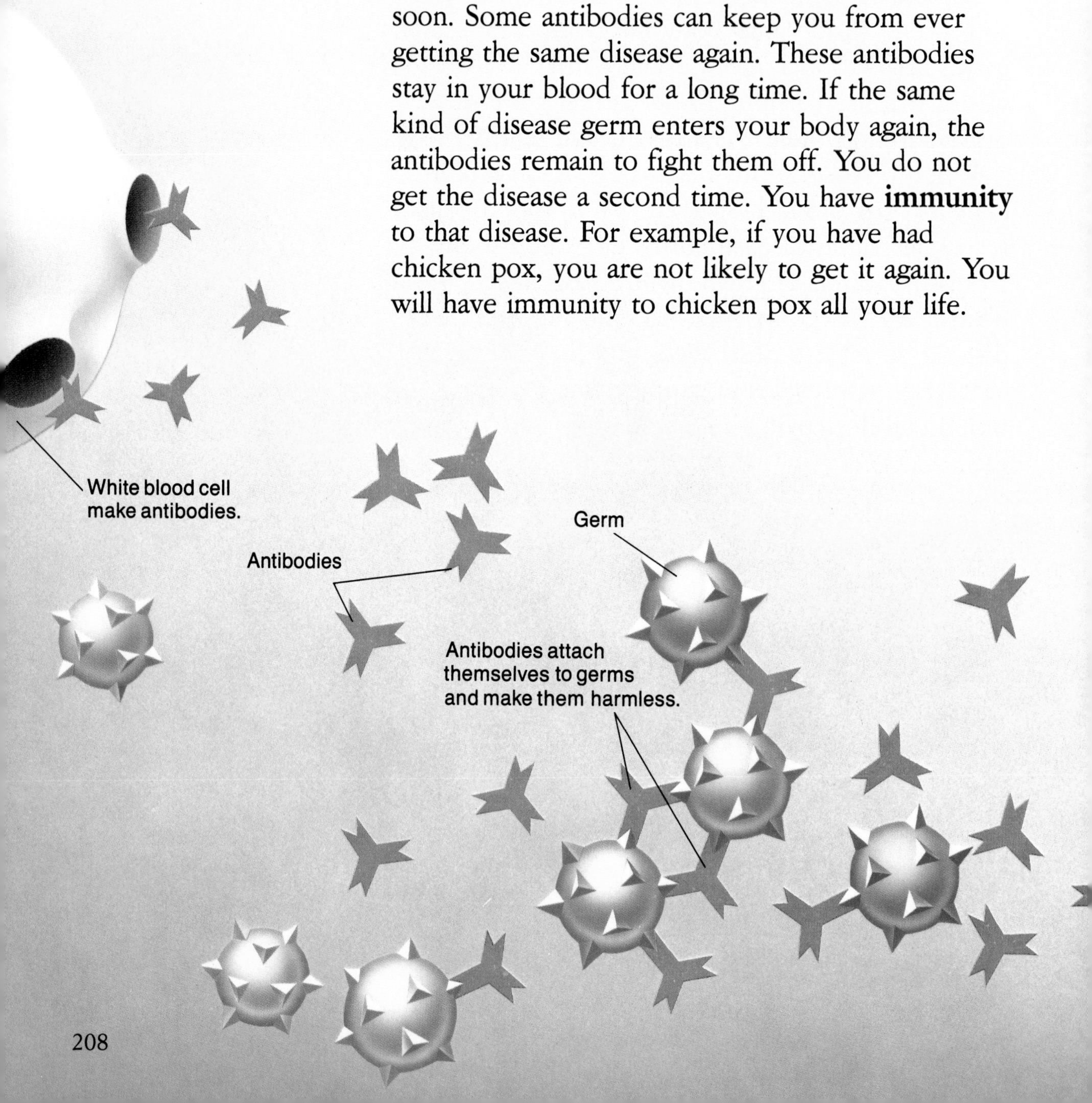
White blood cell
make antibodies.
Germ
Antibodies
Antibodies attach themselves to germs and make them harmless.

What Does the AIDS Virus Do to the Body?

AIDS is a disease caused by a virus that can destroy certain white blood cells. These are the same white blood cells that help fight off disease germs. People with the AIDS virus can get certain diseases because their bodies cannot fight them off.

Usually when a virus is in the body, white blood cells help make antibodies that can kill the virus. However, the AIDS virus is different from most viruses. As the picture shows, the AIDS virus can enter a white blood cell and make more AIDS viruses. Then the white blood cell dies. When other kinds of disease germs get into the body, few white blood cells are left to help win the battle against disease.

Luckily, AIDS is hard to get. It is hard for this virus to get inside the body. People can also protect themselves from getting this virus in many ways. Scientists all around the world are working to find a cure for AIDS.

AIDS (ādz), a disease caused by a virus that can destroy white blood cells that normally help fight off disease germs.

Did You Know?
The AIDS virus is passed from one person to another by exchange of bodily fluids. Bodily fluids are exchanged during sexual contact. Diseases that are spread by sexual contact are called sexually transmitted diseases. Therefore, AIDS is a sexually transmitted disease, or STD. The AIDS virus also can be passed from one person to another by sharing needles used to inject illegal drugs.

Think Back • *Study on your own with Study Guide page 264.*

1. How does your body keep disease germs out?
2. How do white blood cells fight disease germs?
3. How do you get an immunity to a disease?
4. How does the AIDS virus damage the body?

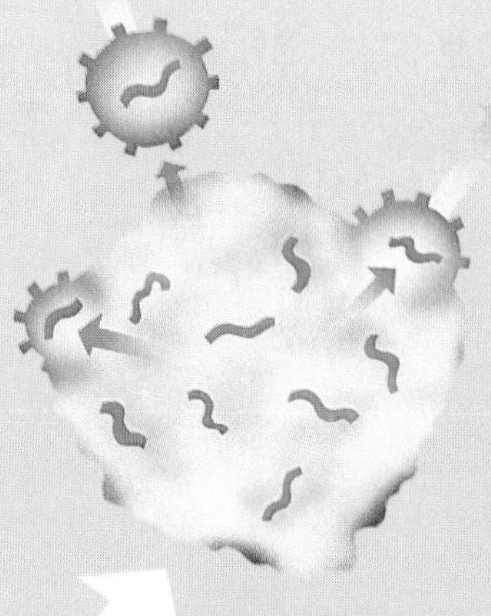

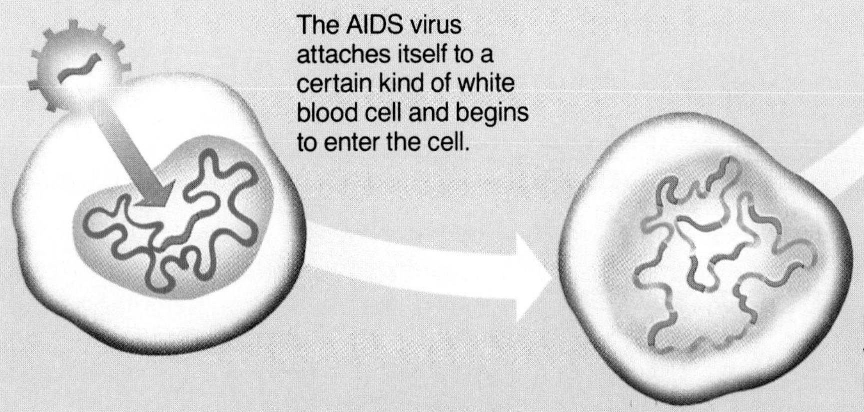

The AIDS virus attaches itself to a certain kind of white blood cell and begins to enter the cell.
Material from the AIDS virus takes over the white blood cell.
New AIDS viruses are made and the white blood cell is destroyed.

Did You Know?

The housefly is one of the busiest spreaders of disease germs. Flies are often found in the garbage and animal wastes that contain germs. Germs stick to the flies' bodies. The flies then spread the germs to food they touch.

3 How Can You Prevent Disease Germs from Spreading?

Did you know that some of the best weapons against communicable disease germs are soap and water? Disease germs can be on your hands and then spread to food, other people, or things you touch. Washing your hands with soap and water will kill and carry away disease germs on your hands.

You should always wash your hands before eating and after using the toilet. At what other times should you wash your hands to keep disease germs from spreading?

Be careful about using things other people touch. People can take germs into their bodies by sharing the same towel or washcloth. Disease germs can also be on eating utensils or glasses. Always use clean eating utensils and do not share them with others.

Suppose you have a cold. How can you prevent the cold from spreading to others? First, you can try to stay away from others while you have the cold. You should use tissues to cover your mouth and nose whenever you cough and sneeze. Then throw the tissues away yourself so the cold germs will not spread to others.

Some disease germs cannot spread to others through food, air, water, or utensils. These germs can only live inside the body and are spread through fluids inside the body such as blood. These germs die easily outside the body. The AIDS virus is a disease germ that works this way. These kinds of disease germs are very hard to get. You cannot get them by touching or being near a person with the disease.

vaccine (vak sēn′), a medicine that contains weakened or dead disease germs or other products and that causes the body to form antibodies.

antibiotic (an′ti bī ot′ik), a medicine that can kill or weaken certain kinds of bacteria.

How Do Medicines Help Fight Off Disease Germs?

Did you know that your body can be made to produce its own protection against some disease germs? A **vaccine** is a medicine that causes your body to make antibodies before you are ever exposed to disease germs. Some vaccines are made from disease germs that have been killed. Others are made from disease germs that are alive but greatly weakened. You can get a vaccine in a shot or in a liquid to swallow.

Instead of getting sick from a vaccine, your body forms antibodies that fight off the dead or weakened disease germs. These antibodies protect you from getting the disease in the future. Sometimes you have to get more than one vaccine for full protection.

Other medicines called **antibiotics** are used to kill or weaken disease germs. People take antibiotics to treat some diseases and keep other people from getting their germs. Antibiotics can kill certain kinds of bacteria. They cannot kill viruses.

Did You Know?
A jet-injector is a machine that can give vaccines very fast. It can give vaccines to 1,000 people in one hour. Sometimes such machines are used when many people need to be vaccinated quickly.

Vaccines help the body to make its own protection against disease germs.

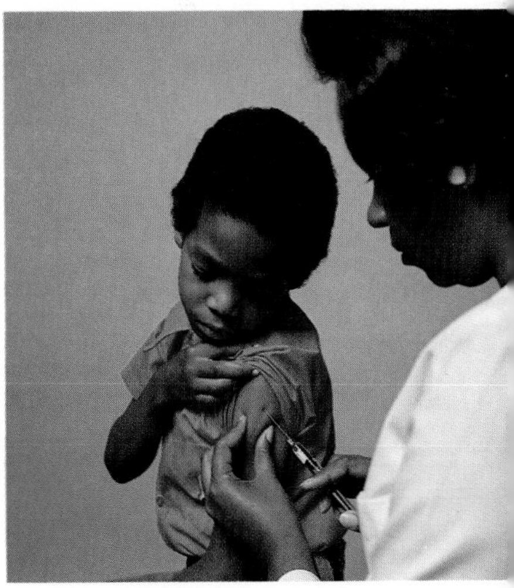

Think Back • *Study on your own with Study Guide page 264.*

1. How can a person help keep disease germs from spreading?
2. How can vaccines protect you from diseases?

noncommunicable (non′kə myü′nə kə bəl) **disease,** an illness not caused by germs and that does not spread to other people.

cardiovascular (kär′dē ō vas′kyə lər) **disease,** any one of several noncommunicable diseases that affect the heart and blood vessels.

4 What Is a Noncommunicable Disease?

Some diseases are not caused by disease germs. Such diseases also do not spread from one person to another. These diseases are **noncommunicable diseases.** The two most serious noncommunicable diseases in the United States today are diseases of the heart and cancer.

What Might Happen When Arteries Are Blocked?

Many diseases harm the heart and blood vessels. Another name for the many different diseases of the heart is **cardiovascular disease.** (The word *cardio* means "heart." The word *vascular* means "blood vessels.") Cardiovascular diseases affect the heart and blood vessels.

One kind of heart disease occurs when arteries become blocked. This disease is atherosclerosis (ath′ər ō sklə rō′sis). It occurs when fatty substances in the blood stick to the walls of arteries.

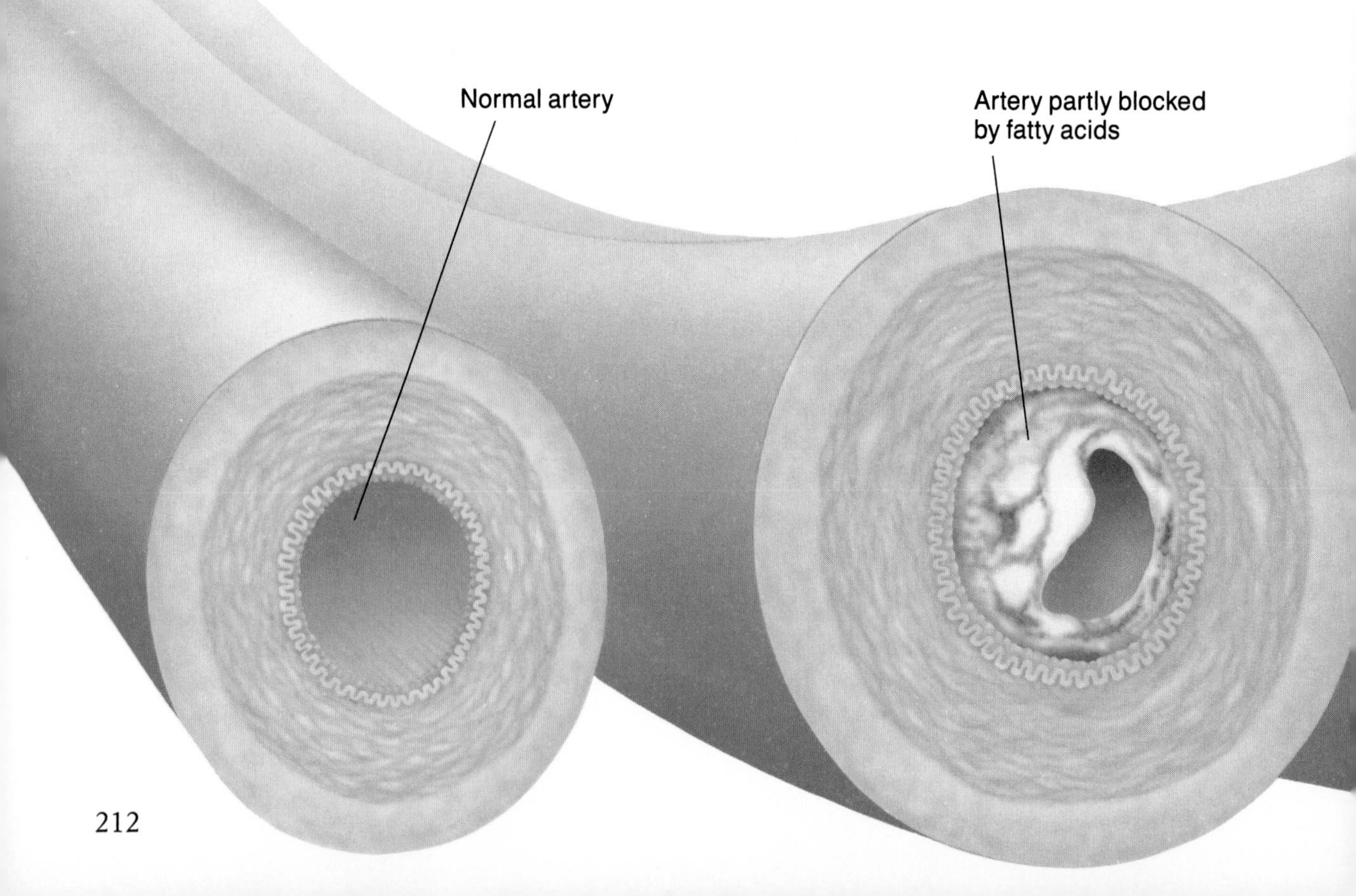

In the pictures you can see a healthy artery and arteries that are partly blocked. The heart must work harder to pump blood through arteries that are blocked or partly blocked.

The disease of blocked arteries might begin in childhood. However, the problems from the disease usually do not appear until many years later. Then the heart might not work as it should.

Research shows that eating less fatty foods might help prevent arteries from getting blocked. Getting regular exercise can also help. People with atherosclerosis can begin to eat less fatty foods and exercise more. The disease might develop more slowly.

Less blood goes through blocked arteries. This means some body cells may not get enough oxygen.

Artery almost completely blocked by fatty substances

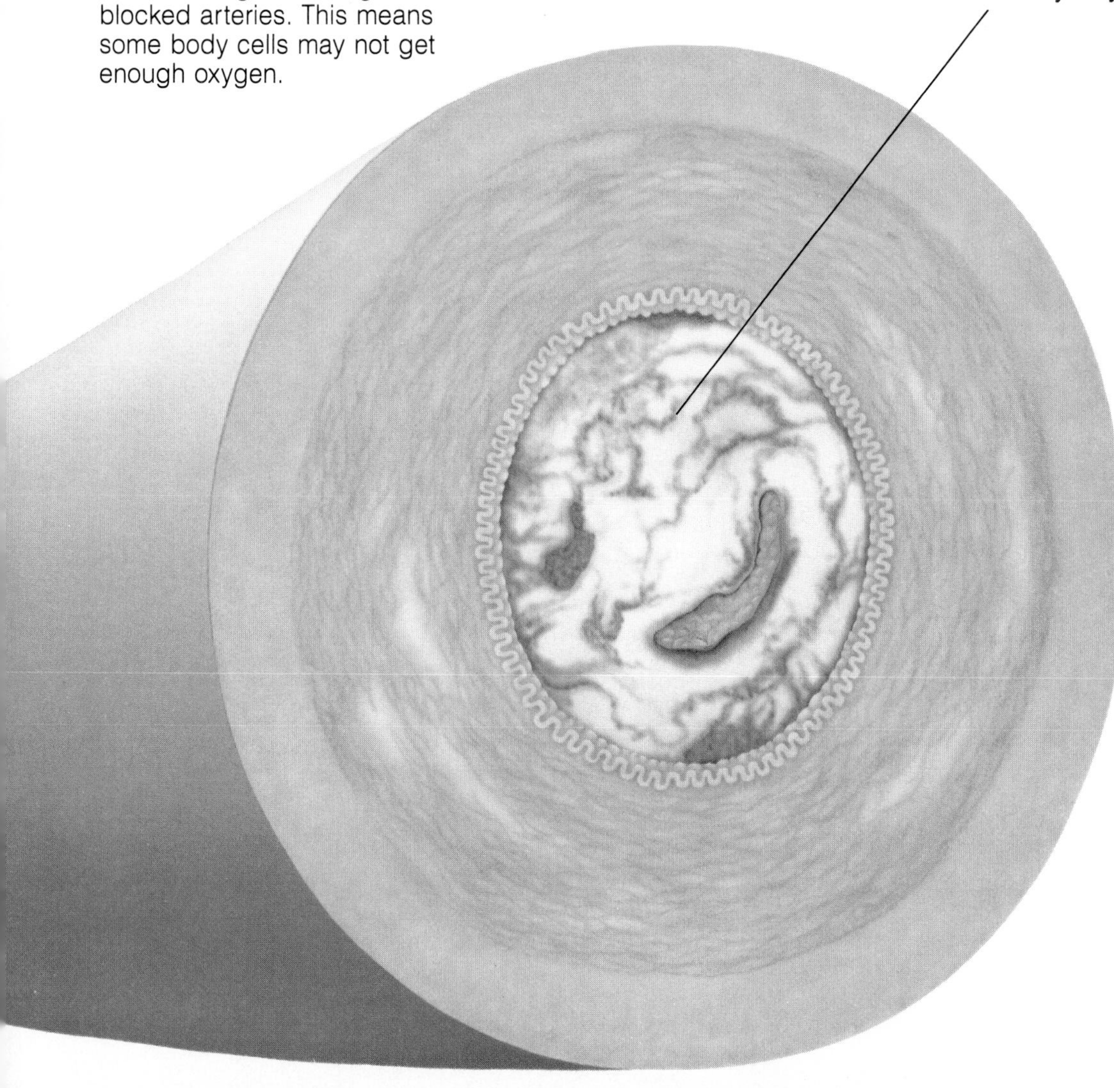

On Your Own
Write a paragraph telling what you know about how having a healthy heart starts when a person is young.

What Is High Blood Pressure?

You might have heard of another heart disease, high blood pressure. In this disease, blood is pumped through arteries with more force than is needed just to move blood through the body. Too much pressure can harm the arteries and the heart over time. A doctor or nurse usually finds this disease during a health checkup.

High blood pressure most often occurs in grown-ups. However, young people also get the disease. The disease can usually be controlled if it is found early. Medicines might be used to lower blood pressure. Changing the foods a person eats and getting more exercise are also suggested.

Doctors believe both younger and older people can keep from getting high blood pressure. Research shows that eating less salt might help. Not smoking also helps. Smoking causes blood vessels to become narrow. The heart has to work harder to pump blood through narrow blood vessels.

What Is Diabetes?

Diabetes is a disease that occurs when the body does not make enough insulin. Certain body cells make insulin. The body needs insulin in order to change the sugar in foods into energy.

Most people with diabetes help control their own disease. They eat fewer sweets and fats. They get regular exercise. Some people with the disease need to take insulin into their bodies. People sometimes get insulin in shots. As yet, nobody knows how to prevent or cure diabetes.

diabetes (dī′ə bē′tis), a noncommunicable disease in which the body does not make enough insulin and cannot use sugars in food as it should.

Helen helps control her diabetes by watching the foods she eats and getting regular exercise. Every day she gives herself a shot of insulin.

cancer (kan′sər), a noncommunicable disease in which cells grow out of control and destroy healthy cells.

arthritis (är thrī′tis), a noncommunicable disease that harms body joints, causing redness, swelling, pain, and often crippling.

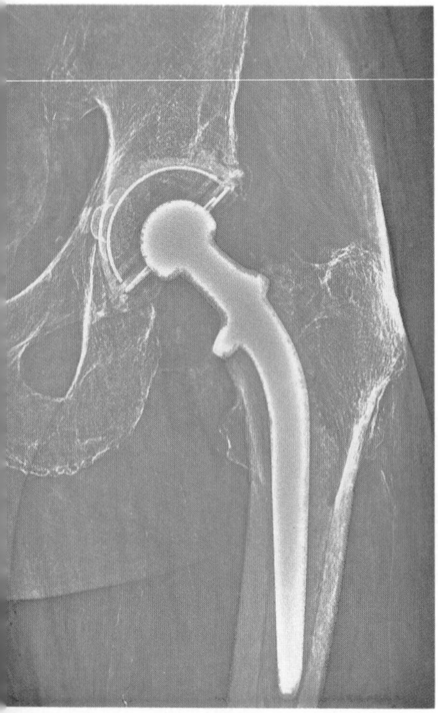

The picture above shows an artificial hip joint.

What Is Cancer?

Cancer is a noncommunicable disease. The many kinds of cancer are alike in one way. With cancer, certain body cells start to grow out of control. These cancer cells are not normal cells. Cancer cells destroy healthy body cells. Then the body cannot work as it should.

In many kinds of cancer, cells form a mass of tissue called a tumor. However, not all tumors are made of cancer cells. Doctors use operations, medicines, and other ways to treat cancer. More than one way might be used. Treatment can cure some kinds of cancers.

Medical research workers are trying hard to find better ways to treat cancer. Workers also try hard to find more ways to cure cancer. Such work is difficult because the exact causes of cancer are not fully understood.

In their work, research workers have learned about some ways people can help prevent two kinds of cancer. One way is not to smoke. Not smoking helps prevent lung cancer. Another way is to avoid staying in the sun for long periods year after year. Avoiding long periods in the sunlight helps prevent skin cancer.

What Is Arthritis?

Arthritis is a disease that harms the joints of the body. The joints might become swollen, stiff, and painful. Some joints might become difficult to move. In most cases, the cause of arthritis is not known.

Older people most often get arthritis. However, some young people also get the disease. Medicines help take away the pain of this disease. However, doctors do not yet know how to cure arthritis. Sometimes an artificial joint, like the one shown, is put in to replace a crippled one.

What Are Allergies?

allergy (al′ər jē), a noncommunicable disease in which a person is sensitive to a substance, such as food or pollen.

A person with an **allergy** is bothered by substances that do not bother most people. The pictures show some of these substances, including certain foods, dust, parts of plants, chemicals, and animal hair. A person with an allergy might have trouble breathing, get a rash, or have an upset stomach. These problems happen after breathing, eating, or touching the substances.

A doctor treats a person with an allergy by trying to find out what food or other substance causes problems. The person might then avoid whatever is troublesome. Sometimes a doctor gives the person a shot so that the troublesome substance bothers the person less.

Think Back • *Study on your own with Study Guide page 265.*

1. What is a noncommunicable disease?
2. What parts of the body do heart diseases harm?
3. What is diabetes?
4. How do cancer cells harm the body?
5. How does arthritis affect the body?
6. What might happen if a person has an allergy to a food?

Health Activities Workshop

Doing More About Diseases

1. Below is a puzzle to solve. Unscramble the letters in the words. You will then have the name of ten diseases. Make two lists. Write the communicable diseases in one list. Write the noncommunicable diseases in another list. Use your own paper.

pmums	olsdc
ulf	betesdia
liopo	lleragies
ceranc	earth sidease
eamsles	rithartis

2. Find out how doctors sometimes help people who have certain heart diseases. You might find out about artificial hearts, for example. An artificial heart might be used until a heart transplant is done. Find a newspaper or magazine article about artificial hearts or heart transplants. Write down some facts you learn. If the article has a drawing, you might copy it. Share your information with your class.

3. You have learned about ways to keep your heart and blood vessels healthy. Make a poster that shows one of these ways. You might tell a way young people can keep healthy now and as they grow up.

4. Make a get-well card for someone who is sick. If the person is in your school, you might write about an event in school. Perhaps the person who is sick is a neighbor or a member of your family. What interesting information could you put on your card?

Looking at Careers

5. Many people have jobs helping people who have diseases. One job is a **nurse's aide.** Nurse's aides help take care of sick people in hospitals and places such as nursing homes.

A nurse's aide works with nurses and doctors. He or she serves food to sick people, helps bathe them, and changes beds. A nurse's aide might take and record temperatures, pulse, and breathing rates.

A nurse's aide must be at least seventeen years old. Most hospitals hire people who have finished high school. Nurse's aides must be in good health and like to take care of people.

Suppose a nurse's aide worked in the part of a hospital that treats sick children. What are some jobs the person might do? Write your ideas on a piece of paper.

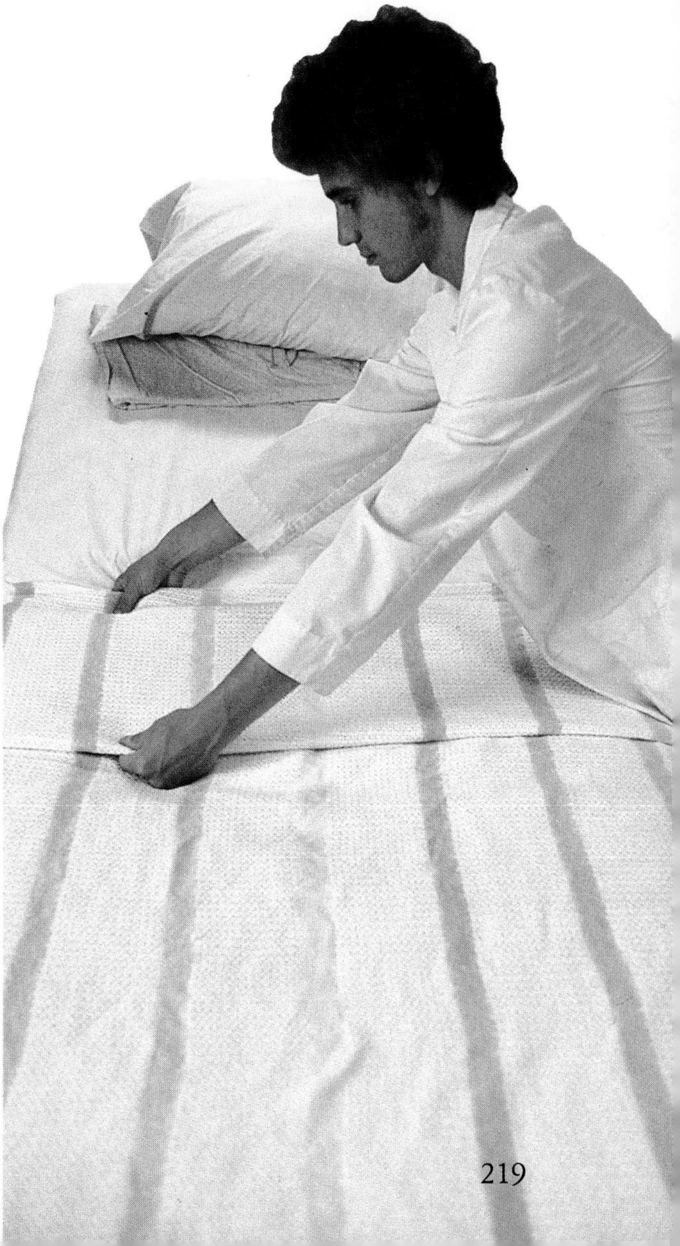

5 How Can You Build a Healthy Lifestyle?

If you have a healthy lifestyle, you have good health habits. The habits can help prevent some communicable diseases and help you be healthy now. Good health habits can also help prevent some noncommunicable diseases later in your life.

Keeping clean is a good health habit. How can this habit help protect you from communicable diseases? Regular exercising helps you become fit. Your heart and lungs become healthier and work better. Exercise also helps prevent some fatty substances from building up in the arteries. Regular exercise can help you avoid overweight and can help prevent heart disease.

Getting enough sleep and rest can help keep you healthy. If your body is rested, it can better fight off disease germs. Your body can work as it should.

Eating the right foods provides what your body needs to grow and work as it should. Food also provides energy to fight disease germs. Eating fewer salty and fatty foods helps keep your heart healthy. Eating less sweet, sugary food helps keep your teeth healthy.

Not smoking is a good health habit too. Not smoking can help prevent lung cancer and some heart diseases. People who avoid abusing drugs also help themselves stay healthy.

Each block on these two pages suggests a way you can build a healthy lifestyle. Explain how each suggested way might help prevent disease.

Think Back • *Study on your own with Study Guide page 265.*

1. How does having a healthy lifestyle help prevent diseases?
2. What are three actions that can help build a healthy lifestyle?

On Your Own
Suppose families could go to a health camp. Write a newspaper ad that would make families want to go to that camp. In your ad, explain how going to the camp might help families build a healthy lifestyle. Include in your ad any activities or equipment to improve health that the camp has.

Having many healthy habits, such as the ones suggested here, helps young and old people alike build a healthy lifestyle.

Exercising After a Heart Attack

Not so many years ago people did not fully understand how exercise could help the heart. Many people thought that if you ever had a heart attack, you could never exercise again. A heart attack occurs when an artery that carries blood to the heart is blocked. The heart can be badly damaged. People used to think that a person who had a heart attack could not live a normal life again.

Dr. White made sure he got regular exercise too.

In 1955 President Dwight Eisenhower had a heart attack. Many people thought the President could not work again even if he got over the heart attack. The President's doctor asked a famous heart doctor to treat the President. The heart doctor was Paul Dudley White.

Dr. White helped the President get better. The doctor made sure the President ate healthy foods and got exercise every day. Dr. White thought that walking and bicycling were very good for the heart.

After a time, President Eisenhower got better. He returned to his work and to a normal life. He still exercised every day and he often played his favorite game, golf. Dr. White had shown the President and the people of the United States that a heart attack need not mean being sick for life. Dr. White's ideas about exercising after a heart attack still help many people get better.

Talk About It

1. What did Dr. White teach the people of the United States about life after a heart attack?
2. How might exercise help keep a person from having a heart attack?

Eating Fewer Fatty Foods

Many people are just beginning to find out how important it is to eat fewer fatty foods. How can it be helpful to members of your family? If you are not sure, read page 213 again before you talk over this important idea.

Some people need to reduce some of the fats in the foods they eat to stay healthy. Listed below are some ideas for these people. Together you and your family might think of other ideas.

- Buy low-fat foods, such as low-fat milk.
- Broil or bake meats instead of frying them in extra fat.
- Take the skin off chicken and other poultry. This part contains much fat.
- Trim extra fat from meat.

Reading at Home

Germs! by Dorothy Hinshaw Patent. Holiday House, 1983. Read how disease germs make you sick. Look at some interesting photographs of disease germs.

The Smallest Life Around Us by Lucia Anderson. Crown, 1978. Try some of the experiments in this book to learn more about germs.

Viruses by Alan Nourse. Watts, 1983. Read what scientists have learned about viruses.

Chapter 8 Review

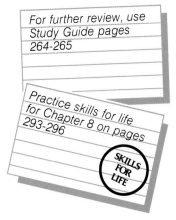

For further review, use Study Guide pages 264-265

Practice skills for life for Chapter 8 on pages 293-296

SKILLS FOR LIFE

Reviewing Lesson Objectives

1. Explain what causes a communicable disease. Tell how disease germs spread. (pages 202–205)
2. State ways disease germs are kept out of the body or killed if they get inside the body. Explain how the AIDS virus can affect the body. (pages 206–209)
3. Explain ways that people can prevent disease germs from spreading. (pages 210–211)
4. Describe what noncommunicable diseases are. Explain how heart disease, diabetes, cancer, arthritis, and allergies affect the body. (pages 212–217)
5. List actions that help build a healthy lifestyle. Explain how a healthy lifestyle can help prevent diseases. (pages 220–221)

Checking Health Vocabulary

Number your paper from 1–14. Match each definition in Column I with the correct word or words in Column II.

Column I

1. an illness caused by disease germs
2. a disease in which the body makes too little insulin
3. a disease that harms the joints of the body
4. a substance made by white blood cells to fight germs
5. a disease that can cause rashes from certain foods
6. protection from having a disease a second time
7. an illness that does not spread
8. a medicine used to kill certain bacteria in the body
9. the kind of germ that causes a cold
10. a medicine that causes the body to make antibodies
11. a disease of the heart or blood vessels
12. a disease in which body cells grow out of control
13. a disease caused by a virus that can destroy certain white blood cells
14. tiny living things, some of which cause communicable diseases

Column II

a. AIDS
b. allergy
c. antibiotic
d. antibody
e. arthritis
f. bacteria
g. cancer
h. cardiovascular disease
i. communicable disease
j. diabetes
k. immunity
l. noncommunicable disease
m. vaccine
n. virus

Reviewing Health Ideas

Number your paper from 1–14. Next to each number write the word or words that best complete the sentence. Choose the words from the list.

air	immunity
bacteria	insulin
cancer	lifestyle
cardiovascular	mucus
cells	skin
divide	vaccines
germs	white blood cells

1. Colds are caused by ____.
2. Viruses and ____ cause communicable diseases.
3. Germs might enter the body through a cut in the ____.
4. Bacteria ____ in the body to make more of themselves.
5. Viruses harm body ____ by breaking and entering them.
6. Disease germs might be carried in the ____ you breathe in.
7. In your nose, ____ traps germs.
8. Inside your body, ____ can destroy germs.
9. Antibodies help a person build ____ to certain diseases.
10. A doctor can give a person ____ against certain diseases.
11. Atherosclerosis is one kind of ____ disease.
12. ____ is a disease that attacks healthy cells.
13. Diabetes occurs when the body does not make enough ____.
14. A healthy ____ might help a person avoid disease.

Understanding Health Ideas

Number your paper from 15–24. Next to each number write the word or words that best answer the question.

15. What are two kinds of disease germs?
16. What do you need to use to see germs?
17. What should you do with tissues used to cover a sneeze?
18. How is the AIDS virus different from other viruses?
19. What medicines sometimes help kill bacteria?
20. In one heart disease, what substances can block arteries?
21. What kind of cancer does not smoking help prevent?
22. What parts of the body are harmed by arthritis?
23. What is one way an allergy can affect a person's body?
24. What health habits can help prevent heart disease?

Thinking Critically

Write the answers on your paper. Use complete sentences.

1. In what ways does not smoking help a person build a healthy lifestyle? Mention three noncommunicable diseases.
2. Not as many young people as older people get heart disease. Why should young people know about heart disease and how to prevent it?

Chapter 9

Working For a Healthy Environment

This girl is planting a tree as part of her town's plan to make it a prettier place to live. How might trees in a community improve a person's health? This chapter describes ways a community works to keep people healthy throughout their lives.

Health Watch Notebook

Make a collage with pictures of things that might be in a healthy and safe community. When your collage is complete, write a sentence about each picture. Explain why you included it as part of your healthy community.

environment (en vī′rən mənt), everything, including places and conditions, that surrounds a person and affects actions and feelings.

pollute (pə lüt′), to make dirty, as for example, to pollute air or water.

1 What Is a Healthy Environment?

Your **environment** is made up of the homes, parks, hospitals, stores, and people around you. Everything that affects what you do and how you feel is part of your environment. A healthy environment provides what you and others need for good health. It takes many people, working together, to keep the environment healthy and safe.

A healthy environment has clean air. Different substances can **pollute** the air. Polluted air is dirty air. People in communities work to keep the air clean because breathing polluted air can cause health problems.

Communities also work to make sure the environment has clean, safe water. Polluted water is not safe to drink or use. Eating fish from polluted water or swimming in it can also harm your health.

Communities also protect the environment from being too noisy. Hearing too much noise can harm your health. For example, hearing very loud sounds for a long time might cause loss of hearing.

Food that is safe to eat is part of a healthy environment. Certain community workers check to see that food in stores and eating places is safe to eat.

You also need places to learn and have fun. While you are enjoying places such as parks, schools, and libraries, you should try to keep them clean. You can clean up garbage that is around you. What else can you do to keep your community clean and healthy?

What parts of a person's environment are not shown in the picture?

Think Back • *Study on your own with Study Guide page 266.*

1. What does a healthy environment provide?
2. How can people keep the environment healthy?

particle (pär′tə kəl), a tiny bit of material.

incinerator (in sin′ə rā′tər), a furnace for burning trash.

Did You Know?
Many factories have machines called scrubbers inside smokestacks. A scrubber works to help get rid of most of the dust and some harmful gases in smoke that could go into the air.

Where might air be heavily polluted from cars, trucks, and buses?

2 What Can a Community Do About Air Pollution?

Air pollution is a serious community health problem. Anything that is burned causes air pollution. Gases and **particles** enter the air during burning. Particles are tiny bits of material so small they float in the air like dust. The gases and particles pollute the air.

Most air pollution comes from cars, trucks, and buses. These vehicles burn fuel in their engines. Gases and particles from the burning fuel go out exhaust pipes and into the air. Smoke from burning trash and smoke and gases from factories also pollute the air. Even blowing sand or dirt can cause air pollution.

Often you know when air is polluted. The air might appear gray or yellow. You might find it hard to breathe. The air might not smell fresh. At other times you cannot see or smell the gases that pollute air.

Air pollution can cause changes in your body. Dirty air can harm your lungs and the tubes that lead to your lungs. Breathing polluted air year after year might lead to lung diseases. Air pollution also makes diseases of the respiratory system worse.

Anyone can feel uncomfortable when air is very polluted. People often have trouble breathing. Their eyes sting and burn. Some people have less energy to work and play.

Many people in a community work together to help solve the problem of air pollution. For example, many communities have laws that do not allow people to burn their own leaves or trash. Instead, all leaves and trash are collected and burned in **incinerators.** Many incinerators have ways to clean smoke before it enters the air.

The incinerator shown here also helps by using trash as fuel. The burning trash heats water in pipes. The water turns to steam, which can be used to provide heat or power to make machines work. Steam can also be used to make electricity.

Certain workers in many communities also check to see that cars, trucks, and buses do not pollute the air. A community might pass laws to have these vehicles checked. Some families share rides and also walk more to use their cars less. How might using cars less help keep air clean?

Think Back • *See Study Guide on page 266.*

1. What causes air pollution?
2. How might air pollution harm health?
3. How can a community help solve the problem of air pollution?

Community workers collect and dump all the town's trash in large bins. In the control room, a person operates the machine that presses the trash together. The trash is then burned to give off steam.

sewage (sü′ij), the wastes carried in sewer pipes and drains.

3 What Can a Community Do About Water Pollution?

Every community has the job of supplying safe water to drink. Many towns and cities get water from nearby lakes, rivers, and streams. Other communities get water from underground wells. Sometimes the water is polluted.

What Causes Water Pollution?

Waste material carried in sewer pipes and drains is called **sewage.** In some communities, pipes carry sewage from homes and other buildings to nearby lakes or streams. Some factories also dump harmful chemicals and oil into lakes and streams.

Laws today prevent factories such as this electric power plant from causing too much water pollution. Such laws help make the water in this lake safer for swimming and fishing.

Chemicals are used on farmland to kill insects or to help crops grow better. Sometimes rain carries these chemicals along the ground and then into nearby lakes and streams.

Wastes and chemicals that enter lakes, rivers, and streams can all cause water pollution. Polluted water is not safe to drink or use. It often has germs from food or toilet wastes. The germs might cause disease. Polluted water often has chemicals that can harm your body.

Once, factories like the one in the picture caused much water pollution. People could not swim or fish safely. Today many factories no longer pollute water in lakes, streams, and rivers. Slowly the water is becoming cleaner.

waste-treatment plant, a place where used water from homes and other buildings is treated before it is put back into rivers and lakes.

water-treatment plant, a place where water from rivers, lakes, and streams is treated so it is safe to drink.

The larger tanks in the picture above are settling tanks. Sewage moves slowly through the tanks so solid material can fall to the bottom. At this plant, the solids are then put into the smaller tanks shown at the top of the picture.

How Do Communities Supply Clean Water?

A community often gets drinking water from polluted lakes and rivers. The pollution in these lakes and rivers can be reduced in several ways.

Many factories treat their wastes to make less pollution in lakes and rivers. The factories deal with the wastes in ways that make them safer to dump into water. Most communities also have **waste-treatment plants** to treat sewage. Sewage from homes and other buildings goes through underground pipes to a waste-treatment plant.

At this plant, sewage moves through special screens that remove solid wastes. The sewage is then put into tanks like the ones at the left. Here grit, sand, and small stones settle out of the water. Finally, a chemical is added to kill disease-causing germs.

Treated sewage is pumped from the waste-treatment plant into a nearby lake, river, or stream. Treated water might be safe for swimming or fishing, but it is still not safe to drink.

Most communities have a **water-treatment plant** to make water from nearby lakes, rivers, and streams safe to drink. Water is filtered at a water-treatment plant to remove dirt. Water is sometimes sprayed into the air. Spraying the water helps remove unpleasant tastes and smells. The water is also treated to kill harmful germs and to remove unsafe chemicals. The last step is for workers to test the treated water to be sure it is safe to drink.

The water-treatment plant, shown on the next page, treats the water for all the people in a large city. Treated water is then pumped through pipes to homes and other buildings in the community. Some treated water is stored in water towers.

Think Back • *Study on your own with Study Guide page 266.*

1. What causes water pollution?
2. How can polluted water harm health?
3. What is done to sewage at a waste-treatment plant?
4. What is done to water at a water-treatment plant?

On Your Own
People in a community can help save water by using it wisely. Write a paragraph about some ways you and your family can avoid wasting water. For example, you might turn off water while you brush your teeth. What other ways can you think of to help save water?

Health Activities Workshop

Learning More About Air and Water Pollution

1. Find out where your community's water comes from. Where is the nearest water-treatment plant? Is extra water stored after it has been treated? If so, find out where. Report what you find out to your class. Make a simple map of the places you learn about.

2. Find out what parts of your school get the most air pollution. Cut four pieces of waxed paper into four-inch (8.16 cm) squares. Tape each square onto a piece of cardboard. Label the squares *A*, *B*, *C*, and *D*. Spread some petroleum jelly over each square of waxed paper.

Put the squares in places where no one will touch them for one week. Put one in your classroom. Put one in a hall. Put one near a door going outside. Put one in a safe place outside.

Collect the squares in one week. If you have a magnifying glass, use it to look at the squares. Describe how each square looks. Which square looks dirtiest? How do you explain any differences you see?

3. Rachel Carson was a scientist who was very worried about how pollution might change the earth. Look for a library book or look in an encyclopedia for information about Rachel Carson. Find out why she was worried about pollution. Write a paragraph about what you learn.

4. Read the following mystery message. Read the lines from left to right. The letters make words. Write the words on your own paper.

BURNI
NGMAK
ESAIR
POLLU
TION

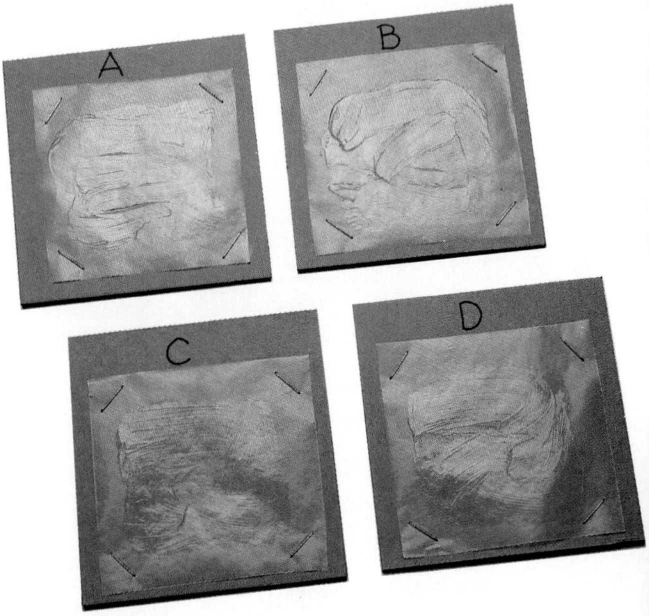

5. Unscramble the following words. You will have four words telling what can cause water pollution. Write the words on your own paper.

iol
agesew
ermgs
icalschem

Looking at Careers

6. Many people work to help solve pollution problems. An **air pollution technician** uses special equipment to measure pollution in the air. A person with this job might work in a laboratory on wheels. An air pollution technician drives the laboratory to different places in a community. The person parks the laboratory near a factory or group of factories.

Air pollution technicians collect samples of air. They put the samples into equipment inside the laboratory to discover what is polluting the air.

The technician reports what has been discovered to a community air-control office. These reports help people plan ways to prevent and reduce air pollution. The reports also help in checking whether air pollution laws are being obeyed.

An air pollution technician goes to a special class for job training. A person might take the class after finishing high school.

Make a list of the places in your community where an air pollution technician would look for air pollution.

4 How Can a Community Reduce Noise Pollution?

If you have ever been to an airport, you can probably imagine the noise the jet in the picture makes. How does this woman who works at the airport protect her hearing from the noise?

Noise is unwanted sound, especially loud sound. Too much noise is noise pollution. Once people thought loud noises in the community were just annoying. Today people know that too much noise harms health.

Some people feel nervous living and working in very noisy places. Noise can upset sleep. Noise can cause some people to get tired easily.

Sudden noise, such as a loud crash, makes the heart beat faster than it should. Working in a very noisy place for a long time or listening to very loud music over and over can harm a person's hearing. The hearing loss might last for a short time or it might last forever.

People have found ways to avoid harm from noise pollution. For example, builders now use special materials on walls, windows, and ceilings. The materials help keep indoor noises from being carried from room to room. The materials also keep outdoor noises from coming inside. Rugs and drapes absorb noise inside buildings. Trees, grass, and bushes are planted around buildings and highways to help absorb noise.

Factories often have loud machines that bother workers and others nearby. Today some factories put noisy machines in special rooms that absorb noise. Factory workers wear ear protectors.

Many communities have laws about noise. In some places, people might not be allowed to play radios too loud. Car drivers cannot honk horns too loudly or too often. Power mowers cannot be used to mow grass in early morning hours. Your community might have other laws to reduce noise.

You can help reduce noise pollution. You can keep radios, stereos, or TV sets turned low. You can close doors quietly. You can talk quietly inside. What other ways can you help keep your environment quiet?

Did You Know?
Sound is measured in decibels. Listening to repeated sounds of 85 decibels or above can harm hearing. A person feels pain in the ears from hearing sounds of 120 decibels or above. The chart shows the decibels of some everyday sounds.

Sound	**Number of decibels**
whisper	20
normal talking	50
loud radio	75
food blender	95
power mower	100
electric saw	110
rock band	115
jet plane	130

Think Back • *Study on your own with Study Guide page 267.*

1. What is noise pollution?
2. How might too much noise harm health?
3. How might a community reduce noise pollution?
4. How can people help reduce noise pollution?

sanitarian (san′ə ter′ē ən), a person who checks to see if food in stores, restaurants, food factories, and dairies is safe to eat.

5 How Does a Community Help Keep Food Safe?

Sanitarians are inspectors from community health departments who work to help keep food safe for people to eat. These people check food factories and restaurants to see that food is handled properly.

A sanitarian checks to see that food in a restaurant is prepared and served safely. For example, meat must be cooked at certain temperatures to make it safe to eat. Certain salads must be kept cold so germs do not grow in them. Dishes must be washed carefully. Why is this important?

Sanitarians also check to see that people who work with food do their work in safe ways. For example, sanitarians help make sure that people who work with food are healthy. Sick people might pass germs to others who eat the food. Sanitarians also check to see that restrooms have soap and warm water. How would this help keep food safe to eat? In food factories sanitarians check to see that machines that touch food are clean. They check to see that floors and walls are clean and free of insects and other animals. Such pests might spread dirt and germs to food.

People who handle food must wash their hands before touching food. Long hair must be tied back or held in a net.

The dairy in the picture is a kind of food factory. At a dairy milk is **pasteurized,** or heated to a high temperature to kill germs. Then the milk is put into sterilized cartons or bottles and immediately refrigerated. Sanitarians check all machines in a dairy to see that everything is clean and working right.

pasteurize (pas′chə rīz′), to heat a substance to a high enough temperature and for a long enough time to destroy germs.

Sanitarians follow several steps if they find unsafe food handling in a food factory or restaurant. They first talk over ways to correct the unsafe handling. They also tell the community health department. Later, this department will close the food factory or restaurant if food is still handled unsafely. Sanitarians visit the places again and check them for safety.

At a dairy milk moves inside pipes to tanks where it is heated. Milk is then cooled and bottled quickly so it does not spoil.

Think Back • *Study on your own with Study Guide page 267.*

1. What do sanitarians check in eating places?
2. What do sanitarians check in food factories?
3. How do sanitarians keep a community healthy and safe?

6 How Does a Community Help People Enjoy Themselves?

A community works to help people stay healthy. A community also provides places where people can have fun, learn, and meet new people. In these ways a community helps people feel good about themselves. How are people in the picture enjoying themselves?

A community might provide parks and playgrounds. People in a community might have special events such as concerts or parades for everyone to enjoy. Some communities have a museum or an art gallery for people to visit.

A community might provide places for activities for people of all ages. A library might have story hours for little children. Older children might go to a community center after school for fun or for help with homework. Older people might go to a place to meet new friends, learn new things, or help young children learn.

Communities often have places that people can get help if they do not feel right. Many communities have hospitals and clinics that treat people if they are injured or sick. Communities might also have places where people can talk with others about their problems and learn how to cope with them. People in communities can also get help if their environment is not clean or safe. By helping to solve health and safety problems, communities help people stay healthy and enjoy themselves.

On Your Own

Sometimes you can tell how people feel about their community. You might hear, "This is a great place to live. I don't want to live anywhere else." Make a list of several reasons why your community is a good place to live.

Think Back • *Study on your own with Study Guide page 267.*

1. What might a community provide to help people enjoy themselves?
2. What might communities have to help people deal with health problems?

Health Focus

Cleaning Up Perth Amboy's Beach

You already know that air and water can be polluted. Did you know that land can be polluted too?

The students from the Flynn Elementary School in Perth Amboy, New Jersey, help clean up one kind of land pollution every year. Perth Amboy is a town along the edge of a beach. Every winter twigs, leaves, and garbage float up onto the beach. In the spring students from the Flynn School clean up the beach. Then people from Perth Amboy have a clean, safe beach to enjoy during the summer.

Cleaning the beach is hard work. All the students rake up the twigs and garbage. Next, they put the garbage in bags and boxes and load them on trucks to be carried away.

The people of Perth Amboy appreciate the students for cleaning up the beach. The students are very proud of their work. They also have another reason to be proud. The students from the Flynn School won an award from the President of the United States for cleaning up the beach. The award goes to young people who help make their community cleaner and safer.

Talk About It

1. How have the students at Perth Amboy helped clean up pollution?
2. What are some ways you could help clean up pollution in your community?

Sharing Ideas About Air Pollution

You know ways a community works to help solve the problem of air pollution. You and your family can also help. For example, if your family has a car, you could follow these suggestions.

- Use the car less often. Walk or ride a bicycle sometimes.
- When possible, leave the car at home and ride a bus or train.
- Consider joining a car pool. When many people ride in a car pool, fewer cars are on the road.
- Keep the family car working well. A car causes less pollution when the engine runs well.

When you have a chance, you might talk with your family about more ways to use cars less.

Reading at Home

Water for the World by Franklyn M. Branley. Crowell, 1982. Learn about ways to use water wisely.

What to Do When Your Mom or Dad Says . . . "Turn Off the Water and Lights!" by Joy Wilt Berry. Learn why saving water and turning off lights helps the environment.

Chapter 9 Review

For further review, use Study Guide pages 266-267

Practice skills for life for Chapter 9 on pages 297-299

SKILLS FOR LIFE

Reviewing Lesson Objectives

1. Identify what a healthy environment provides and why it is important to keep the environment healthy and safe. (pages 228–229)
2. Explain what causes air pollution and how it harms health. Tell ways people in a community try to reduce air pollution. (pages 230–231)
3. Explain what causes water pollution and how it harms health. List two ways polluted water is treated. (pages 232–235)
4. Explain how noise pollution can harm health. List ways a person can help reduce noise. (pages 238–239)
5. Explain how sanitarians work to keep food safe for people in a community to eat. (pages 240–241)
6. List ways a community helps people enjoy themselves and helps solve health problems. (pages 242–243)

Checking Health Vocabulary

Number your paper from 1–9. Match each definition in Column I with the correct word or words in Column II.

Column I

1. a person who checks food for safety
2. wastes carried in sewers and drains
3. to make water, air, or food dirty
4. the place where water is made safe to drink
5. everything that surrounds a person
6. a tiny bit of material
7. the place where sewage is treated
8. a furnace for burning trash
9. to heat in order to destroy germs

Column II

a. environment
b. incinerator
c. particle
d. pasteurize
e. pollute
f. sanitarian
g. sewage
h. waste-treatment plant
i. water-treatment plant

Number your paper from 10–15. Write a sentence using each of the following word or words.

10. air pollution
11. noise pollution
12. community
13. factory
14. polluted water
15. healthy environment

Reviewing Health Ideas

Number your paper from 1–12. Next to each number write the word or words that best complete the sentence. Choose the words from the list.

air pollution	people
community	sanitarians
environment	sewage
incinerators	respiratory
laws	water pollution
noise pollution	water-treatment
pasteurized	

1. Your neighborhood is part of your ____.
2. Exhaust from cars causes most ____.
3. Polluted air can harm a person's ____ system.
4. A community might provide ____ so people do not have to burn their own trash.
5. Wastes from homes and factories can cause ____.
6. One part of keeping water safe to use involves treating ____.
7. Water from lakes and streams is treated at a ____ plant before it is sent into homes.
8. ____ can harm hearing.
9. Many communities have ____ to help keep the environment quiet.
10. ____ check restaurants to see that food is prepared properly.
11. Milk is ____ at a dairy to help keep it safe to drink.
12. A healthy ____ has activities for people of different ages.

Understanding Health Ideas

Number your paper from 13–22. Next to each number write the word or words that best answer the question.

13. What can pollution do to a person's health?
14. How can people keep their environment healthy and clean?
15. How might polluted air affect the eyes?
16. What vehicles can community workers check to help reduce air pollution?
17. What items that cause pollution do some factories add to water?
18. Why does treated sewage from a waste-treatment plant then go to a water-treatment plant?
19. How might noise pollution affect sleep?
20. What might a factory worker wear to protect his or her hearing while working with noisy machines?
21. Who does a sanitarian tell about unsafe food handling?
22. How do communities help people solve their health and safety problems?

Thinking Critically

Write the answers on your paper. Use complete sentences.

1. List three reasons why a community would want to keep a nearby lake clean.
2. How can young people help keep their community safe and healthy?

Using Metric

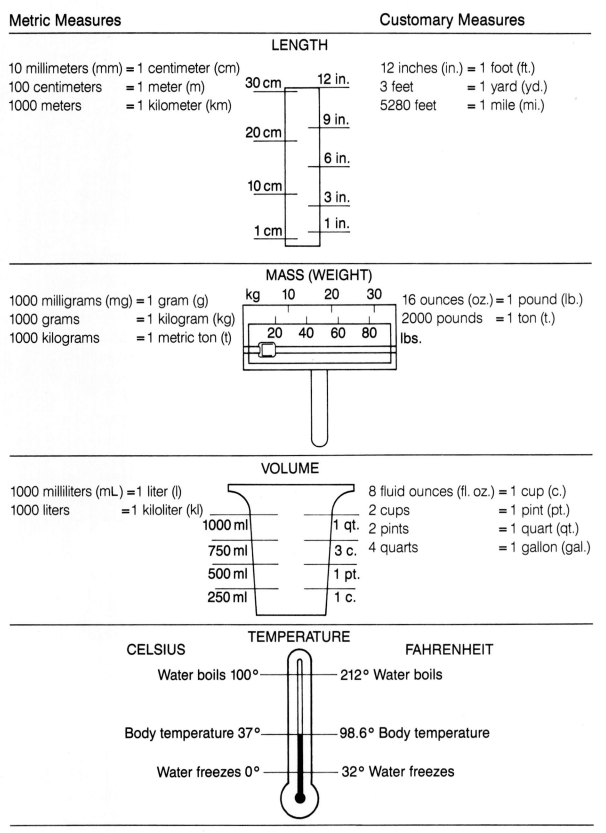

Metric Measures | **Customary Measures**

LENGTH

10 millimeters (mm) = 1 centimeter (cm)
100 centimeters = 1 meter (m)
1000 meters = 1 kilometer (km)

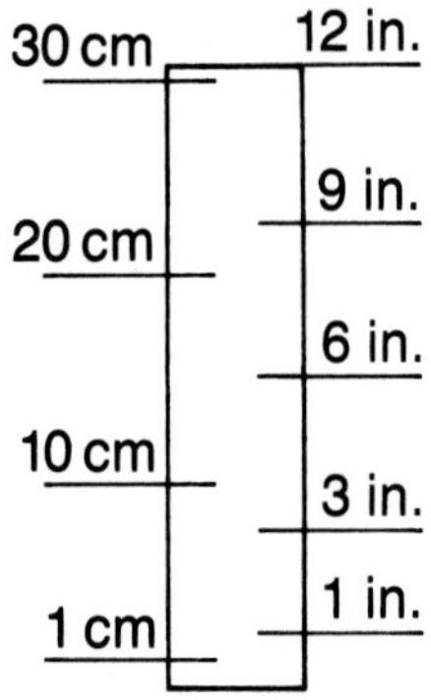

12 inches (in.) = 1 foot (ft.)
3 feet = 1 yard (yd.)
5280 feet = 1 mile (mi.)

MASS (WEIGHT)

1000 milligrams (mg) = 1 gram (g)
1000 grams = 1 kilogram (kg)
1000 kilograms = 1 metric ton (t)

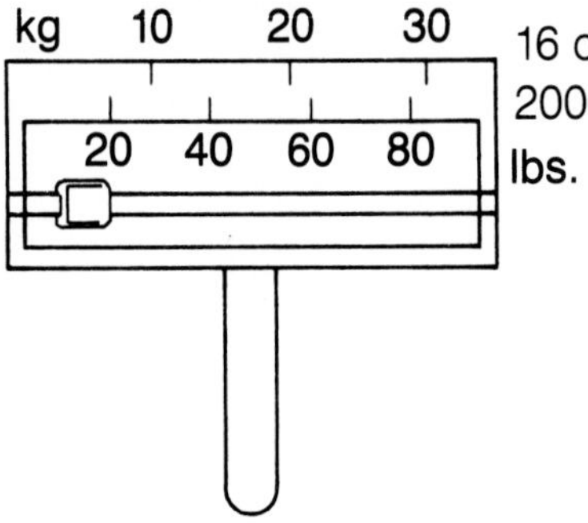

16 ounces (oz.) = 1 pound (lb.)
2000 pounds = 1 ton (t.)

VOLUME

1000 milliliters (mL) = 1 liter (l)
1000 liters = 1 kiloliter (kl)

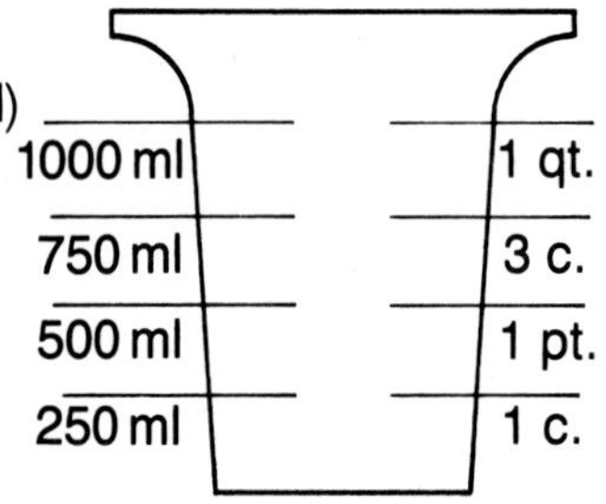

8 fluid ounces (fl. oz.) = 1 cup (c.)
2 cups = 1 pint (pt.)
2 pints = 1 quart (qt.)
4 quarts = 1 gallon (gal.)

TEMPERATURE

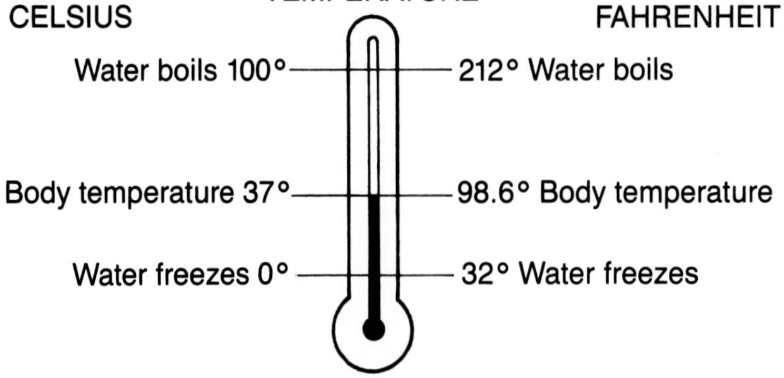

Independent Study Guide

Use the *Independent Study Guide* to review the lessons in each chapter. After you read each lesson, answer the questions to find out what you remember. Answering the questions will help you learn the important ideas in each lesson. You can also use the study guide to help you review for the chapter test.

Chapter 1 Study Guide

On a separate sheet of paper, write the word or words that best complete the sentence or answer the question.

Lesson 1
pages 18-21

1. What are some ways people are different?
2. Something a person does well is one of the person's ____.
3. How does appearance help make a person special?
4. List some strengths people might have.
5. What helps a person understand himself or herself better?
6. A person who feels good about himself or herself has a good ____.
7. People who accept themselves know they have ____ as well as strengths.
8. How might a person with a good self-image deal with a particular weakness that cannot be improved much?
9. How might having a good self-image help a person get along with others?
10. Learning words from a friend who speaks a different language is one way to ____ differences in the friend.
11. How might a deaf person communicate with others?

Lesson 2
pages 24-25

1. ____ such as anger often affect the way the body works.
2. List some body changes a person might have before talking in front of a group.
3. What does it mean if a person says he or she has butterflies in the stomach?
4. How are people different in the way feelings affect them?
5. Feelings that cause body changes usually last a ____ time.

Lesson 3
pages 26-27

1. List two or three reasons people might get angry at one another.
2. How might angry feelings affect the way a person's head or stomach might feel?
3. Who can a person talk to in order to get rid of angry feelings?
4. What usually happens to angry feelings if a person keeps them inside?
5. Describe what a person might do to get rid of angry feelings if the person does not have someone to talk to.

Lesson 4
pages 28-29

1. People who think differently about something might have a ____.
2. Describe two ways people might solve a problem together or settle a disagreement.
3. During a disagreement, people need to ____ to each other.
4. What can be done when disagreements cannot be settled?
5. What is one way to keep some disagreements from taking place, such as disagreements about certain family rules?

Lesson 5
pages 32-35

1. List some kinds of decisions people your age often need to make.
2. Who can help you make decisions?
3. List the five steps people can use to make wise decisions.
4. A person should think about ____ results as well as good results when making decisions.
5. What was the result of Brian's decision?

Chapter 2 Study Guide

On a separate sheet of paper, write the word or words that best complete the sentence or answer the question.

Lesson **1** pages 42-45

1. Every part of your body is made of ____.
2. List five kinds of cells in your body.
3. How are cells grouped in the body?
4. List some of the different tissues in your body.
5. The brain, heart, lungs, and stomach are ____.
6. List two tissues that make up the eye.
7. Organs and body parts that work together to do a job make up a ____.
8. The ____ system moves blood around your body.
9. What system changes the food you eat?
10. The ____ system helps you breathe.
11. What system helps you think and act?

Lesson **2** pages 46-48

1. The heart is made of ____ tissue.
2. What happens when your heart contracts?
3. Where can you feel the pulse?
4. What body parts make up the circulatory system?
5. Where in the body does blood pick up oxygen?
6. Blood carries ____ and nutrients to body cells.
7. Blood travels in ____, veins, and capillaries.
8. What waste does blood take away from cells?
9. What connects veins and arteries?

Lesson **3** pages 50-51

1. Where does digestion begin?
2. What liquids in the stomach help digest food?
3. Partly digested food in the small intestine contains ____.
4. Where is digestion completed?
5. What pushes material along in the large intestine?
6. List the organs and body parts of the digestive system.

Lesson 4
pages 52-53

1. What gas in air do you need to stay alive?
2. Your ____ controls your breathing.
3. Air is drawn into the lungs through the ____.
4. Where are the air sacs in your body?
5. What does oxygen pass into when it leaves the air sacs?
6. ____ carries oxygen to the heart.
7. When does the body get rid of carbon dioxide?
8. List organs and body parts that make up the respiratory system.

Lesson 5
pages 56-59

1. List the five main senses.
2. The ____ reads messages from sense organs.
3. What body parts and organs make up the nervous system?
4. The ____ protects the spinal cord.
5. What is the spinal cord?
6. What do sensory nerves carry?
7. What do motor nerves carry?
8. What parts of your body have nerves?
9. You do not have to think about doing ____ actions.
10. List some actions that go on in your body that you do not direct.
11. A special part of your ____ system controls automatic actions.

Lesson 6
pages 60-63

1. List some ways a person changes as he or she grows to an adult.
2. People grow partly because their bodies make more ____.
3. An adult's ____ are four times longer than a baby's.
4. Each person grows in his or her own ____ way.
5. What happens during the growth spurt?
6. When do girls usually start to grow heavier and taller?
7. When do boys usually start to grow heavier and taller?

Chapter 3 Study Guide

On a separate sheet of paper, write the word or words that best complete the sentence or answer the question.

Lesson **1** pages 70-71

1. ______ needs to be physically fit.
2. What are three ways being physically fit can help people?
3. How might being fit help a person prevent heart disease?
4. Being fit helps keep body organs, such as the heart and the ______, healthy.
5. How does oxygen you take into your body as you breathe reach your muscles?
6. Describe how a fit person's muscles can move.

Lesson **2** pages 72-75

1. List the three kinds of muscle fitness.
2. A person whose muscles can move easily and freely has ______.
3. How might having good flexibility help a person's muscles?
4. A person might test flexibility by doing an exercise called ______.
5. In what ways can people improve flexibility?
6. A person who can lift and carry heavy objects without feeling tired has muscle ______.
7. How might having strong muscles help people do everyday jobs?
8. Doing ten ______ without stopping is a test of a person's muscle strength.
9. In what ways can people build muscle strength?
10. What is muscle endurance?
11. A person might test muscle endurance by doing the ______.
12. The way the body is held as a person sits, stands, and walks is a person's ______.
13. Which kind of muscle fitness directly affects a person's posture?
14. What are three things a person with good posture can do for a long time without feeling tired?

Lesson **3** pages 78-79

1. How does building physical fitness help a person?
2. List some ways to play actively.
3. In addition to playing active games, a person needs to do ____ to build physical fitness.
4. To build fitness, you need to ____ the amount of exercise you do.
5. Why should a person choose activities or exercises he or she enjoys doing when deciding how to improve physical fitness?
6. List three activities that help build flexibility.
7. List three activities that help muscle strength.
8. List three activities that help build muscle endurance.
9. List three activities that help build a strong heart.

Lesson **4** pages 86-87

1. A sport involves a certain amount of exercise and has a set of ____ to follow.
2. What is a competitive sport?
3. A person needs sports ____ to help play sports.
4. List three or more sports skills.
5. A person who wants to learn a sports skill must ____ the skill over and over.
6. How might learning sports skills while a person is young help the person stay fit as he or she grows older?
7. Sports you can do all your life are ____ sports.
8. List three lifetime sports.

Lesson **5** pages 88-89

1. People do not always need to ____ to enjoy playing games.
2. List some ways people can act while playing a game so everyone has a good time.
3. What helpful way can a person who plays a game well act toward a less skillful player?
4. Why should players follow the rules of a game?
5. What is the only way to stay physically fit?

Chapter 4 Study Guide

On a separate sheet of paper, write the word or words that best complete the sentence or answer the question.

Lesson 1
pages 96-97

1. Pedestrians are people who ____ on streets and sidewalks.
2. A ____ often walks or crosses streets without paying attention to safety rules.
3. Where are you most likely to find a marked crosswalk?
4. Before you cross a street, you should look ____, then right, then left.
5. A safe pedestrian obeys traffic lights and ____.
6. If you are waiting for a car to cross in front of you, where is the safe place to wait?
7. Be sure that the ____ in an oncoming car sees you.
8. List two rules for safe walking when a group of people walks on a road with no sidewalk.
9. Wear light-colored ____ when walking at night.

Lesson 2
pages 98-101

1. A bicycle driver should drive on the ____ side of the street.
2. What is the safe way to drive bicycles when two or three people are driving together?
3. What is the safe way to cross a busy street while you are driving a bicycle?
4. A bicycle driver should use ____ signals when turning or stopping.
5. How should a bicycle driver signal that he or she is going to stop?
6. A bicycle driver should watch out for ____ coming into and out of driveways.
7. How can a person safely carry books on a bicycle?
8. What is a safety tip for driving a bicycle over wet, slippery roads?
9. What two parts of a bicycle can be moved so the bicycle fits a particular driver?
10. List three pieces of equipment a safe bicycle has.

Lesson **3** pages 102-105

1. What two skills will a person most likely learn at a swimming class?
2. People should come out of the water during a storm because of the danger of ____.
3. Swim only in a place where a parent or ____ can watch you.
4. What are two safety rules to follow at a public swimming pool?
5. What is the very first action to take if you see someone in trouble in the water?
6. To help rescue a person in trouble in the water, throw out something that will ____.
7. Another way to rescue a person in water is to reach out with a ____, belt, shirt, oar, stick, or rope.
8. To rescue a small child who falls in the water near the side of a pool, what should you do after you lie down?

Lesson **4** pages 108-110

1. Such happenings as falls and sudden illnesses are ____.
2. List two important actions to take in case of an emergency.
3. When you phone for help in an emergency, what should you tell the person who answers?
4. To stop bleeding from a deep cut, press down firmly with a clean ____.
5. What would you tell a friend who had a nosebleed to do?
6. To give first aid for a mild burn, first hold the burned part under ____ water.
7. What first aid is needed if a blister breaks open?

Lesson **5** pages 112-113

1. When home alone, never open the door to a ____.
2. What is the safe way to answer the telephone when you are alone and a call comes for your parent?
3. What phone numbers besides those of safety helpers should you keep near the phone?

Chapter 5 Study Guide

On a separate sheet of paper, write the word or words that best complete the sentence or answer the question.

Lesson **1** pages 120-121

1. During sleep many parts of the body get a chance to ____.
2. What happens to the activity of the heart and lungs while a person sleeps?
3. When do you know you have had enough sleep?
4. Most ten or eleven-year-olds need about ____ hours of sleep each night.
5. How can getting enough sleep help you with your schoolwork?
6. Getting enough sleep helps your feelings by making you less likely to be ____.

Lesson **2** pages 122-125

1. If you look at your teeth in a mirror, you can see first teeth, or primary teeth, and new teeth, or ____ teeth.
2. List the four kinds of permanent teeth you will have as an adult.
3. Teeth are held in the jaw by ____.
4. What covers roots of teeth?
5. The covering of the crown of a tooth is the ____.
6. What do incisors do?
7. Which teeth do the work of grinding food?
8. How do braces help make teeth straight?

Lesson **3** pages 126-129

1. What foods can people limit to help their teeth stay healthy?
2. What helps remove plaque from teeth?
3. How does plaque cause a cavity?
4. Gum disease is often caused by ____, which is plaque that has hardened.
5. During a checkup a dentist looks for ____.
6. A dentist or dental hygienist ____ a person's teeth to remove all the calculus.

Lesson **4** pages 132-134

1. Skin helps protect you by keeping ___ out of the body.
2. How does sweating help you?
3. What happens to blood vessels in your skin when you feel too cool?
4. The outer layer of skin where new skin cells form is the ___.
5. List three structures that are found in the dermis.
6. What kinds of messages do nerve endings in the dermis send to the brain to tell what has touched the skin?
7. What do you remove when you wash your face?
8. List two ways to protect your skin from too much sunshine.

Lesson **5** pages 136-137

1. Name three signs of possible eye problems.
2. If a person has trouble seeing objects clearly, it might be a sign that the person needs ___.
3. A person should work in a room with enough ___ to see properly.
4. Ringing, buzzing, headaches, or dizziness are signs of ___ problems.
5. ___ can protect ears from damage when a person is doing sports activities.
6. Small ___ cells in the ear can be damaged by loud sounds.
7. What should a person do if he or she is having any eye or ear problems?

Lesson **6** pages 138-141

1. List four kinds of health products people make decisions about buying.
2. List three kinds of information usually found on the label of a health product.
3. Give an example of helpful information in an ad for a health product.
4. Give an example of not very helpful information in an ad for a health product.

Chapter 6 Study Guide

On a separate sheet of paper, write the word or words that best complete the sentence or answer the question.

Lesson **1** pages 148-149

1. What happens to food in the stomach when the walls of the stomach move back and forth?
2. The walls of the stomach touch as they move back and forth when the stomach is ____.
3. How does food help the body grow?
4. Food provides your body with the ____ it needs for everything you do each day.
5. ____ is the meal many people need each day in order to do their best work in the morning.
6. How does food help bones, muscles, and teeth?

Lesson **2** pages 150-155

1. Every food you eat contains one or more substances called ____.
2. List the six main kinds of nutrients in foods.
3. Each kind of nutrient helps the body ____ and stay healthy.
4. List the names of the four food groups.
5. The numbers ____ can help a person remember to eat the right number of servings from the four food groups each day.
6. An orange, a serving of green beans, a tossed salad, and a glass of apple juice make up the needed daily servings from the ____ group.
7. List three foods that are in the same group as bread.
8. Cheese and yogurt are foods from the ____ group.
9. A peanut butter sandwich with two slices of bread provides one serving from the bread-cereal group and one serving from the ____ group.
10. A hamburger on a bun with lettuce and tomato and salad dressing has one food from the extra group. What is it?

Lesson
3
pages
158-159

1. Certain ____ are caused by a lack of certain nutrients.
2. Rickets harms the way the ____ grow.
3. What is the cause of rickets?
4. List two foods a person can eat every day that will help prevent rickets.
5. What health problems can scurvy cause?
6. A lack of vitamin ____ causes scurvy.
7. Name three foods people can eat to prevent scurvy.

Lesson
4
pages
160-161

1. Foods made with large amounts of ____ might not have other useful nutrients.
2. Eating foods that have large amounts of sugar can help cause ____.
3. What is one way people might start to limit the amount of salt they use?
4. If people broil meats, chicken, and fish, the foods will have less ____ than if they were fried.
5. A person who eats many different foods daily has a good chance of getting needed ____ each day.

Lesson
5
pages
162-165

1. List two living things other than bacteria that can cause food to spoil.
2. A spoiled food usually looks or ____ unpleasant.
3. If you think a food has spoiled, never ____ the food.
4. Bread, milk, and cheese should be stored in the ____.
5. If a person buys meat and will not cook it for a week, the meat should be stored in the ____.
6. List three foods that can be stored safely on shelves.
7. You might find directions on a food ____ for storing the food after it is opened.
8. What is the first action to take before you eat or prepare foods that others will eat?
9. Put leftover food from meals right in the ____ to prevent them from spoiling.
10. A person should not buy a can of food that is badly ____.

Chapter 7 Study Guide

On a separate sheet of paper, write the word or words that best complete the sentence or answer the question.

Lesson **1** pages 174-178

1. What is a drug?
2. List three ways people use medicines for diseases.
3. A medicine that a person can buy in a food store and is used for a mild headache is an ____ medicine.
4. A person must have an order from a doctor to buy a ____ medicine.
5. Who fills a doctor's order for a medicine?
6. What is an unwanted change caused by a medicine?
7. List three possible side effects from medicines.
8. Call the ____ when a person gets a side effect from taking a prescription medicine.
9. You should take medicine only from a ____ you trust.
10. Each time a person takes medicine, he or she should read the ____ on the medicine.
11. Who should be in charge of giving medicines to a person your age?
12. List two ways to store medicines safely.
13. What does it mean to misuse a medicine?

Lesson **2** pages 180-183

1. Nicotine makes the heart beat faster and the blood vessels become ____.
2. What does carbon dioxide do to a smoker's body?
3. What kind of diseases do people often get when they smoke cigarettes for a long time?
4. What kind of cancer does a cigarette smoker risk getting?
5. What health problems might chewing tobacco cause?
6. People who start smoking find it very hard to stop because their bodies get used to ____.
7. How does tobacco smoke affect other people who are near a smoker?

Lesson
3
pages
184-187

1. The ____ in beer, wine, and liquor changes the way a person thinks, acts, and feels.
2. Describe how alcohol affects the work of the brain.
3. Drinking large amounts of alcohol can cause a person to become ____, sleepy, or quarrelsome.
4. How can drinking alcohol affect a person who then drives a car?
5. What does it mean when a person depends on alcohol?
6. How are other family members affected when one person in a family depends on alcohol?
7. What can people do to get help if their lives are affected by alcohol?

Lesson
4
pages
190-193

1. Marijuana can make a person feel ____, sick, or sleepy.
2. What changes in the way a person thinks or acts might be caused by smoking marijuana?
3. Tests show that marijuana can cause ____ cancer.
4. ____ is a powerful drug made from the coca plant.
5. A form of cocaine called crack is especially dangerous because it causes ____ very quickly.
6. What does it mean to abuse a product, such as a cleaner?
7. What body organs can be harmed from breathing in large amounts of fumes of some glues and paint thinners?
8. Products that give off harmful fumes usually can be used safely by following ____ on the product's package.

Lesson
5
pages
194-195

1. Some people abuse a drug because ____ do.
2. What is the best answer you can give to an offer to try a cigarette or drug?
3. Saying no to abusing drugs is a healthy ____.
4. Why do many adults not smoke tobacco or abuse alcohol?
5. Young people who do not abuse drugs often join friends in healthy ____ instead.

Chapter 8 Study Guide

On a separate sheet of paper, write the word or words that best complete the sentence or answer the question.

Lesson 1
pages 202-205

1. A communicable disease is one that can ____.
2. What causes communicable diseases?
3. ____ are tiny living things that can make you sick when they get inside your body.
4. ____ are the tiniest germs.
5. What are two diseases caused by bacteria?
6. What are three diseases caused by viruses?
7. How do bacteria grow when they get into the body?
8. How might disease germs get into another person's body?

Lesson 2
pages 206-209

1. Your ____ keeps most of the germs around you from getting inside your body.
2. In what two ways can germs get trapped in the nose and throat?
3. How do cilia help get rid of disease germs?
4. White blood cells can ____ disease germs and destroy them.
5. Antibodies help ____ fight disease germs.
6. Antibodies can give a person ____ to a disease so he or she will not get the disease again.
7. The AIDS virus can destroy ____ that normally protect against disease germs.

Lesson 3
pages 210-211

1. How can washing hands before eating or fixing food help prevent germs from spreading?
2. What can a person do to prevent a cold from spreading to others?
3. A vaccine protects you by causing your body to make ____.
4. Vaccines are made from disease ____ that have been killed or that are alive but weakened.
5. Antibiotics can kill certain ____, but not viruses.

Lesson **4** pages 212-217

1. How do noncommunicable diseases differ from communicable diseases?
2. Heart disease and ____ are the two most serious diseases in the United States today.
3. What parts of the body are affected by cardiovascular diseases?
4. ____ is a heart disease in which the heart and blood vessels become blocked.
5. How might people help prevent arteries from becoming blocked?
6. Some research shows that eating less ____ might help keep people from getting high blood pressure.
7. Diabetes results when the body does not make enough ____.
8. Describe two ways a person with diabetes can help control the disease.
9. In the disease cancer, body ____ start to grow out of control.
10. List two ways doctors treat cancer.
11. Arthritis harms the ____ of the body and makes it difficult for a person to move.
12. In what two ways might arthritis be treated?
13. What are two ways an allergy might affect the body?
14. What might a doctor suggest to a person who has an allergy toward a certain food?

Lesson **5** pages 220-221

1. A person with a healthy lifestyle has good health ____.
2. What noncommunicable disease does regular exercise help prevent?
3. Your body can fight off disease germs better if you get enough ____.
4. Eating fewer salty or fatty foods helps keep your ____ healthy.
5. What diseases does not smoking help prevent?

Chapter 9 Study Guide

On a separate sheet of paper, write the word or words that best complete the sentence or answer the question.

Lesson 1
pages 228-229

1. Your ____ is made up of everything that surrounds you and affects what you do and how you feel.
2. What are the parts of a healthy environment?
3. What harm can air, water, and noise pollution cause?

Lesson 2
pages 230-231

1. Gases and ____ pollute the air during burning.
2. List what can cause air pollution.
3. Describe how polluted air might look.
4. Polluted air might not smell ____.
5. Air pollution can harm the organs of a person's ____ system.
6. Polluted air can cause a person's ____ to burn.
7. Many communities collect trash and burn it in ____.
8. How do some communities make electricity from trash?
9. How do some communities help prevent cars from polluting the air too much?

Lesson 3
pages 232-235

1. Where do people get the water they use in homes and other buildings?
2. Waste material carried in sewer pipes and drains is called ____.
3. Sometimes ____ dump wastes such as chemicals and oil into lakes and streams.
4. In what way do chemicals used on farmland sometimes cause water pollution?
5. Polluted water might have germs that cause disease or ____ that can harm the body.
6. Where do communities treat sewage before it is pumped into lakes, rivers, and streams?
7. What is done to water before it enters homes and other buildings to make it safe for people to use?

Lesson **4** pages 238-239

1. Living and working in very noisy places can make some people feel ____ or tire easily.
2. How can noise pollution affect the heart or hearing?
3. How might using special materials in buildings help avoid harm from noise pollution?
4. People who work near very noisy machines wear ear ____ to keep noise from harming their hearing.
5. List three laws that some communities have passed to help prevent noise pollution.
6. What is one way people can help prevent noise pollution in their homes?

Lesson **5** pages 240-241

1. ____ are inspectors who help a community keep food safe to eat.
2. What kinds of places do sanitarians work?
3. What does a sanitarian check for in places that serve food?
4. Why do sanitarians check to see if food factories are free of insects and other animals?
5. Sanitarians check restrooms in restaurants and food factories to make sure they have ____ and warm water.
6. Milk is ____ at a dairy to kill the germs.
7. What does a sanitarian check for at a dairy?
8. What will the community health department do if a restaurant or food factory continues to handle food unsafely?

Lesson **6** pages 242-243

1. What special events might communities have for people to enjoy?
2. A community might provide activities at ____ or community centers.
3. What place might a community have where children could get help with homework?
4. What kinds of problems might be solved by people in places provided by a community?

Skills for Life Handbook

Use the activities in this handbook to learn and practice skills for life. These are skills that will help you deal with events in your life in good, healthful ways. Read stories about how people your age deal with some difficult situations. Then answer the questions about what these people have done or should do.

Feeling Good About Yourself You will learn how people can have a good self-image by thinking good thoughts about themselves.

Deciding What to Do You will learn how to use the 5-step plan and how to judge choices to make responsible decisions.

Dealing with Problems You will learn to deal with problems and uncomfortable feelings such as sadness and anger.

Learning When and How to Say No You will learn when it is important to say no to avoid doing things that may be harmful or wrong. You will learn ways to say no.

SKILLS FOR LIFE

Getting Along and Communicating with Others You will learn ways to get along better with others. You will also learn ways to settle disagreements and communicate better.

Setting Goals You will learn how to set realistic goals and then how to achieve them.

Evaluating Ads and Choosing the Best Product You will learn how ads can influence choices you make. You will also learn how to use ads and labels to judge products in order to choose the best.

Deciding What to Do

When people have a decision to make about a problem, it helps to use decision-making steps. These steps help people sort out different ways to deal with the problem. Before deciding which choice is best, it also helps to think of the value of each choice. The wise choices will meet these guidelines:

1. The choice should be safe and promote health.
2. The choice should be legal and follow the rules of school and community.
3. The choice would be accepted by parents and other family members.
4. The choice shows respect for self and others.

Sam was walking home from school with his neighbor Todd. Todd moved to town only a few weeks ago, so Sam does not know Todd very well yet. On the way home, Todd pulled a cigarette out of his pocket. He offered one to Sam. Sam had to decide what to do.

Sam knew that his choices were to take a cigarette from Todd or to refuse it. He thought about which choice would best fit the decision-making guidelines he learned about in school. Sam decided to refuse the cigarette.

On another sheet of paper, answer the following questions:

1. How did using the decision-making guidelines help Sam reject the other choice?
2. Did Sam make the best choice? Explain.
3. How can Sam's decision affect how he feels about himself?

Getting Along with Others

SKILLS FOR LIFE

Karen and her friend Tammy are in the same classes together at school. They are good friends. After math class they talk about spending Saturday afternoon together at the park.

On Saturday morning, Karen calls Tammy's house to find out when she will be ready to leave for the park. Tammy is not there. Tammy's father tells Karen that Tammy is at Kelly's house and they are going to a movie.

On a separate sheet of paper, write your answers to the questions below.

1. How do you think Karen feels as she hangs up the phone? (List as many feelings as you can think of.)
2. Karen does not want to lose her friendship with Tammy, but Karen wants Tammy to know she was hurt by Tammy's actions. What do you think Karen should do the next time she sees Tammy?
3. What can Tammy do to help Karen feel less hurt?

Feeling Good About Yourself

Kevin wrote this paragraph about his brother:

My big brother, Marc, is a great guy. He is funny and smart. He is also a good brother. Marc taught me how to ride my bike. He helps me with my math homework. Sometimes he even takes me with him when he goes out with his friends. I'm really glad Marc is my brother.

Answer the following questions on a separate sheet of paper:

1. How do you think Marc would feel if Kevin read this paragraph to him?
2. Why does hearing about their strengths make people feel good about themselves?
3. What might someone write about you? Write a paragraph about your strengths that could be written by someone in your family.

Deciding What to Do

Bruce is sitting under a tree at a park with his cousin Rick. They are watching some boys play baseball, and they are talking.

Rick has to use a wheelchair. His muscles and nerves do not work right, so Rick cannot play like other kids his age.

After they are at the park for about twenty minutes, one of the other boys comes over to them. He asks Bruce if he wants to play baseball with them.

Bruce likes playing baseball, but he also likes spending time with his cousin. Bruce also knows that if he plays baseball with the other boys, then Rick will be left out.

Use the *Health for Life* decision-making steps to show how Bruce can decide if he will play baseball or not. Write these on a separate sheet of paper or on your decision-making chart.

Feeling Good About Yourself

Sandra and Gayle are good friends. They live down the street from each other and are in the same fourth-grade class.

Sandra has just told Gayle that she feels funny about how her body is growing. Sandra has begun her growth spurt. She is taller and heavier than many other people her age. Sandra told Gayle that she feels big and fat, and she wishes she looked different.

Pretend that you are Gayle and you are now with Sandra. What can you say to Sandra that can help her feel better about herself? Write three things you could say on another sheet of paper.

Deciding What to Do

SKILLS FOR LIFE

Andrew is a member of the soccer team in his community. He has soccer practice every day after school, and games are on Saturdays. Andrew enjoys playing soccer, but sometimes he gets tired of practicing so much.

One day, Andrew sees a commercial for a special afternoon television program. Andrew thinks the television special looks really good. The problem is that the TV program is at the same time as soccer practice. Andrew is not sure if he would rather go to soccer practice on that day or stay home to watch the TV special.

Andrew has a decision to make. Use your *Health for Life* decision-making chart. Fill in the steps that Andrew could take to help him decide what to do.

Dealing with Problems

Calvin was at Boy Scout camp for the first time. He was having a great time. He was learning how to paddle a canoe, tie-dye a shirt in arts and crafts, and make a table in woodworking. Calvin's favorite activity, however, was team sports. Every afternoon, the camp split up into two groups and played baseball, basketball, or volleyball. The campers played with different people every day. This way, Calvin got to become friends with more people as he played a different sport.

Calvin was at camp almost a week when he broke his arm. Calvin was running along the path that led to the cafeteria when he hit a rock and tumbled over. He fell onto his arm and broke it. Now he has a cast on it and cannot use his arm for the rest of the week he will be at camp.

Calvin is very upset about breaking his arm. He cannot do many of the activities that he has been enjoying at camp. He especially hates watching all the other kids playing team sports. He wishes he could play too.

Pretend you are Calvin's camp counselor. You can see that Calvin is upset, and you want to help him deal with his problem. You know people have to accept their problems in order to deal with them. You also know that doing something else can help a person deal with a problem. On a separate sheet of paper, write what you would say to Calvin to help him deal with his broken arm.

Setting Goals

SKILLS FOR LIFE

Beth began swimming lessons during the summer and discovered that she likes swimming very much. She thinks swimming is good exercise and wants to continue it to increase her physical fitness.

Setting a goal can help Beth improve her swimming endurance. A goal is something a person wants to do or achieve. A good goal is not too hard or too easy. It should also be reachable in ways that are not harmful to others. For example, a person might set a goal of finishing a stamp collection. If that person takes his brother's stamps to complete the collection without asking first, then he has harmed someone in order to reach his goal. What would be a better way to reach this goal?

Beth decides that she wants to improve her muscle endurance, or how far she can go without getting tired. She has learned that swimming is an excellent way to build muscle endurance. Right now Beth can go twelve laps in the pool without getting tired.

Set a goal for Beth and decide on ways for her to achieve it. Answer these questions about Beth's goal on a separate sheet of paper:

1. What is Beth's goal?
2. What will she do to reach her goal?
3. How long will it take?
4. How will she know if she has reached her goal?
5. Will anyone be harmed by Beth reaching her goal? How do you know?

Learning When and How to Say No

Eric and his partner, Scott, are playing badminton in gym class against two other people. They are near the end of the game and are now losing by three points. The score is thirteen to ten.

Just as the other team is about to serve again, Scott whispers to Eric. He suggests they should do something against the rules to help them win.

Eric is stunned that Scott would suggest that they cheat. Eric does not want to break the rules to win. He likes to win, but not by cheating. He knows he would be angry if his opponents cheated against him. He wants to keep Scott as his partner, but only if he will play fairly.

Think about what Eric can say to Scott to show that he will not cheat. Write the conversation between Eric and Scott on a separate sheet of paper.

Deciding What to Do

SKILLS FOR LIFE

Nicole broke her ankle in February when she slipped on an icy street. She got the cast off her leg a few weeks ago. Her ankle feels much better, but it still feels sore if she uses it too much.

Today is a beautiful spring day, and Nicole's friends just pulled in front of her house on their bicycles. They want Nicole to come on a bike ride with them.

Nicole would love to get on her bicycle and go with them, but she is not sure her ankle is strong enough yet. She is afraid that if she does too much exercise on her ankle, it will not heal right.

Look at the *Health for Life* decision-making steps and guidelines for making decisions in Chapter 1. Answer the questions below using another sheet of paper:

1. What are Nicole's choices?
2. What are the good and bad results of each choice?
3. Which choice does not fit the guidelines for making good decisions? Why?
4. What is the best choice Nicole could make? Why?

Communicating Well

When two people are talking to each other, they are both doing work. While one is talking, the other is listening. You might not think of listening as work, but it is. What do you think would happen if people talked but no one listened?

Listening is important work. The listener must pay attention and try to understand what the speaker is saying. If the listener does not understand what the speaker is saying, then the message may be lost.

Listening is especially important if the speaker is talking about safety rules. If the listener does not pay attention, then that person may not know how to be safe. For example, if you are swimming, you should listen to the lifeguard. If you do not listen to the lifeguard, you might be unsafe in the water.

On a separate sheet of paper, write a statement that is a safety message. Then write a sentence explaining what could happen if no one listened to the safety message.

Learning When and How to Say No

SKILLS FOR LIFE

Mario and Paul are good friends. They go to school together. Sometimes they also play together after school. They both like to play checkers and build model airplanes.

Today after school, Paul called Mario and asked if he could come over to work on one of their airplanes. Mario was home alone.

Mario thought about his parents' rules for when he was home alone. Mario's parents told him that no one was allowed to come over without asking them first. It was now 4:20 p.m. Mario knew that there was no way to reach either of his parents. They would both be driving home from work now.

Mario would like to play with Paul, but he knows it would be against his parents' rules. How can Mario say no to Paul without hurting his feelings?

Think of two ways that Mario could say no to Paul. Write these on a separate sheet of paper.

Setting and Achieving Goals

Luiz knows that swimming can be fun and good exercise. He also knows that people have to be careful to be safe in the water. Luiz is already a good swimmer. Luiz decides that he also wants to learn how to keep swimmers safe. He wants to become a lifeguard.

Luiz knows that lifeguards have to be trained to help rescue a swimmer who is in trouble. A lifeguard also has to be a good swimmer. Luiz knows of some classes offered by the American Red Cross that can give him this training.

Becoming a lifeguard is a goal Luiz wants to achieve very much. He knows it will be hard work, but he thinks he can do it. Luiz knows he will be learning important safety skills in his classes.

Pretend you are Luiz and old enough to become a lifeguard. Write a paragraph about what you will do to achieve your goal and how you will feel when you work to achieve it.

Deciding What to Do

Kim is home with her new babysitter Lynne. They are playing checkers and are having a good time. Kim thinks Lynne is really nice.

After three games of checkers, Lynne asks Kim when she is supposed to go to bed.

"You mean my parents didn't tell you?" Kim asks.

"No, I guess they forgot," Lynne responds, "but I'm sure you know when your bedtime is."

Kim looks at the clock and starts thinking. She is not tired yet, but her bedtime is only twenty minutes away. She is thinking that maybe she should not tell the truth about her real bedtime so she can stay up later. Kim knows that getting enough sleep is important, but she is having a good time and does not really want to stop.

Help Kim decide what to do by using the decision-making steps. Write on your *Health for Life* decision-making chart or use a separate sheet of paper. Also write which of Kim's choices best fits the decision-making guidelines.

Getting Along with Others

Parents try to keep their children healthy. They tell them to do things to keep them safe, healthy, and clean. Your parent might have said to you, "Make sure you wash your hands" or "Put on your jacket before you go outside."

Sometimes when children hear parents saying these things, they get upset. Children might not always understand why they should do certain things. When parents and children do not understand each other, they often argue.

Raphael and his mother are driving back from the dentist. Raphael had three cavities. Raphael's mother says to him, "You know, Raphael, it is not good for you to get so many cavities. What could you do to have a better check-up the next time you see the dentist?"

Raphael starts to get upset. "Why do you have to pick on me?", he says. "Do you think I like getting cavities?"

"I'm not picking on you. I'm only saying this because I care about you. I just want you to protect your teeth to keep them strong and healthy."

Raphael says, "Well, OK, but that's not how it sounded to me."

Answer the following questions on a separate piece of paper:

1. Why did Raphael start to get upset at his mother?
2. What was Raphael's mother concerned about?
3. What are two things you could do when you get upset at another person?

Choosing the Best Product

SKILLS FOR LIFE

Heather is at a drugstore with her mother. She remembers that she is out of toothpaste. Heather's mother tells her to pick out a toothpaste for herself.

Heather walks to the aisle that has all the kinds of toothpaste. She is surprised to see so many different brands. Heather has used the same brand of toothpaste for as long as she can remember. She never noticed all the others before.

Heather looks through the long row of colorful toothpaste boxes. Then she notices a display for a new kind of toothpaste. A picture of this new brand of toothpaste is shown below.

Heather sees on the label that this new toothpaste has fluoride. She knows that fluoride is important to have in a toothpaste. It helps prevent tooth decay. Heather looks at the other information on the label. She tries to decide if the information is helpful enough to make her try this new kind of toothpaste.

Look at the information on the toothpaste box below. On a separate sheet of paper, write down all the information from the label that will help Heather decide whether or not to buy the product.

Feeling Good About Yourself

Louisa is very upset. She just got back from the orthodonist's office where she had braces put on her teeth. Louisa was told that she has to wear her braces for two to three years. She does not like them already. She feels that they make her look dumb and ugly. She does not think she will ever get used to them.

Louisa knows that some of her teeth are crooked. She also knows that her orthodontist can help protect her teeth. She has learned that wearing braces helps because they slowly move the teeth into the correct position in the mouth. Louisa understands that having straight teeth makes them stronger and healthier. She also knows that straight teeth will make her look better later on. However, she is still upset about having braces now.

Louisa goes to the bedroom that she shares with her sister Anna. Louisa says to Anna, "I feel so ugly and dumb with these braces. I talk funny too. I'm sure that kids at school will make fun of me because of them."

Anna says, "Louisa, you have to stop thinking only bad things about yourself. Start thinking about some good things for a change."

Pretend you are Louisa. On another sheet of paper, write three positive things you could say to yourself that show you are thinking about yourself in more positive ways.

Deciding What to Do

SKILLS FOR LIFE

Derek wanted to have a tuna sandwich for lunch. He was going to make his own lunch because his parents were outside working in their garden. Also, Derek liked making healthy meals for himself on the weekends.

Derek pulled out the last can of tuna that was on the shelf. He noticed that it had a dent on the side of the can. He knew that it was not safe to eat food from a can that was either dented or bulging out. He learned in his health class that this meant the food inside the can could be spoiled.

Derek was not sure how the can became dented. He knew that if he ate the tuna inside it was possible that he would get sick. He also knew that the can might have become dented by falling on the floor. However, there were no other cans of tuna in the house. If Derek did not eat this tuna, he could not have a tuna sandwich for lunch.

Derek did not want to take the chance of becoming sick. He decided not to eat the tuna.

On a separate sheet of paper, explain why Derek made the right decision. Use the steps from the *Health for Life* decision-making chart in your answer. Make sure you explain what Derek's choices were and what the good and bad results would be for each choice.

Communicating Well

Jackie went to her friend Maria's house for dinner. It was Maria's birthday and her mother made a special meal. Jackie was very happy that Maria had asked her to join in her birthday celebration.

Jackie met Maria's parents and sister soon after she arrived. She thought they were very nice people. They made her feel at home. After a while, Maria's mother called everyone to the dining room table.

A few minutes later, Maria's mother brought out a tray of something that Jackie did not recognize. Maria said it was a Mexican dish that her mother made especially for the birthday dinner.

Jackie knew it was a good idea to try new foods, but she wanted to know what this food was made of before she tried it. However, she did not want to seem rude since she was a guest. Jackie must have had a funny look on her face, because Maria's mother asked her what was wrong. Jackie was not sure what to say.

Write three things that Jackie could say to Maria's mother to find out more about this new food but still show respect. Write your answers on another sheet of paper.

Choosing the Best Product

SKILLS FOR LIFE

Keith knows that one good eating habit is to cut down on salt. He does not add extra salt to foods. He also tries not to eat foods with a lot of salt already in them.

Keith has also been learning about food labels. He learned that when foods list the ingredients, they are listed from most to least. For example, a food that is made with mostly sugar will have sugar listed as the first ingredient on the label.

Since Keith is trying to cut down on salt, he is looking for salt on food labels. Below are the labels for three types of canned green beans that Keith has found at the store.

Look closely at the labels. Write on a separate piece of paper which type of canned beans (A, B, or C) Keith should buy and explain why. Then write a sentence telling what else Keith needs to consider when choosing foods to buy.

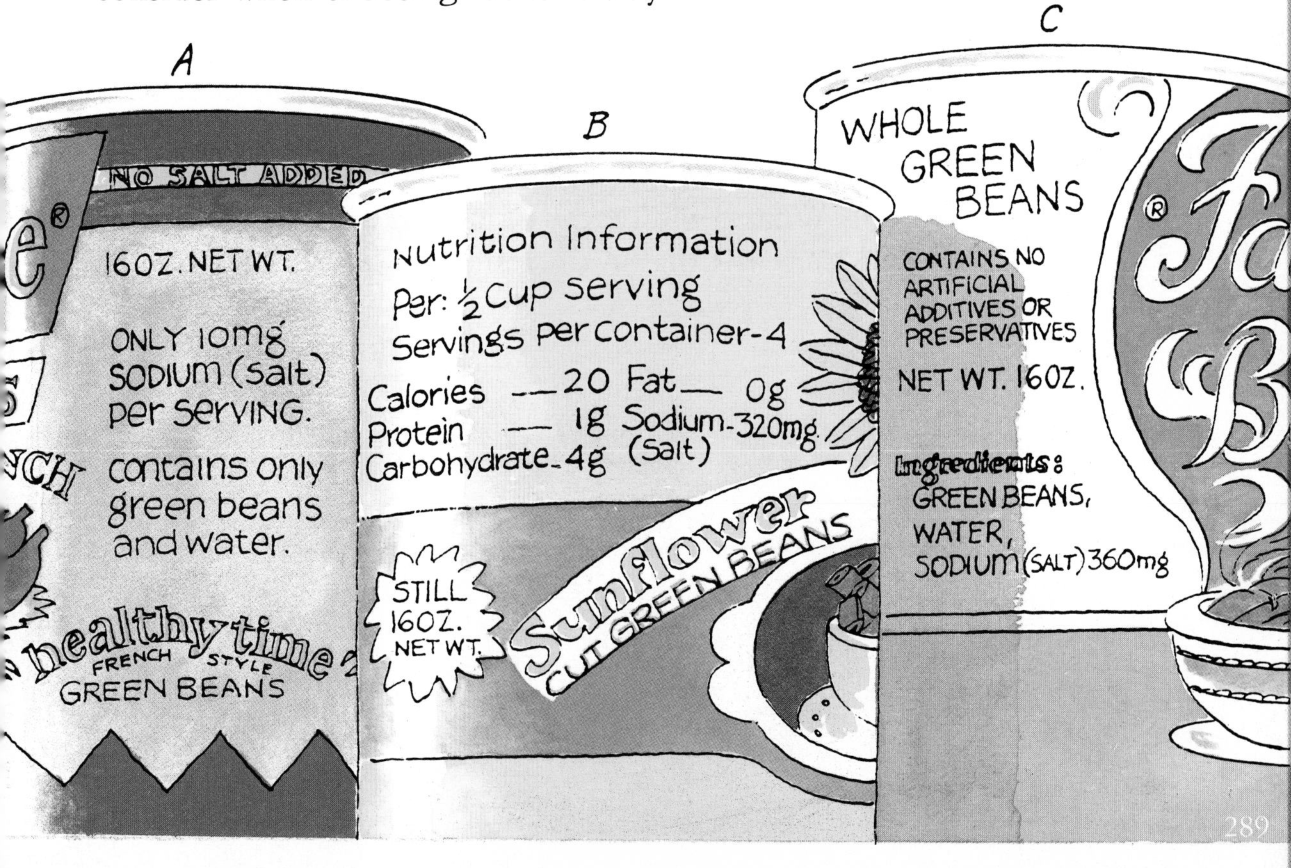

A
NO SALT ADDED
16OZ. NET WT.
ONLY 10mg SODIUM (salt) per SERVING.
contains only green beans and water.
healthytime
FRENCH STYLE
GREEN BEANS
B
Nutrition Information
Per: 1/2 Cup serving
Servings per container-4
Calories --20 Fat__ 0g
Protein -- 1g Sodium-320mg (Salt)
Carbohydrate_4g
STILL 16OZ. NET WT.
Sunflower
CUT GREEN BEANS
C
WHOLE GREEN BEANS
CONTAINS NO ARTIFICIAL ADDITIVES OR PRESERVATIVES
NET WT. 16OZ.
Ingredients:
GREEN BEANS,
WATER,
SODIUM (SALT) 360mg

Deciding What to Do

Aaron is spending the day at Zack's house. They are playing with Zack's train set when Aaron starts to get a headache. Zack's parents are not home.

Aaron tells Zack that maybe he should go home since his head hurts. Zack tells Aaron that he should just take some of his medicine. He said it would make Aaron feel better.

Aaron is not sure what kind of medicine Zack has. Aaron's mother taught him that he should not take anyone else's medicines. He also learned that he should take medicines only from an adult.

Aaron is having a good time with Zack, and he does not really want to leave his friend. However, his headache is starting to get worse.

Aaron has to decide what to do. Answer the following questions about Aaron's decision on a separate sheet of paper:

1. What are Aaron's choices?
2. Which is the safest choice? Why?
3. Which choice would be most accepted by Aaron's parents? How do you know?
4. What could be the results of each choice?
5. What is the best decision for Aaron to make? Why?

Learning When and How to Say No

Aaron has decided that he should not take Zack's medicine for his headache. He thinks he should go home and get some medicine from his mother.

Aaron knows that Zack was only trying to help when he offered his medicine. However, he knows that it would not be the healthful choice.

Aaron knows that when he says this to Zack, his friend might be disappointed. Aaron is afraid that Zack might be mad at him because he wants to leave. He wants to make sure Zack knows that he is going home because of his headache, and not because Zack has done anything to make him upset. Aaron hopes Zack will understand.

Finish the discussion between Aaron and Zack on a separate sheet of paper. Have Aaron explain why he cannot take Zack's medicine and why he thinks he should go home. Also, show how Zack responds to what Aaron says.

Feeling Good About Yourself

Natalie was walking home from a baseball game with some other girls from her neighborhood. The girls all had a great time watching their local team beat their state rivals.

On the way home, two of the girls took out packs of cigarettes from their pockets and began smoking. They asked Natalie if she wanted to smoke too.

Natalie knows that smoking is bad for people's health. She knows it can lead to heart and lung diseases. She also knows that the smoke from cigarettes can be harmful to others who are around a smoker. Natalie does not want to start the bad habit of smoking. Natalie says no to the other girls.

By refusing to take a cigarette, Natalie did something that makes her feel proud of herself. On a separate sheet of paper, write down all the things that Natalie could say about herself that show she feels good about what she did.

Deciding What to Do

SKILLS FOR LIFE

Allison feels like she is getting a cold. Her head feels stuffed up and she has been sneezing all day.

Allison has been trying to ignore her cold because she has plans to go to the baseball game that afternoon. She has been looking forward to this game for three weeks, ever since her father told her about the tickets.

Allison knows that a cold is spread by germs. She understands that she could spread her germs to others and they might get a cold too. She also knows the best way to treat a cold is to rest. She is not sure if she should go to the baseball game, but she really wants to go. She has been really looking forward to spending the day with her father. Allison is not sure what to do.

Answer the following questions on a separate sheet of paper:

1. What are Allison's choices?
2. What are the good and bad results of each choice?
3. Which choice best meets the decision-making guidelines? Why? (See page 34 of your book.)
4. What is the best decision Allison can make? Why?

Getting Along with Others

Laurence's classmate Tyler became ill last month and was absent from school for several weeks. The class found out that Tyler is ill because he has AIDS. While he was gone, the health teacher taught Laurence's class about AIDS. Laurence learned that AIDS is caused by a virus that lives in blood. He found out that people with the AIDS virus can get diseases their bodies cannot fight off. Laurence also learned that AIDS is hard to get and that the virus is not spread by being around someone who has AIDS.

Tyler came back to school today. Laurence sees him in class and decides to tell him that he is glad to see him. Laurence wants Tyler to know that he still wants to be his friend even though he is sick. He also wants Tyler to know that he understands how the AIDS virus works and that he is not afraid to be around him.

On a separate sheet of paper, answer the following questions:

1. What has Laurence learned about AIDS?
2. Why should Laurence not be afraid to see Tyler?
3. What could Laurence say to Tyler to explain how he feels about seeing him again?

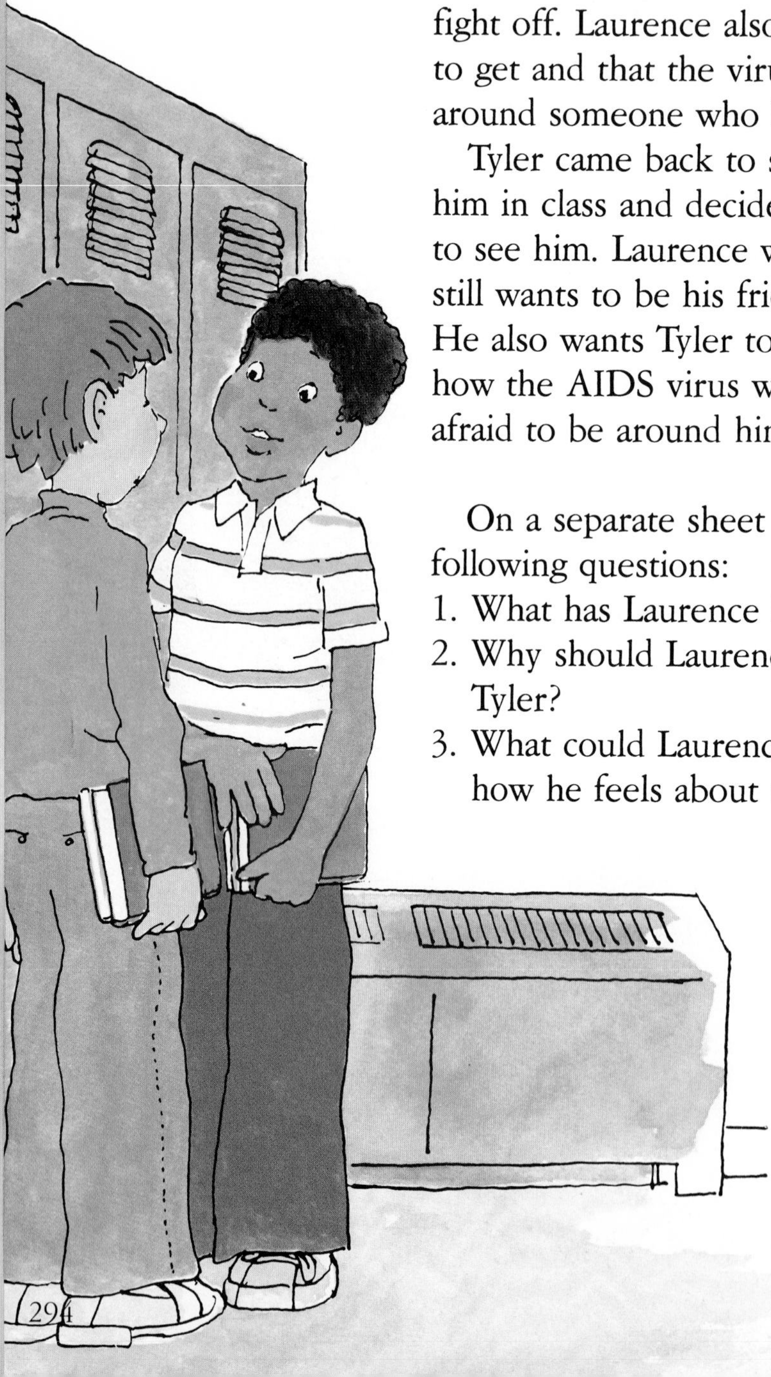

Dealing with Problems

SKILLS FOR LIFE

Darlene's grandmother was not feeling well and decided to go to see her doctor. The doctor did many tests and found out that she has cancer. Abnormal cancer cells have been growing in her body and harming other cells. Darlene's grandmother is getting some treatment to help kill the cancer cells, but she still does not feel well.

Her grandmother's illness is a problem for Darlene's whole family. Everyone is concerned because they do not know if the treatment will kill all the harmful cells and make her grandmother healthy again. It is hard for them to deal with this problem.

Darlene has learned that people have to accept their problems in order to deal with them well. She knows that it is all right to feel sad and upset. Darlene also understands that it takes time to accept and deal with problems.

Darlene decides to do something active to help her stop thinking about her family's problem. She decides to go for a walk with her friend.

On a separate sheet of paper, write three other things Darlene could do to help her deal with this problem.

Setting Goals

Richard has learned about cardiovascular disease in health class. His grandfather had cardiovascular disease and died of a heart attack two years ago. Richard wants to take good care of himself so he can prevent a heart attack in the future. He decides to set a goal.

A goal is something people want to do or achieve. A good goal is not too hard or too easy for a person to reach. A good goal is also specific and can be measured. Then a person can tell if the goal has been reached. For example, a person might set a goal of getting better grades in school. A more specific goal would be to get all A's and B's. The report card will show if the goal has been reached. It is also helpful to set a time limit for reaching a goal. The time limit for this goal would be the end of the grading period.

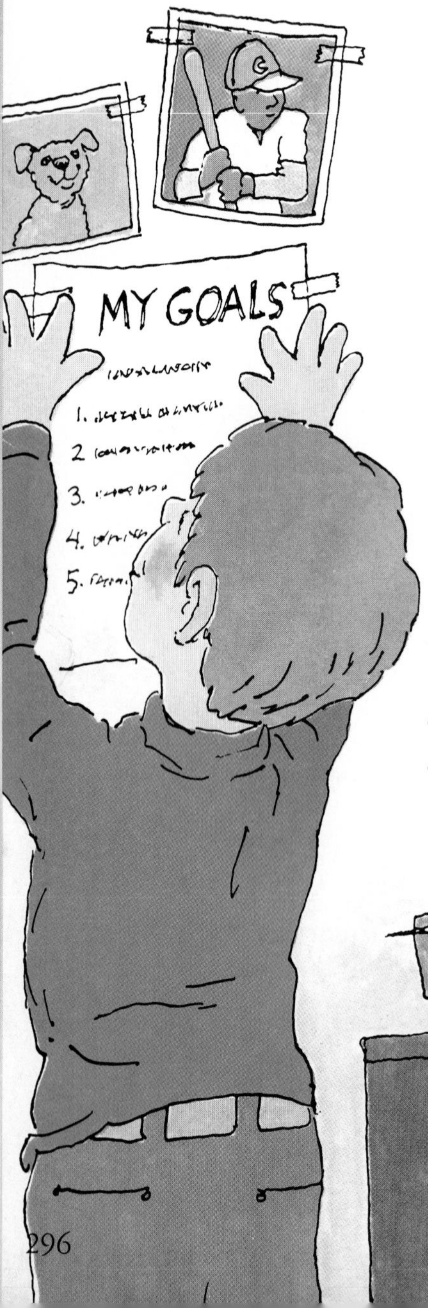

Richard set some goals to help prevent himself from getting cardiovascular disease. However, Richard's goals are not specific. On a separate sheet of paper, change Richard's goals into specific goals. For each goal, write how it can be measured and what kind of time limit could be set for it.

- I will eat healthier foods.
- I will do more exercise.

Deciding What to Do

Ed is a sanitarian who works for his local health department. He and his partner Chris go to restaurants in their town to make sure the people who work there are preparing food safely. They check the machines and utensils that make the food to be sure they are clean. They also check to see that the food is stored safely. They know that if food is not prepared or stored properly, germs can grow in the food. People can get diseases caused by germs that grow in unsafe food.

When Ed and Chris go to different restaurants, they fill out reports about what they have found. Then they give these reports to their boss at the health department. Today Ed and Chris are at a restaurant that is owned by someone Chris knows. While they are doing their inspection, Ed notices that Chris is marking off certain things on his report without checking them first. Ed says something to Chris about this and Chris says not to worry about it.

When Chris and Ed get back to their office, Ed is not sure what to do. He knows that Chris did not fully inspect the restaurant. It is possible that some people could get sick because they did not complete their job. However, Ed does not want to get Chris in trouble.

Answer the following questions on a separate sheet of paper:

1. What are Ed's choices?
2. What are the good and bad results of each choice?
3. Which choice best fits the decision-making guidelines? Why?
4. What should Ed do? Why?

Feeling Good About Yourself

Marsha offered to help some other people in her community clean up a local park. The park was full of litter and had not been properly cared for in a long time. Marsha and others cleared away trash, pulled out weeds, and mowed the grassy areas. They also fixed the swings and the ladder of the slide. Now the park is clean and safe for people in the neighborhood to use and enjoy.

Marsha is glad she offered her time to help clean the park and make it safer. Marsha likes the feeling of helping others in the community. Marsha likes it when she feels good about herself.

Pretend you are Marsha. On another piece of paper, write a paragraph telling how you feel about yourself after this helpful and healthful activity.

Setting Goals

The town where Sara lives planned to hold a meeting to discuss the problem of water pollution in their comunity. The town leaders decided to have a panel of speakers. Each person would talk about the problem from their point of view. They asked the mayor, two scientists, and the PTA president to be on the panel. They also decided that a young person from the local elementary school should be part of the panel.

The school had a contest to choose the student who would be on the panel. The students had to write a short essay. They were asked to explain why pollution is a problem in the community and what could help solve the problem.

Sara learned about the problems of water pollution in health class. She also learned about setting goals. She decided to write her essay about setting goals to help control water pollution. Sara won the contest and became part of the panel at the town meeting.

Pretend you are Sara. On a separate sheet of paper, write a paragraph about how you think water pollution could be controlled by setting goals. In a second paragraph, set specific goal that might help solve the problem of water pollution. Then tell how people could work together to reach it.

Glossary and Index

Glossary

Pronunciation Key

The pronunciation of each word is shown just after the word, in this way: **ab bre vi ate** (ə brēʹvē āt). The letters and signs used are pronounced as in the words below. The mark ʹ is placed after a syllable with primary or heavy accent, as in the example above. The mark ˊ after a syllable shows a secondary or lighter accent, as in **ab bre vi a tion** (ə brēˊ vē āʹshən).

a hat, cap
ā age, face
ä father, far

b bad, rob
ch child, much
d did, red

e let, best
ē equal, be
ėr term, learn

f fat, if
g go, bag
h he, how

i it, pin
ī ice, five

j jam, enjoy
k kind, seek
l land, coal
m me, am
n no, in
ng long, bring

o hot, rock
ō open, go
ô order, all
oi oil, voice
ou house, out

p paper, cup
r run, try
s say, yes
sh she, rush
t tell, it
th thin, both
ŦH then, smooth

u cup, butter
u̇ full, put
ü rule, move

v very, save
w will, woman
y young, yet
z zero, breeze
zh measure, seizure

ə represents:
- **a** in about
- **e** in taken
- **i** in pencil
- **o** in lemon
- **u** in circus

A

abuse (ə büz′), using a drug or other substance on purpose in ways that can harm health.

agriculture (ag′rə kul′chər), the science or job of farming.

AIDS (ādz), a disease caused by a virus that can destroy white blood cells that normally help fight off disease germs.

air sac (sak), a tiny baglike part at the ends of bronchial tubes in the lungs. Oxygen and carbon dioxide pass into and out of blood through the walls of the air sacs.

alcohol (al′kə hol), a drug in beer, wine, and liquor that slows down the nervous system.

allergy (al′ər jē), a noncommunicable disease in which a person is sensitive to a substance, such as food or pollen.

antibiotic (an′ti bī ot′ik), a medicine that can kill or weaken certain kinds of bacteria.

antibody (an′ti bod′ē), a substance made by the body that helps white blood cells destroy disease germs.

appreciate (ə prē′shē āt), to think well of someone or something.

artery (är′tər ē), one of the three kinds of blood vessels; blood flows away from the heart through arteries.

arthritis (är thrī′tis), a noncommunicable disease that harms body joints, causing redness, swelling, pain, and often crippling.

atherosclerosis (ath′ər ō sklə rō′sis), a cardiovascular disease in which fatty substances build up on the inside walls of the arteries.

B

bacteria (bak tir′ē ə), tiny living things, some of which cause communicable diseases.

bicuspid (bī kus′pid), the kind of tooth with two sharp points used to tear and crush food. Adults have eight bicuspids.

blister (blis′tər), a small swelling in the skin that is filled with a watery substance.

blood vessel (ves′əl), any of the tubes that carry blood through the body. Arteries, veins, and capillaries are blood vessels.

C

calculus (kal′kyə ləs), hardened plaque that forms at the gumline, causing gums to pull away from teeth.

cancer (kan′sər), a noncommunicable disease in which cells grow out of control and destroy healthy cells.

capillary (kap′ə ler′ē), one of the three kinds of blood vessels; capillaries connect arteries to veins. Cells receive oxygen and nutrients and get rid of wastes through the walls of capillaries.

carbohydrates (kär′bō hī′drāts), one of the six kinds of nutrients in food; the body uses carbohydrates for energy.

carbon dioxide (kär′bən dī ok′sīd), colorless, odorless gas that is a waste product of body cells.

carbon monoxide (kär′bən mo nok′sīd), a gas found in cigarette smoke that takes the place of oxygen in the blood.

cardiovascular (kär′dē ō vas′kyə lər) **disease,** any one of several noncommunicable diseases that affect the heart and blood vessels.

cavity (kav′ə tē), a hole in a tooth.

cell (sel), the smallest part that makes up a living thing.

certified laboratory assistant (sėr′tə fīd lab′rə tôr′ē ə sis′tənt), A certified laboratory assistant might work with a doctor or medical technologist and might look at blood cells under a microscope.

cilia (sil′ē ə), very small hairlike parts in the nose and throat that can help remove germs from the body.

circulatory system (sėr′kyə lə tôr′ē sis′təm), the body system made up of the heart, blood, and blood vessels. This system moves materials to and from body cells.

cocaine (kō kān′), a harmful drug made from leaves of the coca plant.

communicable (kə myü′nə kə bəl) **disease,** an illness that can spread, usually from one person to another.

competitive (kəm pet′ə tiv), having to do with a contest or game in which one person or team tries to win over the other.

crown (kroun), the part of a tooth you can see above the gum.

cuspid (kus′pid), the kind of tooth with a sharp point used to tear food. Adults have four cuspids.

D

dermis (dėr′mis), the part of skin below the epidermis.

diabetes (dī′ə bē′tis), a noncommunicable disease in which the body does not make enough insulin and cannot use sugars in food as it should.

digestive system (də jes′tiv sis′təm), all the organs and body parts that help change food into a form cells can use.

disagreement (dis′ə grē′mənt), a difference in what people think.

drug, a substance other than food that causes changes in the body.

E

enamel (i nam′əl), the hard, white outer layer of a tooth.

environment (en vī′rən mənt), everything, including places and conditions, that surrounds a person and affects actions and feelings.

epidermis (ep′ə dėr′mis), the outer layers of skin.

exhaust (eg zôst′), the escape of gases from an engine.

F

fats, one of the six kinds of nutrients in food; the body uses fats for energy.

first aid, the first help given to a person who has been hurt or has become suddenly ill.

flexibility (flex′sə bil′ə tē), the ability of muscles to move easily and freely.

floss (flôs), a soft, waxed or unwaxed thread used for cleaning between the teeth.

G–H

gum (gum), the firm tissue around the teeth.

heartbeat (härt′bēt), one complete contraction and relaxation of the heart muscle.

I

immunity (i myü′nə tē), a person's protection from or resistance to disease.

incinerator (in sin′ə rā′tər), a furnace for burning trash.

incisor (in sī′zər), the kind of tooth with flat edges used to cut food. There are eight incisors.

insulin (in′sə lən), a substance made by certain body cells that enables the body to use sugars in food.

J–L

jaywalker (jā′wôk′ər), a person who crosses a street without paying attention to traffic rules.

large intestine (in tes′tən), an organ of the digestive system through which solid waste moves.

M

marijuana (mar′ə wa′nə), a plant that contains many substances, including drugs, that can cause changes in the body when smoked.

minerals (min′ər əlz), one of the six kinds of nutrients in food; the body uses minerals to help the body work as it should.

molar (mō′lər), the kind of tooth with a broad top used to grind food. Adults have twelve permanent molars.

motor nerve, a bundle of nerve cells that carry messages from the brain or spinal cord to the muscles.

mucus (myü′kəs), the wet, sticky substance inside your nose and throat that can kill some germs.

muscle endurance (en dur′əns), the ability to use muscles for a long time without getting tired.

muscle strength (strengkth), the ability of muscles to produce a great deal of force.

N

nervous system (ner′vəs sis′təm), all the organs and body parts that control actions you direct and actions you do not direct.

nicotine (nik′ə tēn′), a drug in tobacco that speeds up the heart and causes the blood vessels to become narrow.

noncommunicable (non′kə myü′nə kə bəl) **disease,** an illness that is not caused by germs and does not spread to other people.

nutrient (nü′trē ənt), a substance in food that the body needs for growth, energy, and good health.

O

organ (ô′gən), several kinds of tissues that work together for a special purpose.

orthodontist (ôr′thə don′tist), a dentist who specializes in moving teeth into proper position.

over-the-counter medicine, any medicine a person can buy without a doctor's order.

oxygen (ok′sə jen), a colorless, odorless gas in air that most living things need to stay alive.

P

particle (pär′tə kəl), a tiny bit of material.

pasteurize (pas′chə rīz′), to heat a substance to a high temperature and for a long enough time to destroy germs.

pedestrian (pə des′trē ən), a person who travels by walking.

physical (fiz′ə kəl) **fitness,** the ability to exercise, play, and work without getting tired or injured easily.

plaque (plak), a sticky, colorless film of harmful bacteria that is always forming on a person's teeth.

polio (pō′lē ō), a communicable disease that destroys nervous tissue in the spinal cord, causing crippling.

pollute (pə lüt′), to make dirty, as for example, to pollute air or water.

pore (pôr), a very small opening in the skin through which sweat leaves the body.

posture (pos′chər), the way a person holds the body while sitting, standing, or walking.

prescription (pri skrip′shən), a doctor's order for a medicine.

product (prod′əkt), an item that is produced; for example, soap is a health product.

proteins (prō′tēnz), one of the six kinds of nutrients in food; the body uses proteins for growth and repair and sometimes for energy.

psychologist (sī kol′ə jist), a person who is trained to help people with feelings, especially troubled feelings that last a long time.

pulse (puls), the push of blood through certain blood vessels.

R

reflector (ri flek′tər), a surface or object that turns back light, such as a disk on a bicycle.

rescue (res′kyü), to save or free a person from danger or harm.

respiratory system (res′pər tôr′ē sis′təm), all the organs and body parts that help the body take in oxygen and get rid of carbon dioxide.

rickets (rik′its), a disease caused by too little vitamin D. The disease causes bones to soften, bend, or become crooked.

ring buoy (boi or bü′ē), a cork or plastic ring used to keep a person afloat in the water until he or she is rescued.

S

saliva (sə lī′və), a colorless liquid made by salivary glands that starts digestion of certain foods in the mouth.

salivary glands (sal′ə ver′ē glandz), the part of the body that produces saliva.

sanitarian (san′ə ter′ē ən), a person who checks to see if food in stores, restaurants, food factories, and dairies is safe to eat.

scaler (skā′lər), an instrument for removing calculus from the teeth.

scurvy (skėr′vē), a disease caused by too little vitamin C. The disease causes bleeding, weakness, and sometimes death.

self-image (self′im′ij), the way a person sees or feels about himself or herself.

sensory nerve (sen′sər ē nėrv), a bundle of nerve cells that carry messages from the sense organs to the brain or spinal cord.

sewage (sü′ij), the wastes carried in sewer pipes and drains.

side effect, any unwanted change in the body that a medicine causes.

skill, an ability gained by practice.

small intestine (in tes′tən), an organ of the digestive system in which food is changed into a very thin liquid.

spinal (spī′nl) **cord,** a thick, whitish cord of nerve tissue that extends from the brain down through most of the backbone.

stethoscope (steth′ə skōp), an instrument used by doctors to hear the sounds produced in the heart and lungs.

strength, something a person is strong in or can do well.

system (sis′təm), a group of organs and body parts that work together to perform a job.

T

tissue (tish′ü), cells of the same kind grouped together.

V

vaccine (vak sēn′), a medicine that contains weakened or dead disease germs and that causes the body to form antibodies.

vehicle (vē′ə kəl), any means of transporting, such as a car, wagon, bicycle, or sled.

vein (vān), one of the three kinds of blood vessels; blood flows back to the heart through veins.

virus (vī′rəs), one kind of disease germ that causes some communicable diseases, for example, colds and flu.

vitamins (vī′tə mənz), one of the six kinds of nutrients in food; the body uses vitamins to help the body work as it should.

W–Y

waste-treatment plant, a place where used water from homes and other buildings is treated before it is put back into rivers and lakes.

water-treatment plant, a place where water from rivers, lakes, and streams is treated so it is safe to drink.

windpipe (wind′pīp′), the long tube in the neck that divides in two and leads into each lung.

yeast (yēst), a living thing that sometimes causes food to spoil and also is used in making bread and certain cheeses.

Index

*A **bold-faced** number indicates a page with a picture about the topic.*

A

B

E

J

L

M

N

O

P

R

S

T–U

V

W

X–Y

Acknowledgments

Page **114:** From "Kids Test Their Safety at Bicycle Roadeo" by Karen Ettinger adapted from *Traffic Safety* November/December 1983.

Page **196:** From "Smokebusters Was Not A Drag" by Jon W. Hisgen, from *WAHPERD Journal* (May, 1985). Reprinted by permission of the author.

Picture Credits

Page **36:** Courtesy *Kids on the Block.* Toll free 800-368-KIDS
Page **55:** Stacy Pick 1984/Stock Boston
Page **77:** Erik Anderson/Stock Boston
Page **90:** Heinz Kluetmeier/SPORTS ILLUSTRATED © Time Inc.
Page **107:** Diana O. Rasche
Page **114:** Courtesy National Safety Council
Pages **126-127:** Ccpyright by the American Dental Association. Reprinted by permission
Page **131:** Steve Smith/Wheeler Pictures
Page **142:** Ira Wyman/Sygma
Page **168:** Bettmann Archive
Page **179:** John McGrail 1985/Wheeler Pictures
Pages **180–181:** © G. T. Hewlett 1972
Page **183:** Courtesy Dr. Francis Howell/Oral Medicine/Scripps Clinic, La Jolla, CA
Page **191:** Don & Pat Valenti
Page **196:** John Hisgen/Pewaukee Public Schools, WI
Page **202(l):** Eric V. Grave/Phototake
(c): Manfred Kage/Peter Arnold
(r): Dr. J. Metzner/Peter Arnold
Page **203(l):** Prof. Luc Montagnier, Institut Pasteur/CNRI/Science Photo Library/Photo Researchers
(c): Martin Rotker/Taurus
(r): Omikron/Photo Researchers
Page **204:** Manfred Kage/Arnold
Pages **206–207:** Dr. James D. Hirsch, Rockefeller University
Page **216:** Lester Kalisher, M.D., St. Barnabas Medical Center, Livingston, NJ
Page **222:** Courtesy Massachusetts General Hospital
Page **231(all):** Cameramann International Ltd.
Pages **232–233:** Eric Kroll/Taurus
Page **234:** Peter Menzel/Stock Boston
Pages **235–237:** Cameramann International Ltd.
Page **238:** John Coletti/Stock Boston
Page **240:** Dan McCoy/Rainbow
Page **241:** Tom Pantages
Page **244:** Courtesy Dr. W. G. Perrine, Perth Amboy Public Schools, NJ

All photographs not credited are the property of Scott, Foresman and Company. These include photographs taken by the following photographers:

James L. Ballard: Pages 16–17, 40–41, 68–69, 94–95, 118–119, 146–147, 172–173, 200–201, 226–227

David Bentley: Pages 18–19, 20, 21, 24, 25, 27, 29, 32, 33, 35, 37, 101

Ralph Cowan: Pages 72, 73, 74, 80, 81, 82, 83, 84, 85

Allan Landau: Pages 22, 49, 54, 60–61, 62–63, 65, 71, 75, 76, 78, 79, 87, 88–89, 91, 97, 98, 100, 102–103, 104, 105, 109, 110, 111, 112–113, 115, 138–139, 149, 150, 161, 166, 169, 174, 176, 177, 178, 194, 195, 197, 214–215, 220–221, 223, 245

Paul LeCat: Pages 151, 152, 153, 154, 155, 156, 157, 158, 159, 160, 162, 163, 164, 165, 236

Diana O. Rasche: Page 31

Ryan Roessler: Pages 120–121, 128–129, 130, 134, 141, 143, 204–205, 210